Praise for
Made in California

"George Geary has chronicled California's place in the legacy of American eating."
—*The New York Times*

"George Geary's *Made in California* takes you on a delightful journey down memory lane. It's a must-read guide for anyone who loves history, food, and California's culture of innovation. Fortunately, you can still visit many of these iconic locations, so plan your road trip now!"
—**Linda Dishman, president and CEO, Los Angeles Conservancy**

"This delicious book serves up more than a feast of information—it's food for the soul of anyone who is hungry for the back stories and glories of California's classic cuisine, iconic kitchens, famous flavors, and tastiest landmarks."
—**Charles Phoenix,**
author of *Addicted to Americana* and *Holiday Jubilee*

"I gained fifteen pounds reading this book, but it was worth it because ten of those went to my brain! A smart, encyclopedic, delightful read worthy of a coffee table, a classroom syllabus, or a car seat as a road-trip companion!"
—**Gustavo Arellano,**
author of *Taco USA: How Mexican Food Conquered America*

"Lots of colorful pictures and informative details will captivate foodies and cultural mavens alike… California public libraries need to have this in their shelves."
—**Andrienne Cruz, Azusa City Library**

MADE IN

CALIFORNIA

VOLUME 2

Published by Prospect Park Books
An imprint of Turner Publishing Company
Nashville, Tennessee
www.turnerpublishing.com

Made in California, Volume 2: The California-Born Diners, Burger Joints, Fast Food & Restaurants that Changed America, 1951–2010

Cover and Book Design by Amy Inouye

Library of Congress Control Number: 2021939980

9781684429189 Paperback
9781684429196 Hardcover
9781684429202 Epub

Printed in Canada
1 2 3 4 5 6 7 8 9 10

To My Mom,
the strongest, brightest, and most positive person I know.

Table of Contents

Introduction

IN 2021, *MADE IN CALIFORNIA* was published to great acclaim. When I first put the book together, I had over a hundred food establishments to highlight. The book would have been over 500 pages. We decided to make two volumes of *Made in California*, and here is the second half, packed with over fifty locations.

I have deep admiration for learning and keeping our history alive. Walking around Europe, you will see buildings with plaques stating what happened or who lived there. Here in California, if a building is over thirty years old, it is demolished; if a chain updates its "look," the building is remodeled to strip away its past. I wanted to at least document the history of these historical food locations with a book.

Today, large food conglomerates test a concept: if it is popular, they start mass expansion or begin with franchises. In years past, a family or small like-minded group had an idea and started with one location and then expanded cautiously. Across the country and sometimes the world, many have enjoyed Panda Express, California Pizza Kitchen, Johnny Rockets, and so many others. Who started their first location? What has made them famous? Where were the original buildings? I wanted to capture the stories of these essential businesses and structures before they were gone forever. And so, I did.

When the first volume was released, I had been interviewed by newspapers and agencies coast to coast, not just in California. I would be asked, "Why do you think California had so many original locations of companies that spread eastward?" The common denominator is the Car Culture of California and that the state has such a diverse population. California is the most populist state in the country to test a concept to the masses.

One of the thrills of writing both books was meeting the founders' children and grandchildren, telling the stories they thought would be lost. I asked the tough questions of the history, and they gave the answers. Sitting down for coffee or a meal with the child of one of the entrepreneurs across from me was a thrill. Listening to the family stories, knowing that their family created hundreds of locations worldwide and jobs for thousands, was remarkable. These are the people that shaped the industry that I share in this book.

I also get asked why such-and-such a location was not included, or why I included a defunct place. Many locations' media and publicity departments would not talk with me, even after having four historical food books. I also included closed chains or chains that merged into others for the history aspect.

In closing, the most challenging part of writing this book was that every time I worked on a chapter, I would start craving the food from those places. Each one of the locations has made a mark on our society and the world. Now you can celebrate with me in this book.

— GEORGE GEARY

Opposite: Farmer Boys growing large fried zucchini sticks

Hof's Hut

ORIGINAL LOCATION: 4828 2nd St., Long Beach
OPENED: September 16, 1951
FOUNDERS: The Hofman Family
CURRENT OWNERSHIP: The Hofman Hospitality Group
CURRENTLY AT THE FIRST LOCATION: Saint & Second Restaurant
There are three Hof's Hut locations in Southern California.

hofshut.com

IN THE LATE 1930S, Sjoukje Hofman, with the help of her husband Dirk, a merchant marine, opened Hofman's directly on the sand in Long Beach off 5th Place. Opening the stand was not simple for Sjoukje; she had to wade through lots of municipal red tape to finally realize her dream.

"The Beach," as the town was called then, was very popular with sunbathers, surfers, and visiting/stationed military; Long Beach was known as the "Waikiki of Southern California" in 1939. Long Beach even had a National Surfing Competition until the breakwater was built starting in 1940; this calmed the waters in East San Pedro Bay, making it into more of a wading pool.

Sjoukje's youngest son Meindert (Harold) worked the stand during the summer months before starting at Oregon State University, where he was awarded a basketball scholarship. Unfortunately, an injury disrupted his basket-

ball career early, so Harold moved back to Long Beach and helped his mom and dad at the stand. The stand was popular and known for 15-cent Hofburgers and Hot Dogs.

In the mid-1940s, Harold took over the stand after his parents passed away. With the stand only open during the summer, only serving takeout, and having no place for diners to sit, Harold started looking toward expansion.

In 1946, Harold found love and married Donna Corbridge; little did she know that she was also marrying into the restaurant business. Knowing that the little stand could not generate enough

Opposite: Hof's Hut Long Beach location, (inset): Hofmans on the beach, 1951, (top): Hof's Hut waitresses, 1950's

profits in the few months it was open, he decided to expand.

The pulse of the beach town shopping district would be a perfect location in which to expand. The corner of Second and St. Joseph streets in the Belmont Shore area of Long Beach was the perfect spot, only a short block from the 800-seat Fox Belmont Theater. The location could seat fifteen diners. Hearty American fare from breakfast to dinner and home-baked goods also packaged to take home were hits from the beginning. The restaurant's grand opening on a foggy and drizzling day in September 1951 became two grand openings. Also, Craig Hofman was born on the opening day of the restaurant. Craig always said he was born into the restaurant business.

As soon as Craig was able, he carried water and drinks to the tables; he worked the soda fountain at age ten. Craig was eighteen and studying at Arizona State University when his father died of a sudden heart attack in their second home in Palm Springs. Donna took over the operations of Hof's Hut, and Craig was summoned home to help his mom in the family business. She expanded Hof's to five locations, while he finished his degree at Long Beach State.

Like many restaurants of the day, hiring female pie bakers was the best way to get those homemade-looking pies. Marie Callender worked for the Hofman family, making pies and baked goods before venturing out on her own and creating the Marie Callender Pie Shops.

> **Hofman Family**
> 1930s–1940s: Dirk and Sjoukje Hofman
> 1940s–1969:   Harold and Donna Hofman
> 1969–1982:   Donna Hofman
> 1982–Present: Craig Hofman

> **Other Hofmans in the Business**
> Brad Hofman: President
> Ryan Hofman: Director of Construction and Facilities
> Ashley Pedersen: Brand Manager
> Dirk Hofman: Executive Bar Manager for Specialty Concepts

In the mid-1960s, Dick Hofman, Harold's brother, retired from the U.S. Air Force as a colonel. Dick franchised two locations from Harold in the Colorado Springs area. He kept the group of

Sjoukje and Harold Hofman at original beach stand 1930's

Hof's Hut Locations and the Opening Years

OPENING ORDER/ YEAR	ADDRESS	WHAT IS THERE TODAY
1st: 1951–2000	4828 E. 2nd St., Long Beach	Saint and Second
2nd: 1953–1971	33 Pine St., Long Beach	Building replaced
3rd: 1955–Present	2147 Bellflower Blvd., Long Beach	Still in operation
4th: 1960–2015	4251 Long Beach Blvd., Long Beach	Medical Offices
5th: 1961	6257 E. 2nd St., Long Beach	Lucille's
6th: 1965–2003	15342 Beach Blvd., Westminster	Asian Restaurant
7th: 1972	4050 W. Chapman, Orange	Lucille's
8th: 1974–2014	7001 Knott Ave., Buena Park	Black Bear Diner
9th: 1975	18850 Douglas, Irvine	Condominiums
10th: 1975	11338 South St., Irvine	Lucille's
11th: 1986–Present	23635 Crenshaw Blvd., Torrance	Still in operation
12th: 1995	10900 Los Alamitos Blvd., Los Alamitos	Moved
13th: 2020–Present	12489 Seal Beach Blvd., Seal Beach	Still in operation

restaurants open for about ten years, and then opened McDonald's franchisees. Although all the Colorado locations were sold and rebranded, the new owner renamed them "the Hut."

With Craig taking over the business in 1982, Hof's Hut grew to thirteen locations. Looking toward the future of the American dining experience, Craig noticed many "theme" restaurants opening with great success, with dining moving away from the typical American coffeehouse. Looking toward the future, Craig embarked on a one-year research trip into the Midwest and Southern states to study barbeque cuisine; he had noticed that the West lacked good barbeque. In 1999, Lucille's Smokehouse Bar-B-Que (page 191) opened to great acclaim. In 2015, the first Hof's Hut was rebranded into the new concept Saint and Second, with a second location in Manhattan Beach, California.

Since 1985, Hof's Hut Hospitality Group has been awarding scholarships through the Long Beach Century Club. The philanthropical work for the community still to this day is an integral part of the Hofman family.

In the spring of 2013, the Hofman Hospitality Group was given the prestigious Long Beach Entrepreneur of the Year award.

Craig's four children all work in the company, making it four generations of Hofmans in the restaurant business. Today there are three remaining Hof's Huts, which keep the original hospitality alive with all the Hofman branded restaurants.

Former Franchised Locations for Dick Hofman

1st: 1968-1974	2202 E. Pikes Peak Plaza, Colorado Springs
2nd:1968-1974	421 S. Nevada St., Colorado Springs
3rd: 1973-1973	21 N. Union St., Colorado Springs

BBQ Stand

SLOGAN: "World Famous Pastrami"

NAME TODAY: The Hat: World Famous Pastrami

ORIGINAL LOCATION: 1 West Valley Blvd., Alhambra

OPENED: 1951

FOUNDERS: Sam and Alvin Anenberg (father and son)

CURRENT OWNERSHIP: C&J Food Company

CURRENTLY AT THE FIRST LOCATION: The first location is still in operation. *There are eleven locations throughout Southern California.*

thehat.com

PROMINENT STREET CORNERS of Main Street USA always housed at least one if not more gas stations. 1925 was no different in the City of Alhambra. Standard Oil had a service station on the northwest corner of Valley and Garfield. The Standard Oil Company in the '20s and then the Signal Oil Company of the '30s and '40s pumped gasoline there for over 27 years. But eventually, Sam Anenberg of nearby Montebello decided to open a BBQ stand after the Fourth of July holiday in 1951 on the gas station property he owned.

After launching several other BBQ stands around the Southland, Anenberg was looking to sell that first one. Finding that the location was perfect for a restaurant, as it was directly across the street from the 1,100-seat Garfield Egyptian theater, John and Catherine Brown purchased the stand and renamed it Johnny Brown's Drive-In in late 1951; they referred to it as Johnny Brown's Hat in the early days. The Browns owned and operated the Hat for over 20 years before selling it to Robert Ryan, a city police officer, and his wife, Alice. Alice cooked and served during the day until Robert came off his patrol shift. The cuisine was all-American fare, with carhops serving thick shakes, hot juicy burgers, and fresh fruit pies on trays.

Like so many towns across America, redevelopment happened fast around the downtown area of Alhambra. Brothers Ronald "Corky" and Joe Conzonire, alumni of Alhambra High School, recalled visiting the drive-in on the weekends with their shiny cars and their girlfriends on their arms. Corky was in the class of 1960, and Joe ten years later. The Hat was the local hangout of all the kids from Alhambra High. Then, the brothers got word that the building was to be sold and a strip mall with a dozen businesses would replace the former gas station turned drive-in. The only way to save their iconic drive-in was to purchase it themselves. Joe was not new to the restaurant business, as he owned a chain of Belly Buster Sandwich locations.

1981 was the turning point for the Hat. The Conzonire family purchased the land and the business, saving it and keeping the memory alive. They now operate the business under C&J Foods

Opposite: The Hat, Alhambra location neon sign

Company. The brothers run the business, while Corky's son, Joe, is the president of C&J Foods and runs the day-to-day operations.

The Hat is known for its pastrami sandwiches, as its neon sign does say "World Famous Pastrami." Each large sandwich is plenty large enough to share; over half a pound of thinly sliced meat is stacked on each roll. Today, the Hat goes through approximately 15 million pounds of beef annually. Other items on the menu are hamburgers, hot dogs, chili, and French fries with cheese, onions, and pastrami packed on top of the heaping pile. The pastrami meat is made from brined brisket, seasoned with a dry rub, smoked, steamed, sliced very thin, and served on a French roll, unlike most delis that use rye bread. The car-hops are gone; you must get out of your car to order and wait. At the rear of the location, you will find tables to enjoy your food. If you order the chili fries, ask for four plates to share with your three best friends.

The family owns all the Hat locations; while expanding, they have kept the menu and look of nostalgia of each place the same as the first in Alhambra. A few new sites have been outfitted with a drive-through window. But I still say you should walk up so you can experience watching the kitchen and all the staff preparing the sandwiches and the piles of French fries. 👨‍🍳

Other Names of the Location

BBQ Stand
Johnny Brown's Drive-In
Johnny Brown's Hat
Hat Drive-In
The Hat

Ownership

1951–1952:   Sam and Alvin Anenberg (Father and Son)
1952–1969:   John and Catherine Brown
1969–1981:   Alice Ryan
1981–Present: Ronald "Corky" and Joe Conzonier (Brothers)

Wrapping a pastrami sandwich in Murrieta

Current Locations

Alhambra
Brea
Glendora
Lake Forest
Monterey Park
Murrieta
Pasadena
Rancho Cucamonga
Simi Valley
Temple City
Upland

The following text appears on the menu board in the image:

featuring
World Famous
PASTRAMI DIP $11.99

COLD SANDWICHES

ROAST BEEF		COLD BEEF	$11.99
BAR-B-QUE BEEF		HAM & CHEESE	$7.59
STEAK SANDWICH		HAM & SWISS	$7.69
GRILLED CHEESE		TURKEY & HAM	$7.59
HOT DOG	$3.99	AVOCADO	$7.59
CHILI DOG	$5.39		

SIDE ORDERS

CHILI FRIES $7.69
ADD TOMATO & PICKLE

FRIES SMALL $3.99 LARGE $4.99
WET FRIES WITH $5.99
ONION RINGS SM $4.19 LG $5.99

DRINKS
COKE CLASSIC · DIET COKE · SPR
DR. PEPPER · WILD CHERRY · ROOT I

FRESH BREWED ICE TE

ORANGE BANG

PINK LEMON O

PINA COLADA B

COFFEE
MILK

Right side panel:

PASTRAMI DIP	$11.99
ROAST BEEF	$11.99
BAR-B-QUE BEEF	$11.99
STEAK SANDWICH	$11.99
GRILLED CHEESE	$4.99
HOT DOG	$3.99
CHILI DOG	$5.39
CHILI TAMALE	$5.99

Far right:
HAMBURGE
DOUBLE BUR
CHEESEBUR
DOUBLE CHEE
CHILIBURG
DOUBLE CHI
PASTRAMI
JR. BURGE
TURKEY B

Fantastic
CHILI FRIES

(top): Kitchen at The Hat, Murrieta location, (bottom): Original location of The Hat, Alhambra, CA

HOT DOGS
BURGERS

Since 1951

Just GOOD FOOD

ACAPULCO
RESTAURANT Y CANTINA

CATERING

SPECIAL EVENTS
PATIO

MILLING

Acapulco y Los Arcos

NAME TODAY: Acapulco's Mexican Restaurant and Cantina

ORIGINAL LOCATION: 2936 E. Colorado Blvd. (Historic Rt. 66), Pasadena

OPENED: 1960

FOUNDER: Ray G. Marshall

CURRENT OWNERSHIP: Xperience Restaurant Group

CURRENTLY AT THE FIRST LOCATION: Office building

There are currently four locations in Southern California.

acapulcorestaurants.com

RAY MARSHALL WAS RAISED in an orphanage in Denver, Colorado. At a young age, he ran away and later found himself in Mexico. He loved life in Mexico; the flavors of the foods tantalized his taste buds. So, he came to Los Angeles and started working in the kitchen at the Biltmore Hotel as the night cook, his first job. He loved to cook, and started making some of the foods he'd tried in Mexico for his co-workers. Marshall also went to many small restaurants in the East Los Angeles area to taste the flavorful foods he recalled from Mexico.

In 1960, Marshall opened the restaurant Acapulco y Los Arcos, which sat on Route 66 (Colorado Blvd. in Pasadena). He slept in the kitchen on a blow-up mattress for the first year. He finally got a thriving business going, and it grew from there. Many had not tasted or even known what Mexican food was. Many thought beans with a lot of cheese and maybe a tortilla was Mexican food. People enjoy foods they are familiar with, ones they grew up eating from their family's kitchen table, but this new kind of food was irresistible.

Because of moving around Mexico in his early years, Marshall's flavor profiles include various northern Mexico regions, from the Nuevo Leon area, with menudo flavors from Sonoran, the pozole soup, and seafood of the Pacific coast area of the state of Jalisco.

Marshall became famous for the then-unheard-of innovation of crab enchiladas. At first, people thought cheese and shellfish seemed like an outrageous idea, but the enchiladas were a huge hit and a sign that Americans were ready for a bit of novelty in their Cali-Mex foods.

Traveling north, Marshall competed in the San Francisco Fisherman's Wharf seafood competition, winning a gold medal for his innovative dish. The *Los Angeles Times* highlighted the event and Marshall's recipe in a multi-page story. The cantina had never been so busy with diners wanting to taste the award-winning enchiladas. Marshall had two versions: Crab Enchiladas Verdes (Green

Opposite: Acapulco sign in Costa Mesa, (inset): Acapulco menu

Costa Mesa patio

Tomatillo Salsa) and Crab Enchiladas Rancheras (Red Tomato Pepper Salsa).

Ray started demonstrating cooking classes in the 1960s in his Pasadena location on less-busy days. He was instrumental in urging fellow California Chefs de Cuisine members to follow his lead in their establishments. This was near the beginning of the trend of the cooking classes that we see today. Marshall also gave back to the communities on specific days every month, where all proceeds were donated locally.

After winning the Fisherman's Wharf event, Marshall wanted nothing more than to compete to show America his style of Mexican food. However, in 1976, the United States Culinary Olympic Team rejected his request to join the team. The team did not feel that Mexican food represented the country; they didn't think a medal would be won with just beans and cheese. After being rejected, Marshall organized his team of himself and three northern California chefs, flying all of them on his dime to Germany. The four chefs worked 18 hours a day for five days of competition to create a display table of 17 classic elegant Mexican dishes. The best U.S. team tied for third place, while Marshall won a gold medal in the individual competition, proving that the U.S. chefs were incorrect when they re-jected him and told him Mexican cuisine was irrelevant. Marshall was a maverick, as he was not Mexican but an American born in Salamanca, New York. He had seen that the top U.S. chefs largely over-looked Mexican cuisine.

Working hard, Marshall opened a total of 38 locations. He was in the front of the house and the field, from demon-strating at the state and local Los Ange-les county fairs to teaching how to cook

Ownership

1960–1985:	Ray G. Marshall
1985–1998:	Restaurant Associates
1998–2018:	Compass Group:
	Bruckmann, Rosser, Sherrill & Co.
	A private equity firm
	Real Mex Restaurants
	Sun Capital Partner, Inc.
2018–Present:	Xperience Restaurant Group

Mexican foods at local schools. He would draw a big crowd as he presented his award-winning crab enchiladas.

In 1985, Marshall, at 72, sold his chain of restaurants to Restaurant Associates, who in turn shortened the name to Acapulco's. Restaurant Associates also streamlined many of the recipes and dishes. With the sale, Marshall created a trust for his wife, Gertrude, and their special-needs son, John. But Marshall was too young to retire fully. Instead, he consulted with other restaurants, maintained his collection of over 3,500 cookbooks, dabbled in investment, and judged food contests.

Most diners only know of salsa that you dip a tortilla chip in. Francesca Carbajal, Marshall's first chef, learned how to make fresh salsa from his mother from Guadalajara: salsa made with pumpkin seeds for chicken and fish dishes, nut salsa for rabbit and game. Like most home cooks, Francesca's mother did not write down recipes and instead cooked by sight and feel. Re-creating the salsas that he knew as a child took a while. When Restaurant Associates became the new owners of Acapulco's, Francesca's salsas were no longer served.

In later years, Marshall hosted many events at his Pasadena home. For example, in June 1985, Marshall hosted the Pasadena Art Workshop Fiesta Fantastica, a chance to view his cookbook collection, some dating back to the sixteenth century.

In 1992, Ray Marshall passed away, leaving a legacy of awards, recipes, and restaurants around the Southland.

Today, Xperience Restaurant Group is the parent owner of the four Acapulco restaurants. 🌮

(bottom): Costa Mesa location 2023, (top): Menu

House Specialties

Fresh, house-made tortillas

Camarones rancheros (Mexican shrimp stew)

Chile verde (pork with hot green chile)

Chilaquiles (eggs scrambled with onions, cheese, and tortillas)

Menudo (tripe soup)

A variety of fresh salsas made daily

Phoenix Inn Chinese Cuisine

ORIGINAL LOCATION: 301 Ord St., Los Angeles

OPENED: 1965

FOUNDERS: Kai Tai and May Chang

CURRENT OWNERSHIP: The Chang Family, third generation

CURRENTLY AT THE FIRST LOCATION: The first location is still in operation.

PRIOR AT THE FIRST LOCATION: Ramona Wine and Liquor Company

There are currently ten food boutiques, two bakeries, and one commissary.

phoenixfood.us

THE IMMIGRATION AND NATURALIZATION ACT OF 1965 (the Hart-Celler Act) abolished an earlier quota system based on national origin and established a new immigration policy designed to reunite immigrant families. Under the new legislation, many immigrants increasingly came from Asia. Looking for a better life and the American Dream, Kai Tai Chang and his bride, May Chang, emigrated from Hong Kong to Los Angeles with four of their five children (the eldest daughter stayed in Hong Kong and still resides there today) in the early 1960s.

Kai Tai did not waste time; the following day, he started looking for work. He knew there was an area close to Downtown LA filled with Chinese restaurants and shops. He came across the Phoenix Inn Chinese Cuisine on the corner of Ord and New High Street, finding work as a chef, as he had been an apprentice chef in Hong Kong. He knew the restaurant would be a busy place for employ-ment, as the establishment's second floor was a hotel, a popular spot for Asians coming to their new homeland, and they needed a place to eat.

Kai Tai worked hard to save money for several years so he could buy the Phoenix Inn business. It was not uncommon for him to work until three in the morning and return a few hours later. May Chang helped with the front-of-the-house operations and brought authentic Chinese dishes to the Phoenix Inn. They were a happy family, raising their children when they came to also

Opposite: Yau Gok (Chinese New Year fried dumplings)

Locations and Year Opened		
Classic Chinese Cuisine	1965:	Los Angeles
Southeast Asia Food	1997:	Alhambra
Phoenix Dessert	2002:	Alhambra
	2012:	San Gabriel
Phoenix Food Boutique	2003:	Arcadia
		South Pasadena
	2004:	Rowland Heights
	2006:	San Gabriel
	2008:	Rowland Heights
	2010:	City of Industry
		Monterey Park
	2015:	Garden Grove
Phoenix Kitchen	2014:	Temple City

(top): Founders Kai Tai and May Chang, (bottom): Phoenix Food Boutique Monterey Park location

Menu Items That Have Used the Same Recipe Since 1965
+ Phoenix Boneless Chicken
+ Chinese Sausage Sticky Fried Rice
+ Minced Pork and Thousand-Year Egg Congee (Rice Porridge)
+ Phoenix House Lobster
+ Steamed Hog Maw with Ginger and Scallion

assist at the restaurant.

Tom Chang, their son, started at USC for business and worked at the restaurant on the weekends. He met Elaina in school and fell in love. They married and worked the weekends together at the Phoenix Inn; they made a great team, just like his parents were.

With a love of Chinese pastry that no one had on the menu at any of the restaurants around town, Elaina started making the pastry for sale at the Phoenix.

As the years proceeded, the old Chinatown of Los Angeles got smaller and smaller and became more of a tourist area than a place where former immigrants from China lived. The Changs knew they needed to make a move. The migration started in the late 1990s from Downtown to Alhambra, less than ten miles away. Opening a second location closer to new Chinese immigrants was in order, and it opened in 1997 on Valley Boulevard to great acclaim. Having an authentic Chinese restaurant from downtown in their neighborhood was precisely what Alhambra needed. Elaina's pastry had become so popular at the two Phoenix Inns that the family knew the desserts could stand independently. Five years later, Phoenix Desserts opened next to the restaurant, specializing in traditional pastries made by Elaina.

Chang's started opening new restaurant concepts for the next four years. First was the Phoenix Food Boutique, marrying both the sit-down restaurant and the pastry concept. Adding additional cities and locations

Dessert Favorites
Kaya Durian Rolls
Mixed Fruit Delight
Mango and Grapefruit Panna Cotta
Mango Pomelo Sago and Silken Tofu
Hot Dessert Soup

(left): House Special Lobster, (center): Ord Street location, (right): Desert spread, (bottom): Kai Tai and May Chang at opening of Alhambra location

resulted in positive results for the company. Realizing they needed a central organizing structure, in 2008 the Changs built their company up-to-date test kitchens and an entire commissary with corporate offices.

Kai Tai passed away in 2015, and five years later May left the company and its growth in capable family hands. Although the foundation of the Phoenix Food Company is family first, its mission is to ensure that employees and customers are always treated like family through a commitment to quality food, exceptional service, and mutual respect.

Tom and Elaina's son Nick finished his undergrad at Cal Berkeley and worked a corporate job for five and a half years, then continued at Columbia for his MBA. He knew, though, that he wanted to work in the family business. Nick is the third generation of Changs working at the Phoenix Food Group.

> **Traditional Chinese New Year (CNY) Dishes That Symbolize Greater Happiness, Health, and Prosperity**
> Nian Gao (Sweet Rice Cake)
> Luo Bo Gao (Radish Cake)
> Yu Tou Gao (Taro Cake)
> Yau Gok (Chinese New Year Fried Dumplings)

To give back to the community, the family of Phoenix Food Group started Project Phoenix, creating hot meals for the front-line workers during the COVID pandemic. They served over 22,000 meals to the underserved in Chinatown and the San Gabriel area.

The company remembers the beginning traditions without forgetting where they came from. Nick will be the one to move the company in the next exciting direction. 🍵

SPIRES

Family Restaurant

Coffee Shop OPEN 24 HRS.

Family RESTAURANT

Spires Family Restaurant and Coffee Shop

SLOGAN: "Making Good Food Easy to Find Since 1965" ◆ "The Pinnacle of Eating"

NAME TODAY: Spires

ORIGINAL LOCATION: 990 S. Euclid (1673 W. Ball), Anaheim

OPENED: August 26, 1965

FOUNDER: John Alex Haretakis

ARCHITECT: Michael E. Gester and Associates

CURRENT OWNERSHIP: Cathie Haretakis

CURRENTLY AT THE FIRST LOCATION: El Gallo Giro Restaurant

There are currently seven locations, all franchised.

spiresrestaurants.com

JOHN ALEX HARETAKIS WAS BORN in the spring of 1929 on the island of Crete in Greece. Living through the Second World War, John, with his mother, boarded the Marine Carp ship for the trek across the Atlantic to Ellis Island for a better life in the United States in April 1947. John was seventeen years old. His father and five siblings had fled the year before. Soon after their arrival, the family left for the West Coast and landed in the Los Angeles area.

Without a formal education, John found work at the Hollywood Roosevelt hotel and then worked at a marshmallow factory. Los Angeles was filled with food-manufacturing facilities with plenty of jobs for the onslaught of immigrants and military personnel coming home from the war. John found his love for the food industry with the hotel and confectionary jobs he held for the next ten years.

In the late 1950s, John's brother-in-law, Pericles (Perry) Korkos, an immigrant from Greece, and John formed a partnership; they opened two Jodys' Coffee Shops, which had a midcentury-looking design, one in Torrance and the second in Redondo Beach. This is where John honed his skills and learned what customers wanted and ate. The coffee shop was open 24 hours a day with daily dinner specials. Despite the name, it was more than a coffee shop or diner; it was a restaurant with good-quality menu items for the middle-income family.

In July 1962, John managed the new Silver Skates Restaurant overlooking the Olympic Skating Rink. The restaurant was a full-service dining, comfort-food location filled with hungry skaters and hockey players.

John's desire for the American Dream of owning a restaurant and building a future for his family grew. So he mortgaged his home, and his suppliers gave him a credit line to start his Spires restaurant.

Opposite: 1970's menu cover

Locations	
1971:	Carson
1971:	Long Beach
1976:	Torrance (2 locations)
1978:	Tustin
1982:	Lawndale
1983:	Ontario

(left): 1970's menu cover with locations, (right): Matchbook cover

John wanted an octagonal building on a street corner so passers-by could see it from all directions. He worked with architecture firm Michael E. Gester and Associates from Orange County to design the distinctive red-tile roof and brown wood sidings, which sits on the corner lot so you can see it from all angles. Inside, the central core is the kitchen, displaying the chefs while they work, with the public space divided into two areas: a coffee shop lunch counter and family dining booths. The colorful décor with large windows throughout make the waiting area very inviting, with memorabilia scattered on the walls. Spires's first location was less than two miles from Disneyland, outside the entertainment area, but close enough for a family to catch a meal before or after a day at the park. John opened his first location in August 1965, only ten years after the theme park's opening.

John's business strategy was to put restaurants in middle-income communities where he knew moderately priced menu items would generate high-volume sales. Spires didn't have just one daily special, but eleven. John created "The Complete Meal Format." Every meal came with soup and salad, a protein, vegetable, starch, roll and butter, and a choice of three desserts: pudding, ice cream, or Jell-O®. In 1982, for cost-cutting reasons, John decreased the portion sizes and the cost of the meals. This prevented waste from the diners.

Keeping open 24 hours a day, Spires would be filled with businesspeople at lunch, families at

(top): Ontario location, (bottom): 2020's menu cover

dinner, and factory and aerospace workers in the early morning.

Many advised John not to open a location in Norwalk, as it had a reputation as a "poor" town. But John believed the blue-collar worker was the backbone of America. Norwalk turned out to be one of his most profitable locations. In addition, John knew that medium-income families were his customers. Therefore, the menu was all-American: chicken, burgers, pancakes, and waffles.

Giving back to the communities that Spires was a part of was essential to John. In 1988, Spires teamed up with the Pediatric-Adolescent Diabetes Research and Educating Foundation (PADRE). The 1,200 employees, from the waitstaff to the kitchen cooks, all bought one-dollar raffle tickets. In addition, two cars, trips to Hawaii and Mexico, and gift cards for meals at Spires were donated. John was also the president of St. John the Baptist Greek Orthodox Church in Anaheim and its annual fall Greek fair.

July 9, 2017, was a sad day for Spires and the Haretakis family as John Alex passed away peacefully at his home. For years, he had always been asked when he would retire, and he would answer "When I die." Before his passing, John started franchising the last restaurants that were still company-owned. The locations were franchised to long-term employees, such as the managers or key employees; someone who had never worked at Spires couldn't buy a franchise. This was John's way of helping others and giving them a chance, just like he had been given when he first came to America.

Spires is still going strong with a complete meal offering for each customer. Cathie Haretakis is the current CEO and owner of the chain. ✕

CARROWS®
RESTAURANTS

CINNAMON ROLL
FRENCH TOAST

California's Classic Kitchen

Carrows Hickory Chip Restaurant

SLOGAN: "Carrows Cares"

NAME TODAY: Carrows Restaurants, Inc.

ORIGINAL LOCATION: 3180 El Camino Real, Santa Clara

OPENED: 1970

FOUNDER: David G. Nancarrow

CURRENT OWNERSHIP: Shari's Management Corporation

CURRENTLY AT THE FIRST LOCATION: Restaurant Chungdam Korea BBQ

The chain merged into Coco's Restaurants in 2023.

carrows.com

DAVID NANCARROW OPENED his first Carrows Hickory Chip Restaurant along the El Camino Real, a 600-mile commemorative route connecting the 21 Spanish missions in California. A 24-hour operation of BBQ dishes and the "Great Western Breakfast," Carrows is known around the area as one of the largest and best breakfast bargains.

David did not stop with just one; the following year, he had a restaurant built from the ground up, a free-standing structure that would be the hallmark of his locations in Goleta, north of Santa Barbara. The approximately 4,400-square-foot building had enough room for 140 diners and a smaller private room for private meetings and clubs to gather. Warm fall colors, deep and sunset orange, were the color scheme; the paneling, tables, and counters were heavy dark and tan woods.

Carrows became a full-service, West Coast family restaurant chain specializing in traditional American meals and a variety of specialty items, many of which were inspired by Carrows's Santa Barbara heritage. Though the company started in Santa Clara, David called Santa Barbara the home of Carrows. Generous portions, good value, and friendly, attentive service in a comfortable atmosphere give Carrows a unique appeal.

The Carrows menu was always current but not trendy. It featured signature recipes reminiscent of Santa Barbara, such as its Southwest Crispy Rolls, Beef Stew in a Bread Bowl, Southwest Chicken Salad, Mile High Sandwiches with sliced meats stacked, and Shrimp Scampi Pasta. From

Ownership

1970: David G. Nancarrow
1985: W.R. Grace & Co.
1987: Restaurant Enterprises Group (REG) Inc.
1994: Family Restaurants Inc. (FRI)
1996: Advantica Restaurant Group
2002: Catalina Restaurant Group
2006: Zensho Co., Ltd.
2015: Food Management Partners
2018: Shari's Café & Pies

Opposite: 2020's menu of Carrows

The last Carrows location in Cerritos, CA closed in 2023

hearty breakfasts, such as Grandma's Cinnamon Loaf French Toast and the Mega Skillet, to lunches and dinners that rival the quality and flavor of those found at casual dinner houses, Carrows offered great-tasting food in generous portions. In addition, specialty menus were provided for seniors, kids, the gluten-intolerant, and those preferring lighter fare.

In 1985, with just shy of a hundred locations, David Nancarrow sold Carrows to W.R. Grace & Company, which had a restaurant division that included many chains from the West and East, such as Jojo's, Taco Villa, El Torito, Charley Brown's, Bristol Bar and Grill, Coco's, and Houlihan's Old Place.

Two years later, an executive management team from W.R. Grace created a new company called Restaurant Enterprises Group Inc. (REG). They purchased Carrows from the parent company and expanded their locations and menu items. They hired a corporate chef, Heather Gardea, in 1991, who introduced innovative new menu items for the chain in keeping with the fresh California flavor.

REG acquired 160 former Bob's Big Boy locations and converted 60 into Carrows, with the rest converted to other concepts that REG had in their portfolio. It took about two years, from 1992 to 1994, for the conversions to occur.

Succeeding the conversions, REG sold Carrows to Family Restaurants Inc. (FRI), including other chains: Coco's, Jojo's, El Torito, and the Casa Gallardo chains. Finally, in May 1996, both Carrows and Coco's, with over 300 locations, were purchased by Advantica Restaurant Group. The brands were very similar since Coco's also started in a Southern California beach town (Corona Del Mar); they became known as "sister" brands.

In July 1998, Carrows introduced a new menu featuring a wide assortment of Santa Barbara-inspired creations. In addition, the menu featured cover art by local Santa Barbara artist Jennie Oppenheimer.

Unit Numbers	
1970:	1
1971:	2
1972:	8
1973:	18
1974:	28 (first outside of Califonia, in Arizona and Nevada)
1975:	36
1977:	50 (first Kansas location)
1978:	64
1984:	89 (seven Western states)
1985:	98
1992:	100+
1994:	160
2000:	141
2021:	3
2023:	0

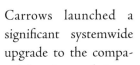

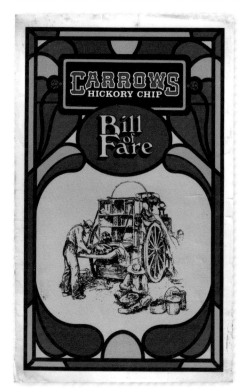

(left): Original Carrows Hickory Chip Restaurant menu from Santa Clara, CA, (right): Cinnamon French Toast Breakfast, (bottom left): Western Burger, (bottom right): Fresh Peach Pie

Carrows launched a significant systemwide upgrade to the company's interiors and signage the following year.

Chef Heather Gardea's creations earned many awards for the company. For example, the signature Mile High Pot Roast Melt sandwich was selected by the editors of *Restaurant Business News* as the standout winner in the Menus 2000 "Best in Class Award." It was also mentioned as a "clever reinvention of an American classic."

In 2000, Carrows started a community-based caring program, supporting local schools and youth organizations. They also reintroduced themselves to local communities by offering an unparalleled service guarantee: "Best service in town or your meal is free." This three-day promotion featured company executives interacting with guests one-on-one as they provided over-the-top service. The promotion took place every weekend at a different Carrows location nationwide. Each individual restaurant worked with the local schools and non-profit organizations through fundraiser days and pie donations.

On June 14, 1991, David Nancarrow passed away in his beloved Santa Barbara. After selling Carrows, David had opened two other restaurant concepts, Jeremiah's Steak House (with a dozen locations), a mid-range steak-house concept from Santa Barbara to Palm Springs, and the Elephant Bar chain.

For over 20 years, the "sister" brands Coco's and Carrows have been merged, purchased, sold, and bought by several restaurant groups. In spring of 2023 the last Carrows in Cerritos, California closed its doors. 🍰

Naugles

SLOGAN: "Prepare food fresh. Serve customers fast. Keep the place clean!"

ORIGINAL LOCATION: 4407 Brockton Ave., Riverside

OPENED: 1970

FOUNDER: Richard M. (Dick) Naugle

CURRENTLY AT THE FIRST LOCATION: Del Taco

Naugles merged into the Del Taco brand in 1988. There are three Naugles operating in name only in Southern California.

nauglestacos.com

RICHARD (DICK) NAUGLE WAS BORN in Kansas and has had the entrepreneur bug since he was seven. During the summer months, he set up a Coca-Cola stand in the city courthouse yard, which expanded to ice cream the following year. He rented a milk truck and converted it into a horse-drawn ice cream truck.

Fourth grade was the last year of formal education for Dick, as he was bored with schooling. For several years, the Naugle family moved around the Western states, and Dick worked in many facets of food service. In the late 1950s, Dick was promoted to manager of the Food Services Facilities in eleven Western states for the Army and Air Force Exchange Service. After working in Europe for the AAEFS, he was tired of traveling, which also put heavy stress and a burden on his family life. He returned home to Riverside.

Once home, Dick started designing restaurants and selling equipment for the immense expansion of post-war neighborhoods and cities. Dick converted the Del Panther (sister restaurant to Del Taco) in Corona, the first fast-food drive-thru restaurant operation in Southern California. You could drive through and pick up food; the team moved three cars a minute. In 1964, Dick opened the first Del Taco drive-thru in Corona. He also developed and designed the warehouse for Red-E-Foods, Inc., the supplier for Del Taco. While at Del Taco, Dick created "Family Night" on Wednesday nights; the other executives renamed it to "Taco Night." Dick had wanted the focus on family, not tacos, but the new name stuck. In 1970, Dick left Del Taco and opened the first Naugles in Riverside, on the corner of Brockton and 14th Streets.

Dick's drive-thru was, in a word, "speedy," like the McDonald brothers in nearby San Bernardino, with fast service. Unlike today when you drive through and order a meal, the employee would streamline the speaker-and-ordering process with a brisk "Order please"—no long conversations, like "How is your day?" or "Is there anything else?" The words "Thank you" come when change is given and the food passes to you. Dick was not the first to use the speaker system (this honor is held by In-N-Out

Opposite: Naugles Stanton, CA location, (top): 1980's Stanton arcade token

1980's Naugles menu from El Centro, CA

Burger in Baldwin Park), but he was the first to use it to increase the speed of the ordering process for the customer.

Dick knew that his menu was not authentic Mexican food but more like Spanish cuisine. So, he decided to go with a twin-kitchen concept of American foods (hamburgers and French fries) and the Spanish kitchen (tacos, burritos). He also started family night at Naugles.

Naugles was known for the freshness of the ingredients and the large portions. The word "macho" in food gave the impression of massive, large, and robust—plus, it was a Spanish word. Dick started calling larger food servings "macho": Macho Cheese Burrito, Macho Taco, and other macho things. Taco Bell began using the word "monster" in the same way Naugles used "macho."

The buildings of Naugles needed to be larger than other fast-food locations, as they required space for both a drive-thru and a dining room; the buildings were about 2,400 square feet in size. Dick always had children's and breakfast menus for the early risers and hearty meals for the late diners.

Ownership

1970: Dick Naugle
1979: Harold Butler
1984: Collins Foods International
1988: Anwar Soliman of AWR II Acquisition Corp.
1990: Wayne W. Armstrong
1995: Converted to Del Taco locations.

In 1979, with three successful locations, Dick sold his small chain to Harold Butler, the co-founder of the Denny's restaurant chain. Expanding the Naugles chain, spending more on the décor of the dining rooms and the food quality than other fast-food restaurants, Harold knew his chain would prosper. So, in 1981, Harold offered a public sale of 1.1 million shares of stock to help with debt and expansions. With over 275 restaurants in nine states, Harold sold the chain to Collins Food International; today, Collins Foods operates Sizzler, Taco Bell, and Kentucky Fried Chicken locations in Europe and Australia. At one point in the mid-1960s, Collins Foods owned the Sizzler brands and over two hundred Kentucky Fried Chicken locations.

In 1988, Anwar Soliman purchased two Mexican food chains, Naugles and Del Taco, to merge them into one, creating a powerhouse of Mexican fast-food locations to compete with Taco Bell. Anwar felt the quality of the food and menu of both Naugles and Del Taco would rival McDonald's and outshine Taco Bell.

Anwar only held onto the two for a few years, converting many of the Naugles into Del Taco locations. Although Anwar increased the menu's pricing, decreased the items' size, and cut the sites that were open 24 hours, new owner Wayne Armstrong extended the hours back to 24 hours and cut prices.

(top): Merchandise for sale—trucker cap, insulated coffee thermos and coffee cup, (bottom): 2023 menu board

In 1995, the Carson City, Nevada, Naugles was the last location to be converted to a Del Taco location. As a result, the Naugles brand and trademark were not renewed.

In 2015, blogger Christian Ziebarth and two friends won a judgment from the Trademark Trial and Appeal Board. They acquired the trademark from Del Taco that had expired and opened a pop-up Naugles "test" kitchen in Fountain Valley, California. The three opened on Saturday, July 25, 2015, and were overwhelmed by fans hearing of Naugles on social media. Running out of food and ingredients, the three focused on only weekend hours. Today, there are three Naugles open in Orange County. The menu is like the old brand; the old recipes are still Naugle family secrets, so the new Naugles only have the name in common. The menu offered now is entirely different. 🌮

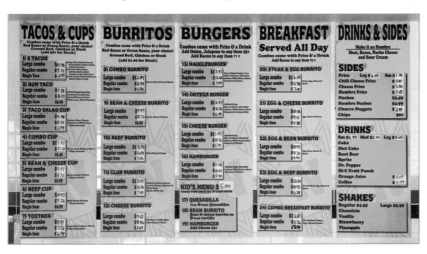

Togo's Submarines

SLOGANS: "Fast Service Not Fast Food" (1978) • "True to the Sandwich" (2018)
"How Far Would You Go for a Togo's" (2018)

NAME TODAY: Togo's

ORIGINAL LOCATION: 336 E. William St., San Jose

OPENED: July 1971

FOUNDER: Michael (Mike) Timothy Cobler

CURRENT OWNERSHIP: Southfield Mezzanine Capital

CURRENTLY AT THE FIRST LOCATION: California Burrito

Today, there are currently 159 locations in five states. All but five are franchised, and thirty are still co-branded with Baskin-Robbins Ice Cream.

togos.com

IN JULY 1971, MIKE CO-BLER, a student, purchased a small submarine sandwich business named Togo's Submarines across the street from San Jose State University for $19,000 ($140,000 in 2023 dollars) from the owner, who resided in Oregon. Mike operated the little

Ownership

1971–2007:	Mike Cobler (as Franchisor)
1971–2015:	Mike Cobler (as Franchisee)
1997–2007:	Allied Domecq Quick Service Restaurants
2007–2015:	Mainsail Partners with Tony Gioia
2015–2019:	(David Nazarian) Nimes Capital
2019–Present:	Southfield Mezzanine Capital

building that was only big enough for three employees as "Submarines to Go," specializing in big, meaty sandwiches that were affordable and fulfilling for the nearby college students. One day when returning to the small building, he noticed that the word "Submarines" had fallen from the neon sign. It was too costly to replace, so Mike kept what was left of his sign and started calling the business Togo's.

In the first two years, thirteen different sandwiches were introduced, including the "gourmet" fruit avocado on turkey, which had not been popularized on sandwiches yet. On the menu board, the new sandwiches were all numbered sequentially as they were introduced.

Then, on January 17, 1974, Mike opened his second location to great fanfare in Campbell. He named it "Togo's Eatery." Mike expanded the menu, added locations, and transformed the business. A few years later, he became a full-fledged franchisor and opened MTC Management Inc. He also offered a fully equipped store franchise for $40,000 ($291,000 in 2023).

In 1977, Mike found bakeries that would supply fresh bread to his locations seven days a week. This was important, to have the freshest ingredients and products available to his sites.

When you have a great concept, you get copycats. In nearby Santa Cruz County, Gary Tucci opened up Tucci's Sandwiches, copying Togo's menus and décor and attempting to duplicate the

Opposite: 1983 *Corvallis Gazette Times* ad, (top): 2020's Togo's logo

Sandwiches Introduced by Decade

THE 1970s
SANDWICHES:
+ Avocado & Cheese
+ BBQ Beef
+ Capicola
+ Ham, Turkey, Salami & Cheese
+ Pastrami
+ Roast Beef
+ Salami & Cheese
+ Tuna
+ Turkey & Avocado
+ Turkey, Salami & Cheese

THE 1980s
SANDWICHES:
+ Roast Beef & Avocado

THE 1990s
SANDWICHES:
+ Turkey & Cranberry

THE 2000s
SANDWICHES:
+ Calzone
+ BBQ Chicken Ranch
+ Steak & Mushroom
SAUCES:
+ Honey Dijon
+ Herb Mayo
BREAD:
+ Dutch Crunch
+ Onion Herb
+ Rustic White
WRAPS:
+ Wheat
+ Spinach
+ Tomato

THE 2010s
SANDWICHES:
+ Hot Pretzel Sandwich
+ Turkey Bistro
+ Pretzelrami
+ Chicken Dijon
+ Brewpub Chicken
+ BBQ Chipotle Chicken
+ Buffalo Chicken

THE 2020s
SANDWICHES:
+ Cheese Steaks
+ Cheese Steak Melt
+ Chicken Cheese Steak Melt
+ Pastrami Cheese Steak
+ Caprese Sandwiches
+ Caprese Chicken
+ Caprese Italian
+ Caprese Veggie

(top): South Corona location signage,
(bottom): First location, San Jose, CA

unique recipes and sandwich ingredients. Mike Cobler sued Tucci for damages, and a restraining order was issued. Less than a year later, Tucci sold off the deli, and the new owner turned it into a mini-market.

With three sandwich sizes and a made-to-order six-foot sandwich, Togo's sandwiches fit the bill for all consumers. The sandwiches came with shredded lettuce, sliced beefsteak tomatoes, dill pickle chips, onions, peppers, creamy mayonnaise, olive oil, and protein in small six-inch size and large sizes: 16 inches, family size 36 inches, and party size, which was the six-foot sandwich mentioned above.

On August 4, 1997, Mike sold Togo's to Allied Domecq to form combo locations with Dunkin' Donuts and Baskin-Robbins Ice Cream stores. Allied felt that combining the three brands into one place would enhance the sales of all three brands: Dunkin' Donuts for the morning rush, Togo's for lunch, midday, and dinner traffic, with Baskin-Robbins for dessert.

During the first years of the new century, Togo's added other sandwiches with various sauces and bread to choose from. The sauces lasted only a couple of years, but some of the bread can still be ordered. In 2009, mini sandwiches were offered for the light eater or someone who wanted to pair them with soup. The Daily Deal sandwich began, as did the offering of gift cards. The #71 (Pretzelrami) was assigned the number of the year the company had been founded, since it was a new signature sandwich.

Mike Cobler did not use the new social-media platforms for advertising or TV/radio commercials, as he felt word of mouth was the best form of advertising. In 2011, Togo's fortieth anniversary brought a fresh new look to the brand, from new uniforms for the team members to new bright packaging with a new logo and store remodels.

On September 2, 2014, Mike Cobler sold all his remaining franchised stores to the parent company, making them all company-owned locations. The following year, the company was sold to Nimes Capital. Many changes to the Togo brand came into play. Coca-Cola became the exclusive drink brand with their new Freestyle machines, which could dispense over 160 different beverages. All proteins in the regular-size sandwiches were increased to four ounces. The brand received a complete overhaul from the stores to increase speed of service.

Over the years, the Togo's brand has included three store models: a stand-alone individual location, a co-branded location with Baskin-Robbins (Togo's and BR), and the newest non-traditional small site for a gas station or rest stop. In 2018, the 3.0 store design was launched to streamline customers' ordering process and to provide welcoming dining areas.

The most recent acquisition of Togo's was in March 2019 by Southfield Mezzanine Capital; precisely one year later, the international pandemic closed all the locations nationwide. Unlike many other fast-food chains, Togo's did not have a drive-thru. Each site increased or added delivery and curbside pick-up options. Offering complete family meals and value offers skyrocketed their sales and helped their communities. 2021 was for celebration: customers could once again visit inside the locations to have their custom sandwich made by a team member; and store openings in Las Vegas and Reno, Nevada, were just in time for the company's fiftieth anniversary.

Working and thinking outside the box, in 2022, a new Togo concept was introduced in Winter, California, as the first Togo's inside a Chevron gas station. This will be the first of many smaller convenient locations. The build-out is smaller, less costly, and very profitable for those stopping for fuel.

The "True to the Sandwich" brand promise has been in effect from Day 1, from the founder to today's current owner; Togo's products are made with high-quality ingredients, locally baked artisan breads, hand-mashed California Hass avocados, and the highest quality meats and cheeses. ❧

National Sandwich Restaurants

Year	Restaurant	Location
1956	Jersey Mike's	Pt. Pleasant, NJ
1964	Blimpie	Hoboken, NJ
1965	Subway	Bridgeport, CT
1971	Schlotzsky's	Austin, TX
1971	Togo's	San Jose, CA
1977	Potbelly	Chicago, IL
1981	Quiznos	Denver, CO
1983	Jimmy John's	Charleston, IL
1983	Lee's Sandwiches	San Jose, CA
1985	Penn Station	Cincinnati, OH
1987	Erbert & Gerbert's	Eau Claire, WI
1989	Milio's Sandwiches	Madison, WI
1994	Firehouse Subs	Jacksonville, FL
2004	Earl of Sandwich	Orlando, FL

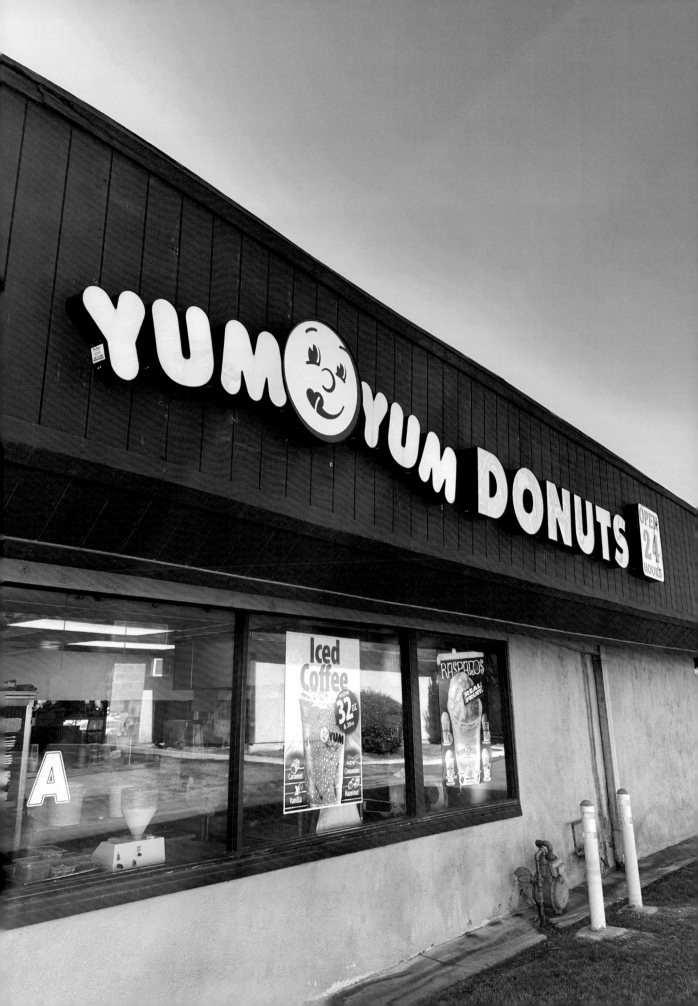

Yum Yum Donut Shops Inc.

ORIGINAL LOCATION: 2633 (2619) N. Figueroa St., Los Angeles

OPENED: April 27, 1971

FOUNDER: Philip C. Holland

CURRENT OWNERSHIP: A subsidiary of Yum-Yum Donuts, Inc.

CURRENTLY AT THE FIRST LOCATION: The first location is still in operation.

There are currently ninety-three locations in California.

yumyumdonuts.com

IN THE SOUTH CYPRESS PARK area of Los Angeles in 1971, Philip C. Holland opened Yum Yum Donuts in what was formerly an Orange Julius location. Prior to the opening, Philip knew he needed to learn the ins and outs of donut manufacturing and the business. He traveled to Winston-Salem, South Carolina, and called on Vernon Rudolph, the founder of Krispy Kreme Donuts, for help. At the time, Winchell's Donuts was the leading donut shop chain in the West. As a result, Yum Yum modeled themselves after Winchell's regarding the stores' product offerings, size, and layout.

Before opening the first shop, Philip Holland remembered an establishment he saw on his daily commute to Grand Central Station in New York City named the Yum Yum Coffee Shop. He felt it was a happy, easy-to-remember name. So he named his new donut shop Yum Yum. The logo of the licking lips and smile was created with the help of a local sign company.

After opening three locations in two years, Holland found that he needed to bring in an equal partner. Frank Watase fit the bill and started opening stores with Holland quickly. Within two years, by 1975, 15 other shops had opened. With the number of stores growing in such a short time, Watase and Holland started looking for a warehouse to manu-facture and distribute the stores' products. They quickly leased a 10,000-square-foot warehouse.

After only six short years, in 1981,

> ### Yum Yum Donuts Mission Statement
> + To use only the freshest ingredients
> + To make each Yum-Yum with tender loving care and art
> + To satisfy the discriminating taste of those who demand the best
> + To bring smiles and satisfaction as you enjoy your tasty Yum Yum donuts.

Opposite: Norco, CA location, (top): Donut bag.

Concept drawing of Yum Yum

Yum Yum's distribution center had outgrown its walls. Phil and Frank decided to buy a building this time. The facility was four times the size of their first building. They moved all manufacturing and distribution operations to this space in the City of Industry.

The California Exposition and State Fair in Sacramento awarded Yum Yum Donuts excellence in products for their donuts. In 1988, Yum Yum introduced "cholesterol free" donuts—a first in the industry—and was awarded a gold medal.

Time Line of Store Openings

1971: First store open
1973: Three stores open
1975: 15 stores open
1989: 80 stores open
2004: 71 stores open
2019: Total 191 stores open
(Winchell's and Yum Yum total)
2022: Total 263 stores open
(Winchell's and Yum Yum total)

Norco, CA location

After 18 years, in 1989, Holland retired and sold his interest in Yum Yum to Watase. Watase's son Lincoln joined the company as vice president.

In 1991, Yum Yum spun off the remanufacturing division into a separate company called Quality Natural Foods, Inc. (QNF) and in 1999 moved into a large distribution center. QNF manufactures bakery mixes, jellies, bagels, croissants, hot cocoa, and other products for Winchell's and Yum Yum locations. Most of the manufacturing is in the private packaging for external customers.

On June 3, 1992, Yum Yum opened its first franchised store in Baldwin Park. After four years with Yum Yum Donuts, Lincoln Watase was promoted to president of Yum Yum Donut Shops, Inc. Today, after 40 years with Yum Yum Donut Shops, Lincoln is still the president. Frank passed away in 2020 at the age of 96.

In 1998, Yum Yum added bagels and bagel sandwiches to their menus by purchasing the small East Coast Bagel chain of eight bagel shops in Orange County, California. With the purchase, a frozen bagel plant was included.

With so many shops needing a facelift, Yum Yum started remodeling interiors with new seating, tile, signage, showcases, and a coffee bar in 2001, resulting in higher sales per store.

Yum Yum's sold off the bagel shops and plant after only five years to focus on the purchase of Winchell's in October 2004, creating the West Coast's largest donut chain with over 196 locations in six Western states, Guam, and Saipan. Today there is minimal co-branding inside the stores. ❀

Oldest Locations Still in Operation

1971: 2633 (2619) N. Figueroa
1987: 1834 Marengo Street
       724 N. Highland Ave.
       1608 Hoover Ave.
       1976 La Cienega Blvd.
       3351 Whittier Blvd.
       5921 Atlantic Blvd.

Don José Mexican Restaurant

NAME TODAY: Rodrigo's Mexican Grill (2017)

ORIGINAL LOCATION: 1230 E. Katella, Orange

OPENED: July 17, 1972

FOUNDERS: Roderick (Rod) and Patricia Showalter Fraser

CURRENT OWNERSHIP: Rod Fraser Enterprises

CURRENTLY AT THE FIRST LOCATION: The first location is still in operation.

Ten locations are currently open.

rodrigos.com

RODERICK FRASER, A WORLD WAR II veteran pilot from Oregon, met Patricia Showalter from Orange, California, at a USO dance. They married in 1944. After his service, the couple resided in Orange, which had a downtown square surrounded by orange orchards. Looking for a business to thrive in, Rod decided on a liquor store just off the town traffic circle that had been a tire shop and then a gas station. Rod opened 23 Rod's Liquor stores over several years around the Southland.

Rod and Patricia expanded into restaurants by opening one of the first Marie Callender's in Los Angeles on Pico and La Cienega in 1972; six years later, they opened other Callenders in Houston, Texas. In addition, Rod and Patricia expanded their portfolio by partnering with Don Callender, the owner of Callenders with restaurants in Garden Grove, El Toro, and Rancho Mirage.

With the restaurant business knowledge and their oldest son Rick, Rod and Patricia signed a licensing agreement with Don José Restaurants. The Adams Street Huntington Beach Don José was doing a great business. The Frasers opened their first Don José Restaurant on Katella Boulevard in Orange on July 17, 1972. Many customers mistakenly thought the same company owned them. The opening celebration was exciting; the food was simple, fresh, and authentic, created by their chefs from Jalisco, Mexico. They used their recipes to create the fresh taste they wanted their customers to enjoy and to bring them back for more.

Over time, locations opened one after another. Rick recollects that at one point, they were opening two Don José locations in the same week: Torrance and Riverside. He thought Riverside would be a relaxed, friendly, and calm opening, with Torrance probably hectic. Instead, Riverside was not so easy and Torrance opened quietly. You never know how restaurant openings will go. After 23

Opposite (top left): Hostess Ladan Razavi ready to seat you at your table, **(top right):** Chalupa Plate, Carnitas Plate, Churros, **(bottom):** Orange, CA location, **(left):** Roderick (Rod) Frazer, **(right):** Patricia Showalter Frazer

openings of Rod's Liquor stores, five Marie Callender's, and 21 Mexican Restaurants, the Frasers know how to open multi-unit establishments.

Every Fraser child and grandchild starts working in the family restaurants practically when they begin to walk, from busing dishes to hosting to waitstaff. This teaches them responsibility and hard work at a young age. Today the company is comprised mostly of family or those married to a Fraser. The longest-serving employee is Linda Fraser, the design supervisor; she started as a hostess in 1972, two years later marrying Rick. Today, they refer to her as the CEO: Chief Emotional Officer. During any holiday, Linda's décor can be seen at each restaurant. Many families call in the fall asking when the Christmas tree will be up so they can take their annual holiday picture with their family. Today, the family gathers for events at Rick and Linda's home.

> **Top Dishes**
> + Combo Plate (Two Entrees, Rice and Beans)
> + Street Tacos
> + Chimichangas (mini crispy burritos, chicken or chile)
> + Fajitas

> **Top Drinks**
> + Margaritas (over a dozen varieties)
> + Skinny Margaritas

Over the years, the Frasers had seven children, and today there are 25 cousins in the third generation, many of whom work in the family business. Still, it is difficult to walk into one of the restaurants and tell if the team members are blood relatives or not; everyone is treated like a family member.

Because of the longevity of the company and the generations of workers, Don José has been the scene for family celebrations, from wedding parties to graduations to birthday parties. The Frasers ensure that everyone who comes through their doors becomes family.

The first seven locations were built and decorated with dark woods and features, a look that was popular in that day. The eighth location went a little more modern with skylights and large windows. After the positive reaction to the new look, the older restaurants were remodeled to reflect the bright sunny look and feel.

The mid-1970s brought a new era in dining and evening entertainment. When disco was popularized with the movie *Saturday Night Fever*, Don José did not sit back and watch other restaurants in the area add a dance floor and DJ. Instead, many locations were outfitted with the new disco look in the bar area. Don José discos were popular with area groups such as the Wheel of Friendship (45+) and the 49 and Holding social groups. This lasted about five years before they were turned back into dining space.

> **Corporate Structure and Fraser Family Involved**
> Founders: Roderick (Rod) Fraser and Patricia Showalter Fraser
> CEO: Roderick (Rick) Fraser II
> COO: Roderick (Rod) Fraser III
> VP Marketing: Suzanne Fraser Fish
> Marketing team: Matthew Fraser Coulter, Melinda Fraser Magana, Suzannah Fraser Bohning
> Restaurant Manager: Patrick Fraser
> Corporate Executive Chef: Allan Aguinaga

Award-winning Sizzling Fajitas still float throughout the dining rooms, tantalizing all your senses. First you hear the sizzle, then you see the steam drift off the platter being delivered to the patron, smelling the aroma. If you place an order for them, you get to taste the beautiful meats and vegetables grilled to perfection. Of course, all the food is fresh, from the tableside guacamole to the salsas made garden-fresh.

Tragedy hit the Fraser family on September 11, 1981; flying back from Las Vegas, Ron Fraser and his son-in-law Suheil Salloum were killed when their twin-engine Cessna crashed into the Swing Auditorium on the National Orange Show Grounds in San Bernardino. Salloum was the husband of Ron and Patricia's daughter Suzanne, a student at Cal State Fullerton, and worked as a bartender at Don José.

After the tragedy, Rick became the president of Ron Fraser Enterprises and took over most of the day-to-day operations. At the same time, the matriarch, Patricia, continued as vice president and was involved with all decisions and staffing.

In 1985, Rick tested a name change to Ricardo's from Don José, but nobody seemed to notice the trial name. Still, the name could not be trademarked because it was so common, so they stayed with Don José until 2017. Then they embarked on a complete company rebranding with a name change to Rodrigo's—a name that could be trademarked and a fitting name for the founder Ron. Even with a new name and new signage, the food is the same and the chain is still run by the same family; only the name has changed.

In summer 2020, Rodrigo's, like so many restaurants, utilized outdoor spaces for dining at safe distances during the global pandemic. The following spring, the company introduced Allan Aguinaga as the corporate executive chef. Aguinaga was born and raised in Orange County and worked in various restaurants. Today he oversees the chefs at each location, menu development, product control, and the creation of seasonal menus for all sites.

You will find your favorites, from traditional dishes to street tacos and dozens of premium tequilas and wines. But, of course, margaritas have been and always will be the drink of choice for south-of-the-border meals. Rodrigo's has an array of tequilas and flavors to make up a margarita for everyone's taste. 🌮

Primary Shareholders of the Seven Siblings (Birth Order)

Roderick Anthony Fraser II
Cheryl Ann Fraser Coulter
Suzanne Fraser Fish
Brent Ronald Fraser
Brian Paul Fraser*
Kathleen Carol Fraser
Lisa Lorraine Fraser
Deceased

Restaurants Owned

MARIE CALLENDER'S:
1969: Los Angeles (Pico & La Cienega)
1973: Garden Grove (Brookhurst)
1975: Houston, TX
1975: El Toro
1980: Rancho Mirage

DON JOSÉ (1972–1992)
Don José Orange
Don José Laguna Hills
Don José Tustin
Don José Huntington Beach
Don José Fullerton*
Don José Anaheim*
Don José La Mirada*
Don José Artesia*
Don José Northridge on Corbin*
Don José Northridge on Balboa*
Don José Las Vegas*
Don José Montclair
Don José Azusa*
Don José Torrance*
Don José Riverside
Don José Anaheim Hills
Don José Moreno Valley Rodrigo's
Rodrigo's Corona
Rodrigo's Temecula
Closed

Hamburger Mary's Organic Grille

SLOGAN: "Eat, Drink and Be Mary" ✦ "Open-air Bar and Grille for Open-minded People"
NAME TODAY: Hamburger Mary's Bar and Grille
ORIGINAL LOCATION: 1582 Folsom St., San Francisco
OPENED: April 1972
FOUNDERS: Jerald "Trixie" Jones, "Heavenly" Heidi Steffan, Jan Hill, Tom Mulvey
TNT (Trixie and Tooloose) Food and Beverage Corporation
CURRENT OWNERSHIP: Ashley and Brandon Wright
CURRENTLY AT THE FIRST LOCATION: The Willows Gastropub—they serve a "Mary" burger out of respect.

There are currently fourteen locations in eight states.

hamburgermarys.com

IN THE EARLY YEARS OF THE 1970s, San Francisco became a melting pot for the outcasts and the socially marginalized of the nation; they were attracted by a greater tolerance and acceptance of diverse cultures in the city. As a result, it grew as one of the world's largest accepting cities for the lesbian, gay, bisexual, and transgender communities. In 1972, Jerald and Heidi Jones opened Hamburger Mary's on the ground floor of a 1980s dilapidated Victorian building in the south of the city's Market area, a restaurant that became a haven for these communities. A wooden sign hung over the entry that warned the intolerant: "Enter at Your Own Risk."

If you were moving to San Francisco, your first stop would be Hamburger Mary's for work if you needed a job or information about where housing was available. Award-winning novelist Armistead Maupin's "Tales of the City" regularly mentioned that Hamburger Mary's reputation was probably why many made the restaurant their first stop.

In 1973, Rose Christensen, 17 years old, had left Milwaukee's cold winters to live with friends in San Francisco. She took a part-time job as a cook at Hamburger Mary's, worked her way to assistant manager, and finally became the last owner of the original location (which closed in April 2001).

The early years of the Folsom location did not rely on drag shows like the new franchised locations, but rather featured musical acts, comedy acts, and karaoke nights. Hamburger Mary's was a place you could take your parents visiting from out of state without a problem. You would see socialites, outcasts, oddballs, journalists, leather men, and musicians there. The punk rock clubs were close by and loved the "come as you are" open policy. Judging was not allowed; the staff made everyone feel at home. About 50 percent of the revenue was from the bar, with Bloody Marys as the most popular drink.

Opposite: 2020's logo at Ontario, CA location

Ownership of the Original Location
1972–1978: Jerald Jones, Heidi Steffan, Jan Hill, and Tom Mulvey
1978: Tom Mulvey
1978: Jerald Jones: Company locations and franchise rights
2001: Closed and became the Willows

Often, locals would say that if you wanted to know what San Francisco had been like in the 1970s, go to Hamburger Mary's. The inside was a kind of museum. The walls were filled with art bulletins over the top of the publications. The décor was peculiar, with baby bottles sitting on the tables with the nipples cut off to dispense cream for coffee. The name lived up to itself, as the hamburgers won many awards from around the bay: thick, large (a third of a pound), and juicy. The French fries were hand-cut, served in generous portions. The menu was described many times as a 1960s coffee shop. Breakfast was served all day. When Hamburger Mary's first opened, the owners tried to create an organic restaurant, but its name soon changed.

"Reliable, Friendly & Fun" was the original Mary's motto. "Water served on request only, and if you order it, you better drink it!" was an early message on their menus (obviously due to the California drought of the early seventies).

Hamburger Mary's falls into many categories: dive bar, restaurant, burger joint, coffee shop, music venue, karaoke bar, and community space. Because Mary's could not be put into one box, it won many awards over the years. Also, so many different kinds of people would stop in.

In November 1989, Jerry Jones passed away in Hawaii, where he owned the Honolulu Mary's location. His ownership of the Hamburger Mary's franchises changed hands several times after his death. In 2007, twins Brandon and Ashley Wright, who operated and owned the Chicago and Milwaukee locations, became the owners of the Hamburger Mary's franchise. They have grown the brand from 12 places to the current 14. In 2016, the twins went undercover in their sites for the hit show *Undercover Boss*. All locations are mainly opened in cities and areas that are accepting of diversity. Shows are a big part of the experience, with the Drag Bingo nights one of the most popular. Of course, not every server is in drag, but you never know who you will get. Excitement, fun, and lots of great entertainment are what the locations are all about. Each Hamburger Mary's is unique

(top): Mary statuette, (bottom): Ontario, CA location

to its community. Although the menus from corporate are more of a template, the one thing that all Mary's have in common is the logo, name, and experience.

By 2001, most original patrons and owners had passed away or moved on. Rose managed many of the business responsibilities and raised her teenage daughter. It was time to sell. The remaining business partners also wanted to sell; the business sold instantly. On April 23, 2001, Mary's held a "last-call party." The iconic art bulletins were supposed to be included in the sale, but the last employees swapped copies for the originals. Although the replicas were later auctioned for a charity fundraiser, some former employees still own pieces of the sources.

Today, the Willows, a pool/bar hamburger restaurant, is in the original space; they serve a "Mary" cheese-and-grilled-mushroom burger on their menu. 🍔

Burger and Menu Item Names
Mary Burger
Proud Mary Burger
Sloppy Mary Burger
Buffy, the Hamburger Slayer
Mary Tyler S'mores

(top left): Coaster, (top right): 1980's menu, (bottom): Original Folsom Street San Francisco location

Numero Uno Pizza: Pizza, Pasta & More

SLOGAN: "One Bite and We Gotcha"

NAME TODAY: Numero Uno

ORIGINAL LOCATION: 9545 Reseda Blvd., Northridge

OPENED: 1973

FOUNDER: Ron Gelet

CURRENT OWNERSHIP: N U Holding Company

CURRENTLY AT THE FIRST LOCATION: Strip mall

There are currently seven locations, all in Southern California.

Each location has its own website.

RON GELET GREW UP in a working-class neighborhood in Chicago. In 1970, Ron was transferred to California while working for a pharmaceutical firm. Loving the Chicago Sicilian-style type of deep-dish pizza, Ron could not find a proper pizza in Southern California. So, he started developing recipes in his kitchen with his wife. He accidentally created an iconic dough, and it has become a favorite of pizza lovers.

Soon after he created his dough, looking for a space with little funding, Ron found a place on Reseda and Plummer streets in Northridge. Ron gave his notice from his pharmaceutical job. Since funds were lacking, Ron and his friends started working together to prepare the restaurant for its first guests.

Numero Uno proved popular, with lines out the door. Ron looked to find other locations; the famed La Cienega Restaurant Row became the street for a second location, and he opened a few more sites with subsequent focus on franchising.

Within six years, *Los Angeles Magazine* called Numero Uno Pizza the best in Los Angeles. Ron claims that he brought the traditional deep-dish pizza to Southern California.

Their pizzas are mainly crust, sauce, and toppings. Any pizza company can put toppings on a crust, but the crust and sauce must be unique. Numero Uno's crust is soft yet crispy, with a bit of sweetness. The crust is now made by outside food manufacturers, with only Ron and his wife knowing the formula. This is to keep the crust consistent throughout the locations.

Ron's practice was to only work in the main office for one day a week. The other days, he would be on location testing the pizzas and ingredients, making products, and hearing from customers firsthand what they wanted.

In 1986, actor Joe Santos, who acted on the hit shows *Rockford Files* and *The Sopranos*, helped create a hit advertising campaign. He would promise "You don't love it; you don't pay." Ron said that only 50 customers took him up on the offer during the five-month campaign. Besides new media

Opposite: Numero Uno Lawndale, CA location, (top): BBQ Chicken Pizza, (bottom): Numero Uno logo

campaigns, they redecorated the dark wood and brass 1970s look to a lighter, fresher look with pastels and neon appearance. The menus also had been changed from one page that looked like a slice of pizza to a traditional bistro look. This is the same time California Pizza Kitchen (page 145) started hitting the market; Ron would mention how those "nouveau" pizzas were flavorless, with a thin cracker crust and hardly any sauce.

With over 60 locations (49 company-owned, 11 franchised) in Southern California in 1986, Numero Uno had 14 percent of the state's pizza sales. Ron collected 10 percent of the gross sales from franchisees, with three percent of gross sales going to advertising.

A few years after opening, Ron expanded his menu from pizzas to other Italian specialties such as lasagna, chicken parmigiana, and spaghetti with meatballs. In 1989, Numero Uno made one of its most significant changes by introducing a thin-crust pizza. Now, diners had two types of pizza to choose from. Unfortunately, offering the thin-crust pizzas only amounted to ten percent of the pizza sales.

Location Numbers	
1978:	9
1979:	16
1980:	18
1981:	22
1982:	33
1983:	44
1984:	49
1985:	50
1986:	59
1997:	76
2022:	7

The ad campaigns for Numero Uno in the 1990s were well known. The Pizza Family Pak brought in new customers and families that had not tried his restaurant. For $12.95 ($42.00 in 2023 dollars), this package included a medium-size pizza, one and a half pounds of spaghetti, a bucket of salad, and garlic bread. All-you-can-eat spaghetti was a popular offer that brought in families on a budget.

The two most popular pizzas are the Slaughterhouse Five (mozzarella cheese, pepperoni, mushrooms, onions, green peppers, and tomatoes) and the Works (pepperoni, sausage, meatballs, black olives, mushrooms, onions, green peppers, garlic, and anchovies).

In the early 1990s, the Los Angeles 1992 riots, the 1994 Northridge earthquake, and a recession hurt sales and store openings; many stores closed. Numero Uno sold off company-owned locations and closed others. However, they held on to 45 franchised locations, mainly in the San Fernando Valley. With phones ringing non-stop at the corporate headquarters from creditors, the company set up payment schedules and began selling international franchises. In 1994, Ron brought in Dan Rouse as vice president of operations. Dan had previously worked at the famed large Chicago pizza chain Giordano's. Dan was hired to expand the brand and see it grow like Giordano's. In 1996, Numero Uno posted its first small profit in years.

Going international created a steep learning curve. At the opening of the first international store, in Shenzhen, China, they discovered that customers looked at the pizza shop as American, not Italian. On the first day, an employee was arrested for walking up and down the street wearing a sandwich board advertising the new opening. They needed a special license to do that kind of advertising.

Filipinos had to be hired for the new Kuwait locations, as Kuwaitis would not work for the

Numero Uno
Southern California Locations
Granada Hills
Ladera Heights
Lawndale
North Hollywood
Simi Valley
Tarzana
Wilshire Los Angeles

going wage. The menus there were stripped of pork and alcohol products for cultural reasons, plus an Islamic cleric had to bless the ingredients before opening the store. With the introduction of South Korean locations, customers needed the pizzas to be scaled back on the amount of cheese, and bottles of ketchup would be on the table for use on the pizzas. After a short time, the China location closed for the lack of interest in American pizzas, and Kuwait followed soon.

In 1997, Numero Uno Pizza Holding Company purchased Oregon's ten-store chain, Original Sandwich Express & Bakery Restaurants. Ron felt that a sandwich company attached to his pizza would be a win-win in sales, as 80 percent of pizza sales were in the evenings and 80 percent of sandwich sales were in the daytime, thus covering the day with two types of food products to sell. But unfortunately, this business move did not pan out for the pizza company.

The same year, Ron left the company, but he still owned the formula for the pizza dough, which franchisees paid to use. The dough is shipped to the locations frozen. Numero Uno pizza dough is unique and distinctive; once you have enjoyed a pizza, you know the taste and aroma of its sweet dough.

In August 2013, Ron, with his son Joe Gelet, took over the ownership of a pizzeria in San Clemente close to his home. They updated the menu of Izza Pizzeria with the famous Numero Uno dough, a thin dough, and a special of the day on Mondays, donating sales percentages to non-profit groups, to half-off bottles of wine on Thursdays.

Numero Uno has significantly downsized from 76 units at its peak to seven locations today; Dan Rouse owns the parent company (N U Holding Company), and Ron Gelet is semi-retired, helping his wife in her real estate business. ◢

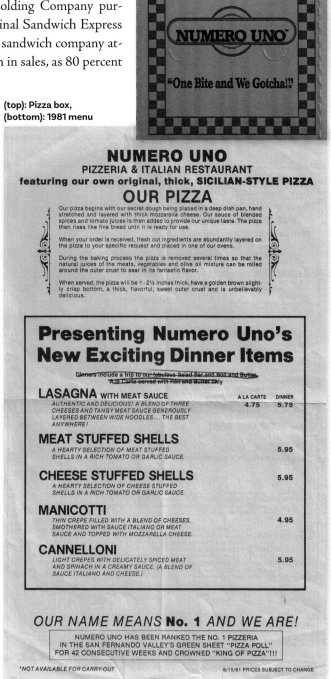

(top): Pizza box, (bottom): 1981 menu

NUMERO UNO
PIZZERIA & ITALIAN RESTAURANT
featuring our own original, thick, SICILIAN-STYLE PIZZA

OUR PIZZA

Our pizza begins with our secret dough being placed in a deep dish pan, hand stretched and layered with thick mozzarella cheese. Our sauce of blended spices and tomato juices is then added to provide our unique taste. The pizza then rises like fine bread until it is ready for use.

When your order is received, fresh cut ingredients are abundantly layered on the pizza to your specific request and placed in one of our ovens.

During the baking process the pizza is removed several times so that the natural juices of the meats, vegetables and olive oil mixture can be rolled around the outer crust to sear in its fantastic flavor.

When served, the pizza will be 1 - 2½ inches thick, have a golden brown slightly crisp bottom, a thick, flavorful, sweet outer crust and is unbelievably delicious.

Presenting Numero Uno's New Exciting Dinner Items

Dinners include a trip to our fabulous Salad Bar and Roll and Butter
A la Carte served with Roll and Butter only

	A LA CARTE	DINNER
LASAGNA WITH MEAT SAUCE *AUTHENTIC AND DELICIOUS! A BLEND OF THREE CHEESES AND TANGY MEAT SAUCE GENEROUSLY LAYERED BETWEEN WIDE NOODLES... THE BEST ANYWHERE!*	4.75	5.75
MEAT STUFFED SHELLS *A HEARTY SELECTION OF MEAT STUFFED SHELLS IN A RICH TOMATO OR GARLIC SAUCE.*		5.95
CHEESE STUFFED SHELLS *A HEARTY SELECTION OF CHEESE STUFFED SHELLS IN A RICH TOMATO OR GARLIC SAUCE.*		5.95
MANICOTTI *THIN CREPE FILLED WITH A BLEND OF CHEESES, SMOTHERED WITH SAUCE ITALIANO OR MEAT SAUCE AND TOPPED WITH MOZZARELLA CHEESE.*		4.95
CANNELLONI *LIGHT CREPES WITH DELICATELY SPICED MEAT AND SPINACH IN A CREAMY SAUCE. (A BLEND OF SAUCE ITALIANO AND CHEESE.)*		5.95

OUR NAME MEANS **No. 1** AND WE ARE!

NUMERO UNO HAS BEEN RANKED THE NO. 1 PIZZERIA IN THE SAN FERNANDO VALLEY'S GREEN SHEET "PIZZA POLL" FOR 42 CONSECUTIVE WEEKS AND CROWNED "KING OF PIZZA"!!!

*NOT AVAILABLE FOR CARRY-OUT   6/15/81 PRICES SUBJECT TO CHANGE

NUMERO UNO
"One Bite and We Gotcha!"

The Big Yellow House

SLOGAN: "Just Like Going to Grandma's for Sunday Dinner"

ORIGINAL LOCATION: 108 Pierpoint Ave., Summerland

OPENED: June 17, 1973

FOUNDER: Great American Restaurants

CURRENTLY AT THE FIRST LOCATION: Empty building

All locations have been closed.

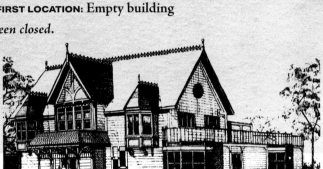

SUMMERLAND, CALIFORNIA, initially named Ortega Rancho for the hill it sat on, overlooked the Pacific Ocean south of Santa Barbara. In 1883, spiritualist Henry L. Williams, a real estate developer, felt the area had summer-like weather the entire year, so he changed the name to Summerland and started subdividing his town into smaller parcels. The following year, Williams built a large house off the main highway.

In 1971, John and June Young purchased the home and painted it bright orange and sunshine yellow. June had previously founded Santa Claus Lane, a roadside street three miles south with holiday shops and foods to attract tourists traveling down the highway toward Los Angeles. The neighborhood of Summerland was upset over the bright color on the large house, but the city did not have an ordinance to prevent the unwanted color.

The Youngs leased the house to W. N. Filcher, owner of the recently closed Green Gables restaurant that had been in downtown Santa Barbara. They kept the house the same paint color. Many of the staff from the original State Street location came south to work at the restaurant. The Pacific Ocean features views from the large plate-glass windows providing sunsets, while patrons feasted on continental cuisine.

Two years later, Great American Restaurants (GAR) took over the lease from Filcher and reopened the restaurant as the Big Yellow House. Larry Hatfield, Dale Marquis, and Sam Battlestone (son of the founder of the Sambo's coffee shop chain) each had 14 percent ownership, with 45 percent held by Invent West.

The Big Yellow House would not be their first venture into the food-service business. The Feed Store Restaurant had opened in a former grain and feed store in Santa Barbara as a steak and seafood restaurant in 1974. The Big Yellow House opened in Fresno, California, the first of many the following year. Although this location was the first to open, the building was a nondescript former restaurant; they painted it bright yellow to reflect its new name. After long daily lines, they increased

Opposite: Original Summerland, CA location, (top): Logo, (bottom): Architectural drawing of Victorian Big Yellow House

the seating in the dining rooms to help with the crowds. The meals were simple yet plentiful. Everything was served family-style on giant platters and bowls brought to your table. The menu stayed the same, with a few rotating main dishes.

Two former train stations (Santa Cruz and Livermore) came up for restoration and repurposing in the following years. GAR saw these as a great space for new restaurants. They did not name them Big Yellow Houses but focused on their being former train stations by calling them the Old Santa Cruz Railway and the Old Livermore Railway. The logos matched that of the Big Yellow House; the décor was that of an 1890s train station, with the same cuisine as the Big Yellow Houses.

In 1977, a Big Yellow House was built from the ground up in Modesto. Huge signs posted at the construction site excited the locals. The building was a two-story house painted bright lemon yellow with white trim and shutters. Crowds formed early on opening day and did not stop. The company touted the location as "Just like Grandmother's House." The building was filled with antiques and replicas filling in where an antique could not be found. The dishes were also mismatched, just like you would find at your grandmother's house. The dining-room chairs were of all sorts of sizes and looks. From the entry, looking up, you would see a breathtaking chandelier ten feet tall and six feet wide and an oak staircase reaching the second level.

Locations in Order of Openings, Address, and What Is at the Site Today

Summerland	108 Pierpoint Rd.	Original Victorian House
Fresno	1440 E. Shaw	Still standing: A.D. Deli (non-Victorian)
Santa Cruz	123 Washington St.	Demolished
Livermore	20 S. "L" St.	Moved to 2500 Railroad St.
Modesto	3105 McHenry	Still standing: Medical Office (first-Victorian)
Palm Springs	150 E. Vista Chino	Still standing: 7/11 Store (non-Victorian)
Sacramento	1788 Tribute Rd.	Demolished
Costa Mesa	3010 Harbor Blvd.	Demolished
Brea	1639 Imperial Blvd.	Still standing: Restaurant
Marion, Iowa	1655 Blairs Ferry	Still standing: Medical Office
Monrovia	725 W. Huntington	Demolished
Santa Rosa	3785 Cleveland	Demolished
Dublin	6960 Amador Plaza	Demolished
Stockton	2659 W. March	Demolished
National City	1908 Sweetwater	Still standing: Medical Office
Reno, NV	4990 S. Virginia	Still standing: Vacant
Montclair	9395 Monte Vista	Demolished
Cerritos	11105 E. 183rd St.	Demolished
Mission Viejo	28381 Marguerite	Demolished
Garden Grove	9100 Trask Ave.	Still standing: Restaurant
Milpitas	1181 E. Caveras	Still standing: Medical Office
La Mesa	5130 Baltimore	Demolished

The Mistlin Buick-Honda dealership in Modesto gave away two free meals with every new car purchase. Mistlin sold many new Buicks with that ad campaign. As soon as your new car was delivered, you drove down the street to have dinner in the Big Yellow House.

Imitation is the sincerest form of flattery—until Longfellow's Big Green House, less than a thirty-minute drive down the coast to Ventura, opened only a year after the Fresno location. Longfellow's had a tagline, "Chicken, Steak, and Chocolate Cake," and heavy advertising. Guests confused the two restaurant brands by asking at Big Yellow House locations, "Where is our chocolate cake?" Longfellow's opened about half a dozen locations and closed within six years.

Between 1977 and 1981, eighteen Big Yellow Houses opened from San Diego County to the Bay area; all but two were built as vast Victorian buildings. Lines formed early in the day for the all-you-can-eat meals. The fried chicken was always on the menu with a rotating second main dish, a cheese-and-cracker appetizer, corn chowder, salad, two vegetables, mashed potatoes and gravy, soup, and salad, and a "cornbread girl" would deliver the sweet cornbread with honey butter to your table personally. Being a family establishment, once you walked into the parlor, you would see a large old-fashioned scale with dollar amounts instead of weights. This reflected what you would pay for children under 12.

In July 1980, the Cerritos location was somewhat difficult to open. After the Victorian building was completed, the city council did not like the brightness of the yellow building. They forced the restaurant to change to a cream color with yellow trim. Like a homeowner's association, the city had to approve colors that would go on their home or outside buildings.

The Modesto location closed in 1980, as it never recovered from a health and safety code violation two years before, where 17 Parent-Teacher Association members from the local school district dined for lunch and became ill.

While opening Big Yellow Houses, in 1978 GAR opened two Strawberry Tree Coffee Shops (one in Redondo Beach and one in Camarillo) with an extensive dessert display case under the hostess stand, packed with desserts all made with strawberries. Unfortunately, they only lasted one year before being sold.

One of GAR's final efforts was opening Penroy's Old Fashioned Eatery, a full-service menu and dining experience in downtown Santa Cruz; also, all the Big Yellow Houses added additional menu items to their menus besides all-you-can-eat chicken dinners. Unfortunately, this move clogged the kitchen and service. In addition, a more extensive menu with many choices delayed the ordering.

In 1983, GAR filed for Chapter 11 on behalf of the Big Yellow House Restaurants. Don Turner, the vice president of operations, purchased three Northern California locations (Milpitas, Sacramento, and Santa Rosa). Turner updated his restaurants with new furnishings but kept the Victorian look and updated his menus to offer a full menu with the choice of the All-You-Can-Eat Fried Chicken meal. In addition, he added appetizers that were unique for the time, such as potato skins and chicken strips, plus fresh fish offerings. These locations lasted a few more years before also closing. The Executive VP of GAR, Gene Bevilaqua, and his wife Kay assumed the lease on the original Summerland House location and continued to serve family-style meals for a few more years.

A restaurant chain that was only in operation for eleven years with 23 locations, the Big Yellow House had a social impact on the family dining industry. Two of the original Victorian houses are still (different) restaurants; three are now medical offices; many others have been demolished. The newest building in Riverside is empty, if you have a great recipe for fried chicken. ✸

Famous Amos Cookies

SLOGAN: "Famously Delicious Cookies"

ORIGINAL LOCATION: 7181 Sunset Blvd., Los Angeles

OPENED: March 10, 1975

FOUNDER: Wally Amos

CURRENT OWNERSHIP: Ferrero SpA

CURRENTLY AT THE FIRST LOCATION: Bossa Nova Brazilian Cuisine

PRIOR AT THE FIRST LOCATION: House of Pies

All retail stores have closed. The product has changed drastically; you can buy it in localized stores such as membership, markets, vending machines, etc.

famous-amos.com

WALLY AMOS WAS BORN in the panhandle of Florida in the summer of 1936. Wally's parents divorced, and he then moved to New York City at the age of 12 to live with his Aunt Della Bryant, who was a great influence on Wally's love of baking by teaching him how to make cookies with just a bowl and wooden spoon. He dropped out of a food vocational high school shortly before graduation and joined the Air Force.

After his military service, he started working as a mailroom clerk in the famed William Morris Agency in New York City, advancing to become the first African American talent agent in the racially tense 1970s. He represented some of the most prominent African American talent coming up the ranks, including Marvin Gaye, Diana Ross, and the Supremes. Eventually, Wally left the agency and opened his own.

In 1974, Wally and his three sons took a driving trip out West to see the Grand Canyon and Hollywood, clear his mind, and figure out his next professional move. Once at the A&M Records offices, he took some cookies to his friend B. J. Gilmore, Quincy Jones's secretary. As they sat eating cookies and talking about the next moves for Wally, B. J. spoke about opening a cookie store. Wally liked the idea, as it wasn't in show business, but funds were a factor. B. J. thought for a moment and said he knew the owner of Tommy's Hamburger. She was optimistic that he would be interested in investing. After that, Wally took cookies to casting agents, producers, and the like as "goodwill" gestures; the cookies became his "hook," so Hollywood was aware of the tasty cookies.

In 1975, Wally found a former House of Pies on the north side of Sunset and Formosa in the heart of the Hollywood area of Los Angeles. With investments from singers Marvin Gaye and Helen Reddy and her husband, Jeff Wald, Wally promoted

Opposite: Wally Amos outside of his Sunset Blvd. location, (top): Logo, (bottom): Historical plaque

First Famous Amos Locations
7181 Sunset Blvd., Hollywood
18670 Ventura Blvd., Ventura
239 Santa Monica Mall, Santa Monica
1140 Court "C," Tacoma, Washington

"The Cookie" as a client, just like his days at William Morris. Roland Young, the creative director at A&M Records who mainly designed album covers, asked to create graphics for Wally. He thought of first having his three sons' pictures on the bags and boxes, but Roland came up with serious graphics: script of the Famous Amos words with Chocolate Chip Cookies underneath.

Wally's philosophy was about the Cookie and "Friend of the Cookie." He wanted anyone associated with the brand to be dubbed a Friend of the Cookie. Wally understood that using a little oven like his home oven and mixing the dough in a bowl by hand would not suffice. He would also have to buy the ingredients in mass quantities.

He befriended a veteran food salesman named Leo. Leo became a Friend of the Cookie. After learning about the new equipment and food products they would need to open, Wally put together a proposal. He was used to buying 2.75 oz. packages of pecans, and

Cookie Products
Famous Amos Chocolate Chip Cookies
Famous Amos Chocolate Chip Walnut Cookies
Famous Amos Oatmeal Walnut Cookies
Famous Amos Oatmeal Chocolate Chip Walnut Cookies
Famous Amos Toffee Chocolate Chip Cookies

Print ad

now he would have 30-pound boxes. The first time he opened the large box of pecans, Wally ran his hands through the golden roasted nuts, feeling that they were little pieces of gold ready to enhance his soon-to-be-famous cookies. He came up with $25,000 as his start-up budget, $20,000 to get the store open, and the other $5,000 to help it run until profits started to come in.

In his formal proposal to investors, Wally had the packaging of the various cookie flavors, such as Chocolate Chip with Pecans, Chocolate Chip with Peanut Butter, and Peanut Butterscotch with Pecans. He also placed cookies at the end of the proposal, so investors could taste the cookies they were investing in.

Tony Christian, a neighbor and an artist, was at Wally's house sampling cookies and chocolate peanut butter. Indicating what he wanted for his Sunset store's grand opening, Wally hired Tony as the creative designer; Tony was now a Friend of the Cookie. Tony created the vision for the shop and the marketing materials; he made a vignette of Wally's original mixing bowl and spoon in a glass case.

Wally's passion was promotion and cookie baking. He created a similar recipe to his Aunt Della's but with more chocolate chips, pecans, and pure vanilla. He hand-delivered (he did not have the funds to mail them) most of the invitations to the grand opening himself, which would be worthy of a premiere in Hollywood. The Cookie became a celebrity with headshots taken and a biography.

Wally's mixing the dough in the sizeable 60-quart mixer and hand-scooping it by teaspoons onto baking sheets took him into the night to prepare for the event. Many times during the night, friends would stop by. He called it quits at five in the morning when his newly appointed staff showed up. He went home to rest and ready himself for the afternoon's grand opening party.

It was like a Hollywood premiere on March 10, 1975, with valet service for anything from Hondas to Rolls Royces, a red carpet, and the media cameras and paparazzi. Los Angeles Mayor Thomas Bradley declared it "Chocolate Chip Cookie Day." Cookies and milk were served with champagne to create a festive Sunday afternoon.

The next day's opening time for the store was set at 11:00 a.m. News spread fast; hours earlier, a line formed down Sunset around to Formosa to the west side of the building. The cookies were a hit.

But many in the music industry who had tasted Wally's homemade cookies before the store found these new ones slightly different in taste. It took him time to rectify this. He could not figure it out at first, so he took some baked cookies on a trip to his Grandma Julia's home. She figured it out with the first bite: there was too much salt in the recipe. Too much salt will throw the entire balance of the cookie off, she said, and it had.

Wally traded his tailored suits from his agency days for his signature style of a Panama hat and Island print shirt. Today his outfit resides in the Smithsonian American History Museum in the Business Americana Collection. His infectious smile became "the face that launched a thousand chips."

Small bag of cookies

Cash flow was still sparse; there were many failed robbery attempts at his Sunset location, as cash was not plentiful at the store. But many newspaper stories were being written about this newfangled cookie company. Gourmet buyer Wes Gardner at Macy's in San Francisco was very interested in carrying the cookies in a pre-packaged form. Wally was not set up for wholesaling his product, so he enlisted Sid Ross, who had been his coffee salesman, as the new director of wholesale.

He also started selling to Jurgenson's gourmet grocery store in Pasadena. Having to deliver the cookies, he decorated a Volkswagen rabbit with his logos. It would deliver up to San Francisco and Pasadena, which he named "The Commuter Cookie." Another store opened in Studio City, and then Tarzana. Tarzana's opening party invites had a bag that said "You and this bag are entitled to be filled up at Famous Amos in Tarzana." The party was a hit. The store had high sales for the first week, but then these gradually declined. The lease was for three years, and then they closed the location.

Meanwhile, Wally was approached by Bill

Ownership of Famous Amos

1975–1985	Wally Amos
1985–1988	Bass Brothers Enterprises
1988	Robert Baer and Jeffrey Baer
1988–1992	The Shansby Group
1992–1998	President Baking Company
1998–2001	Keebler Company
2001–2019	Kellogg Company
2019–Present	Ferrero SpA

Nelson, asking to open a location in Tucson, Arizona. This time, Wally looked at the sites personally. After the Tarzana closing, he remembered the first rule that everyone in retail should adhere to: location, location, location. But he still decided to open in Tucson. The opening had over a thousand guests. The first weeks were great, and then again, there was a backsliding of sales. He had forgotten the business lesson: his location was horrible, so he finally closed the store.

In May 1976, Wally traveled to New York to present his cookies. He showed up in a personalized light brown jumpsuit with a giant cookie embroidered on the back. Wally was the best at promotions! After many meetings, Bloomingdale's signed on. Soon after, a press conference announcing the deal included a Famous Amos cookie placed on a blue satin pillow in front of the Bloomie's boardroom.

Now what was the best way to get the cookies from Los Angeles to New York? Wally thought of

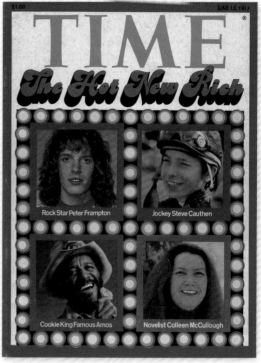

June 13, 1977, *Time* magazine cover

next-day shipping, which would need an East Coast commissary. A location was found in Nutley, New Jersey. In time they also renamed the street Chocolate Chip Way. The Bloomingdale's deal was only for a year and was not renewed because Macy's Herald Square in New York approached them to sell the cookies in their new Cellar Food Boutique. Wally thought both locations could sell his packages of cookies, but Bloomingdales pulled out of their deal.

Starting in 1977, Wally was invited to ride in Macy's Thanksgiving parade for four years. Macy's was not as big as today, so only the few who had the Cellars sold the cookies. *Time* magazine put Famous Amos on the cover of their June 13, 1977, issue, boosting sales even more. Neiman Marcus later carried the cookie: when that deal happened, Wally drove in on an armored truck to deliver the cookies.

Feeling that he now had a voice, Wally wrote the Famous Amos Story in 1983. He focused on before and after his life as the King of Cookies on Sunset.

In 1985, revenue was down, and the company was losing money. In 1988, Shansby Group, a corporation, purchased the Famous Amos Cookie brand. They successfully shifted the brand from a high-end specialty product to a lower-priced cookie suitable for mass production. The recipe had changed so much, with preservatives and stabilizers, that it was nothing like its former self.

While living in Hawaii in 1991, and unhappy that his name was associated with what he claimed was an inferior product, Wally launched another cookie company called Wally Amos Presents: Chip & Cookie. He flaunted that his company was the only company producing the original Famous Amos Cookie of the past. The Shansby Group's lawyers acted swiftly with a cease-and-desist order, as he had violated his agreement by using his likeness on the packaging of any food product. So Wally changed

the name of his Hawaiian cookie business to Uncle NoName Cookie Company and opened a mail-order division and two retail locations on the islands.

In 1988, the Famous Amos brand was sold to the Keebler Company; now, the cookies were packaged for fast food, vending machines, and multi-package units for school lunches. Keebler hired Wally Amos to resume his brand-ambassador and spokesperson roles. In 2001, Keebler was sold to the Kellogg Company. After 18 years, Ferrero USA, Inc., owner of Ferrero chocolates, Tic-Tac Mints, and the world's favorite hazelnut spread Nutella, currently owns the Famous Amos Brand.

During his years in Hawaii, Wally launched several food stores and companies. His last is the Cookie Kahuna. Wally Amos currently resides in Columbia, South Carolina, working on his previous venture, Aunt Della's Cookies. Besides baking cookies and muffins, promoting literacy is his passion. The 86-year-old high school dropout has penned ten books and, for 24 years, served as a spokesperson for Literacy Volunteers of America. President George H. W. Bush gave Wally the Literacy Award in 1991. He currently serves as chairman of the Read It LOUD! Foundation. 🍪

(top): Print ad, (bottom left): City of Los Angeles historical plaque, (bottom right): Original Sunset Blvd. location

Roscoe's House of Chicken and Waffles

NAME TODAY: Roscoe's

FLAGSHIP LOCATION: 1514 N. Gower, Los Angeles

OPENED: December 1975

FOUNDER: Herbert (Herb) Hudson

CURRENTLY AT THE FIRST LOCATION: The flagship location is still in operation.
There are currently seven locations in Southern California.

roscoeschickenandwaffles.com

THE 1930s IN HARLEM, New York, brought supper clubs and dancing to the Black community. However, many restaurants and supper clubs in the area were still open after the dancing and music stopped. So, was it dinner or breakfast the tired revelers wanted? Richard "Dickie" Wells, also known as the "Harlem Playboy," was a high-paid tap dancer at the famous Cotton Club. He also did extra work, being a gigolo for many high-profile women. Realizing that he needed a backup plan, Dickie opened Dickie Wells Supper Club on 133rd Street in Harlem, just a few blocks from the famed Apollo Theater. Dickie conceived the combination of dinner (fried chicken) and breakfast (waffles) for the cravings of hungry late-night crowds. Dickie served his Chicken and Waffles with coffee or a shot of bourbon, and it soon became an iconic dish in the neighborhood. Other supper clubs in the area also started serving this new inventive dish, and, within a few years, the concept went nationwide in soul-food restaurants.

Herbert (Herb) Hudson, a former foreman with General Motors, arrived in the Los Angeles area with plans to open a restaurant. Herb knew he wanted to open a restaurant like Wells's supper club, but a West

Opposite: Chicken and Waffles Specialty, (top): Logo, (bottom): Diners enjoying breakfast

Leonard Pitts and Stevie Wonder having lunch at the Hollywood location

Coast version. Using the power of the African American–focused *Los Angeles Sentinel* newspaper, Herb educated the community with the idea that his fried chicken and waffles were an East Coast specialty with a West Coast twist. He also used his connections to attract music-industry folks to eat in his restaurant.

When you dine at Roscoe's, you are not a customer but part of the family. Their syrup cannot be purchased; it's only made for "family" members to enjoy at the restaurant. When you dine at Roscoe's, you may be seated near a president, a senator, a mayor, an "A"-list movie star, or even a tourist just off a plane from LAX. In 1995, Roscoe's catered their largest "family meal," feeding 6,000 people at the Billboard Music Awards.

Unlike many fried-chicken restaurants, Roscoe's pan-fries each piece like a grandmother of 1930s Harlem would have. It's not deep-fat frying. All the vegetables are fresh and never frozen, such as corn on the cob and mixed greens; if they are not in season, they are not served. Even fresh oranges are squeezed for juice. Likewise, potato salad is made fresh and not from a carton.

In 2000, Herb heard that someone had opened a chicken restaurant in Manhattan 3,000 miles away using a logo like his with a chicken standing in front of a waffle, the name having a slightly different spelling; Rossco's. Herb did not think much of it; being from New York, he knew he would not be back. Then the owner of Rossco's, Darrell Johnson, opened another location in 2008, but this time closer to the Bronzeville neighborhood of Chicago. Herb this time acted with a lawsuit for trademark infringement. It only took Johnson a few weeks to change the name and signage to Chicago's House of Chicken and Waffles. Herb wanted to expand to the Windy City in the future and knew others would confuse the two. Rossco's even had drinks with the

Southern Sides
Candy Yams
Biscuits
Red Beans
Mac and Cheese
Grits
Coleslaw
Greens
Cornbread

same names, like Sun Set and Sun Rise.

President Obama, during his time in office, loved to stop at restaurants unannounced; in 2011, he visited Roscoe's before a fundraiser in Westside Los Angeles. Unfortunately, he didn't realize how close he was to the event when he got back into the presidential limo; he started eating his order (Number 9, The Country Boy) and dripped a little grease on his tie in a rush to finish his meal before the event. After the president visited, Roscoe's changed the name of the Number 9 to the Obama Special (three wings, waffle, and potato salad or fries). President Obama was not the only person to have a dish named after them; Natalie Cole has Natalie's Special on the menu, simply "two fantastically prepared waffles."

In 1992, Herb created and opened Good Herb Records; his ads in the local newspaper would advertise "All new talent is welcome to audition." Unfortunately, his venture did not last too long after only signing a handful of vocalists.

The late *Los Angeles Times* food writer Jonathan Gold was a fan of Roscoe's and wrote about the dishes, such as the Stymies Choice (a mountain of chicken livers drenched with gravy, sitting on grits with double fried eggs on the top) and the Hot Water Corn Bread, as some of his favorites. Both are still on the menu to this day.

With the flagship restaurant on a side street sandwiched between Sunset and Hollywood Boulevards and many TV and movie production studios, Roscoe's was mentioned in and starred in many mainstream and independent films. Of course, this also brought actors and staff to their tables.

Many foods are served at Roscoe's besides the dish that made them famous, from Red Beans and Rice to Banana Pudding. Be assured that you will not go home hungry. 🍗

Flagship location of Roscoe's Chicken and Waffles, Hollywood, CA

Porto's Bakery & Café

SLOGAN: "To Bake Life's Memories for Generations to Come"

ORIGINAL LOCATION: 2919 Sunset Blvd., Los Angeles

OPENED: October 1976

FOUNDERS: Rosa and Raul Porto Sr.

CURRENT OWNERSHIP: The Porto Family

CURRENTLY AT THE FIRST LOCATION: Retail store

There are seven locations in Southern California.

portosbakery.com

ROSA AND RAUL PORTO were passionate and determined to make a better life for their family without losing their heritage from their homeland, Cuba. The 1960s were difficult for Cubans; Fidel Castro and his regime took over the country, and the revolution began. Rosa and Raul saw the changes and requested to migrate to the United States for their family's safety and better life. Unfortunately, because of the request, which was not granted, they were stripped of their careers, and Raul was forced into a labor camp cutting sugar cane for eight dollars a month. Rosa knew she had to step up. With her natural gift of creating Cuban baked goods, she started baking cakes and selling them to her neighbors and locals to support her family and three children.

Obtaining ingredients for Rosa's sumptuous Cuban pastries and cakes was complicated. Supplies had to be bartered or purchased on the black market, as you could not simply walk into a grocery store to pick up the needed items. It was illegal to have a private business; if Rosa had been caught, she would have been jailed for 20 years.

Opposite: Raul and Rosa Porto outside of their first location, Silver Lake, CA, (top): Logo, (bottom): Raul and Rosa at the West Covina grand opening, 2019.

Generations of the Porto Family

FOUNDERS:
Raul Porto
Rosa Porto

2ND GENERATION:
Beatriz (Betty) Porto,
   Vice President of Community Affairs
Margarita Porto, Vice President
   of Catering and Custom Cakes
Raul Porto Jr., President and CEO

3RD GENERATION:
Adrian Porto, Back of House Manager,

Porto children Margarita, Raul Jr. and Beatriz (Betty) with birthday cakes

If a neighbor ordered a cake and Rosa needed four eggs for the cake, she would tell you to bring eight. She was great at bartering.

After ten years, the Porto family's request for exile was finally approved in 1971. The family arrived without jobs or money. Instead, they landed in the Echo Park area of Los Angeles in search of a better life for themselves and their three young children. The Portos knew that coming to America was the right decision.

Once arriving in Los Angeles, Raul found work at the Van de Kamp's bakery plant near Glassell Park, in the packing department. Rosa attempted to find a job; but at every bakery that she applied to, she was turned down. (In later years, her daughter found out that Rosa had been sabotaging her own applications, as she did not want to work for anyone but herself.) Not wanting to give up her passion, she baked cakes in her family home for income, using the bedrooms as cooling places for the pastry. Many Cubans found out about Rosa's cakes and baked goods through word of mouth. After only five years and a $5,000 loan, the family opened a storefront bakery in the Silverlake area, about a ten-minute walk from their home. After six years, the 300-square-foot bakery had outgrown its space. They moved to Glendale, California, in 1982, where they still have a Porto's forty years later. The bakery has moved up and down the same street for redevelopment.

In 2006, they expanded to open a Porto's in Burbank. With both locations open, more people were introduced to Cuban delicacies. Raul and Rosa found that Cubans were not the only ones who enjoyed the delicious pastry. Porto's made a name for themselves with the film and TV studios nearby, and on-set craft services and studio events started using Porto's. It was great quality pastry at a great value. The Burbank location is within a five-minute drive of the Hollywood/Burbank Airport,

Years of Bakeries and Locations

1960–1971	Cuba	Manzanilla, Cuba
1972–1976	Home Kitchen	824½ Robinson, Los Angeles
1976–1982	First Retail Bakery	2919 Sunset Blvd., Los Angeles
1982–1986:	Glendale #1	330 N. Brand Blvd., Glendale
1986–1992:	Glendale #2	327 N. Brand Blvd., Glendale
1992–Present:	Current Glendale Location	315 N Brand Blvd., Glendale
2006–Present:	Current Burbank Location	3614 W. Magnolia Blvd., Burbank
2010–Present	Current Downey Location	8233 Firestone Blvd., Downey
2017–Present	Current Buena Park Location	7640 Beach Blvd., Buena Park
2019–Present	Current West Covina Location	584 S. Sunset Ave., West Covina
2022–Present	Current Northridge Location	19467 Nordoff Street, Northridge
2025–Present	Current Downtown Disney	1580 Disneyland Drive, Anaheim

and many stop in before their flight to take the pastry to their destinations.

With lines from opening to closing, Porto's had to expand. Daily, guests would ask a team member when they would open a Porto's in their neighborhood. Today, when you walk into Porto's, you will see long lines, you'll be greeted by one of the 1,600 team members, and your wait will be short. They have mastered the art of satisfying the demand.

Every Porto's bakery has three significant areas: Coffee Bar, Café, and Bakery. A team member will direct you to the area that will be the quickest at fulfilling your purchasing needs. The Coffee Bar offers a limited variety of top-selling pastries and sweets along with a full menu of house coffees (hot, over ice, and blended), hand-crafted juices, teas, smoothies, and shakes, and even some classic Cuban sodas. The Bakery and Café lines offer the full menu via both lines; however, the showcase is longer in the Bakery lines, so you see a lot more visually. If you already know what you want to buy, you should wait in the Café line, as guests tend to move a bit quicker through this line, though you can still order pastries, sweets, and whole cakes. The Bakery line is recommended for guests who want to see all the offerings and might need more time navigating the menu.

Every Porto's bakery is unique to its neighborhood. When you step into the Burbank location, you will not feel as if you are in a chain or in one of the other locations. The Glendale location was formerly a fabric store and, in the 1930s, a small Sears store before it moved across the street to a more prominent location. Porto's expanded the location and took over the businesses next door to create the Café side, which was a Numero Uno (page 57) pizza restaurant. The Burbank location was a Thrifty Drug Store. The Downey location was a former commercial bank. Buena Park was built from the ground up after demolishing two small motels, the Golden State and the Palm Inn.

(top): Fresh Fruit Tart, (bottom): Downey, CA location

It is the largest of all Porto's locations at 25,000 square feet and has a dining capacity of 207. The West Covina location that you can see while speeding east on Interstate 10 was previously a Red Onion Restaurant before a new Porto's was built on that space from the ground up. Northridge's location was a former Sears Auto Center.

Porto's Bake at Home was introduced in 2018. The Porto family created a central kitchen to supply the Bake at Home concept. The Central Kitchen also houses Porto's freezing, shipping, and test kitchens. The new service was created because so many guests would take home boxes of Porto's sweet and savory pastries. Today, the Bake at Home product line consists of over a dozen items, from appetizers to entire cakes. Porto's does not use any third-party delivery service for frozen products; you can only buy the products from Porto's website.

Porto's Secret Recipe (Core Values)

1. FAMILY: Our team, guests, and our bakeries are all about family and tradition.
2. QUALITY: An uncompromised approach to excellence is baked into everything we do.
3. COMMUNITY: We are committed to making a sweet and positive impact in the communities we call home.
4. INTEGRITY: We choose to do what is right, not what is easy.
5. PASSION: We are on a never-ending pursuit to improve everything we do.

(top): Betty with customers at Northridge, CA grand opening, (bottom): Northridge bakery case

From opening to closing, the pastry cases are packed. In the last hour of the day, the display will look as it did when opening, with offerings just as fresh as the morning pastries. Every location bakes throughout the day, so everything is as fresh as possible for the customer.

Not only are the owners multigenerational, but so are the team members and the customers. It is not unusual for Porto's to have baked the wedding cake, birthday cake, and any other celebration cake for the same family. Many of the team members' parents, siblings, and other family members have worked at Porto's.

Each location donates day-old pastry to a neighboring non-profit in need. For example, the Union Rescue Mission in Downtown Los Angeles has received day-old Porto's goods from the beginning.

Many of the products are closely associated with Porto's. The Potato Rolls and Chicken Croquette are the best in the country. You cannot find anything comparable. Many companies claim that they use the best ingredients, but Porto's really does—and they have done so since opening for business. If the product changes, the customer will tell them. When a new Porto's opened, the quality was the same as when Rosa made the baked goods from her home kitchen in Cuba. The most infamous

Top Items
TOP SELLING CAKE: Milk' N Berries Cake

TOP 5 SWEET:
1. Cheese Rolls
2. Dulce de Leche Besitos
3. Refugiado (Guava & Cheese Strudel)
4. Guava Strudel
5. Chocolate Chip Cookies

TOP 5 SAVORY:
1. Potato Ball
2. Meat Pie
3. Chicken Empanada
4. Cheese & Spicy Peppers Potato Ball
5. Chicken Croquette

pastry is the Refugiado, a guava-and-cheese strudel. These are the flavors of Cuba, and the pastry is named to remind customers how the Portos got to America.

In the early 1990s, Rosa semi-retired to help care for her seven grandchildren, since her three children began taking more active roles in the company at that time. Rosa retired fully in 2005 and Raul Sr. in 2007, but she still advised her children about the company's direction regarding new business products. Sadly, a few weeks before Christmas 2019, Rosa passed away. Raul Sr., in his early nineties, visits the Glendale location a few times a week and is always at any grand openings.

Today Southern California has seven full-service Porto's bakery cafés. The latest to open is Downtown Disney in Anaheim. A full-service restaurant and bakery with table service that serves favorites, classic menu items, and new selections was created for the Disney location. It will be the first time California-Cuban dishes will be served at Disneyland.

The easy way would be to franchise or start selling frozen products in the local grocery stores, but Porto's will wait until the right time before changing their standards. Many more locations are planned; but until the papers are signed, you will have to visit one of the current ones. 🧁

(top): The Porto children (Betty, Raul Jr., and Margarita) holding a picture of their parents at the grand opening of the Northridge location, (left): Parisian Cake, (right): Potato balls

Chuck E. Cheese's Pizza Time Theater

SLOGAN: "Where a Kid Can Be a Kid"

NAME TODAY: Chuck E. Cheese

ORIGINAL LOCATION: 2445 Fontaine Rd., San Jose

OPENED: May 17, 1977

FOUNDER: Nolan Bushnell (Atari Restaurant Operating Division)

CURRENTLY AT THE FIRST LOCATION: The first location is still in operation.

CURRENT OWNERSHIP: CEC Holdings

There are 570 locations in nineteen countries and forty-seven states.

chuckecheese.com

THE FATHER OF ELECTRONIC GAMING and founder of Atari, Nolan Bushnell, opened the first Chuck E. Cheese's Pizza Time Theater in San Jose in 1977.

Bushnell wanted to use his electronic mind to create a space of wonderment and fun for all ages. But creating an interactive restaurant of games, fun, and a show was no easy task. Bushnell wanted a stage with animatronic characters doing a show instead of employees dressed up. This would cut down on labor and costs in the long run. But finding a company to create animated puppets was not an easy task. Harold Goldbrandsen, the owner of Fantasy Forest Manufacturing, mostly created college mascot costumes but said he could figure out how to make an animatronic costume. Using a friendly rat as the character could work, but naming him was difficult; Rickey Rat was a contender, but this name was too close to Mickey Mouse of Disney. Bushnell finally decided on Chuck E. Cheese as the name of the pizza restaurant and the primary mascot. Chuck E. Cheese was also a three-smile name. You smile three times while saying it.

Chuck E. Cheese was to be more than a pizza restaurant; it would be a place for the entire family to have an evening out, with a large indoor arcade, a fun pizza menu, and an animatronic show. Placed around the restaurant would

Opposite: Kids playing at the Charleston, South Carolina opening, (top): Unicorn Churros, (bottom): Chuck E. Cheese

The Original Pizza Time Players

Chuck E. Cheese: Rat

Crusty: Baseball-playing cat

Billy "Banjo" Boggs/Renamed Jasper T. Jowls: a hillbilly dog

Pascal: The Italian Chef

Warblettes: a trio of singing magpies

Helen Henny: Hen

Madam Oink: Pig

Foxy Colleen: Fox

Dolli Dimples: piano-playing hippo

Mopsy sisters

be large picture frames with Chuck E. Cheese and the cast of the Original Pizza Time Players. These performers would create excitement and would entertain guests while they waited for their pizza.

Opening in a building that had formerly housed a brokerage firm, Bushnell soon realized that the size was too small (only 5,000 square feet). He knew a successful location would need to be much bigger. With the success of the first location, Bushnell started looking for a second; he knew it had to be even larger than the first one. Across town, at a former Shopper World grocery store location with a whopping 19,000 square feet, he knew he could have over 100 games of pinball and be the largest pizza restaurant in the country.

Partner Warner Communications wanted out of the restaurant business after just over one year; they wanted to focus only on video games. So, in June 1978, Bushnell purchased the concept from Warner. Since then, Chuck E. Cheese has had many owners and parent companies. In 1984, Bushnell resigned, and Brock Hotel Corporation acquired the chain. When Australian investors came calling, wanting to franchise, they stated that a name change would be in order. Using the name Chuck in Australia refers to "up-chuck" or throw up. The

(top): Kids in the arcade, (middle): Birthday Party Pizza Pack, (left): Irving, Texas location, (right): Exterior of Chuck E. Cheese

Australian market used Charlie Cheese's Pizza Playhouse as a replacement. Today, CEC Holdings is the parent company.

In 2012, revenues were struggling company-wide. A rebranding of some of the characters took place; Chuck E. Cheese became a softened rock-star mouse instead of a rat. A few years later, the company tested half a dozen Midwest locations with a new design concept: upscale décor and an open kitchen. In addition, they expanded the food choices to appeal to adults and families instead of hosting kid parties. They also changed one of the stages into a dance area.

Pizza has always been the focus of Chuck E. Cheese, with chicken wings, a salad bar, sandwiches, and an array of desserts, with many locations also serving alcohol. However, Chuck E. Cheese had to maneuver through the 2020 COVID-19 pandemic without opening its doors to the public. Instead of changing the food choices, Chuck E. Cheese started a ghost kitchen called Pasqually P. Pieplate to service orders through food-delivery systems.

Today, you will not see the animatronic rat that made the chain famous, but someone in costume will be walking around greeting kids and adults alike in over 570 locations in 19 countries, making kids smile as they say Chuck E. Cheese.

(top): Birthday girl showing award card, (middle): Bike riding in the arcade, (bottom): Award redemption area

Claim Jumper Restaurant and Saloon

SLOGAN: "Great Food, Friendly Service, and Good Value"

NAME TODAY: Claim Jumper

ORIGINAL LOCATION: 10900 Los Alamitos Blvd., Los Alamitos

OPENED: September 27, 1977

FOUNDERS: Carl and Craig Nickoloff (father-and-son team)

CURRENT OWNERSHIP: Landry's Inc.

CURRENTLY AT THE FIRST LOCATION: Nick's Deli II Restaurant

There are eleven locations in four states.

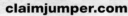

claimjumper.com

THE AMERICAN DREAM for so many is starting a successful business and buying a home for your family. Nicholas (Papa Nick) Nickoloff did just that and succeeded tenfold.

Papa Nick was born in Sophia, Bulgaria, and immigrated to Michigan with a dream of owning a restaurant. With old-world knowledge and family recipes, Papa Nick operated the Pullman Lunch Restaurant, a food truck, and a billiard hall in Pontiac, Michigan. He and his wife had a son, Carl, in the 1930s, and they moved to a warmer climate on the West Coast. They opened the Lookout Drive-In on Pioneer Boulevard in Norwalk. Carl hosted many car clubs at the drive-in as he was also the timekeeper at the Dry Lakes Raceway, and he opened Nick's Patio Restaurant on Olympic Blvd., close to Downtown Los Angeles.

Carl was practically born in a restaurant with a spatula in his hand. Working with his father in the new ventures was in his blood. Father and son teamed up to open a Googie-style coffee shop in the up-and-coming area of Long Beach at Cherry and Wardlow streets. The opening ribbon-cutting picture doesn't only have the father-and-son team, but also includes grandson Craig donning a chef's outfit at the young age of six. Naming the café Nik's without the "c" was a cost-effective measure, as the sign company charged per letter, and Papa Nick felt that the name of the café would still be pronounced the same.

Nik's and the Viking Room served full meals with wines and an array of desserts and satisfied a hungry community for twenty years. After Papa Nick passed away in 1972, Carl and Craig managed Nik's until 1980, when they closed it to focus on opening Claim Jumper Restaurant locations. Nik's and Claim Jumper restaurants operated concurrently for three years.

Carl and Craig dreamed of opening a large restaurant in the Los Alamitos area with a steak-and-seafood menu and huge portions at a very fair price. Looking for a location that would work, Carl found a closed Kaplan's Deli on Los Alamitos Blvd. Theming the restaurant around the Gold Rush of 1849 with antiques and the old Western feel would prove a success. The new restaurant name

Opposite (top): Carl Nickoloff at Los Alamitos during pre-opening construction, (bottom): Nick Nickoloff at Los Angeles food stand, (top): Matches, (bottom): Employee name tag

would not be the family name like former establishments, but was named Claim Jumper. A cowboy kneeling with a gold panning dish became the logo. Success was an understatement. Hungry diners from miles around flocked to the new restaurant. The restaurant's theme is the Gold Rush and the miners of the day.

Claim Jumper Locations, 1977–2006

The company had restaurants in California, Colorado, Washington, Arizona, Nevada, Oregon, Illinois, and Wisconsin. All restaurants listed below had signed leases. At the same time, Craig helmed Claim Jumper, but not all had been built and opened by mid-2006 when he departed.

UNIT/LOCATION NUMBER	OPENING YEAR	UNIT/LOCATION NUMBER	OPENING YEAR
#1 Los Alamitos, CA	1977	#25 Tempe, AZ	2000
#2 Laguna Hills, CA	1984	#26 Tukwila, WA	2000
#3 Fountain Valley, CA	1984	(still operating)	
#4 Santa Ana, CA	1985	#27 Roseville, CA	2000
#5 Puente Hills, CA	1988	#28 Scottsdale, AZ	2002
#6 Buena Park, CA	1989	#29 Las Vegas, NV	2001
(still operating)		#30 Reno, NV	2000
#7 Irvine, CA	1991	#31 Fresno, CA	2005
#8 Corona, CA	1991	#32 Henderson, NV	2004
#9 Carlsbad, CA	1993	(still operating)	
#10 Temecula, CA	1992	#33 Costa Mesa, CA	2003
#11 San Diego, CA	1993	(still operating)	
(still operating)		#34 Lynnwood, WA	2004
#12 La Mesa, CA	1995	#35 Tucson, AZ	2005
(still operating)		#36 Lombard, IL	2006
#13 Rancho Cucamonga, CA	1994	#37 Thousand Oaks, CA	2005
(still operating)		#38 Fremont, CA	2006
#14 Brea, CA	1994	#39 Hoffman Estates, IL	2006
#15 Monrovia, CA	1994	#40 Wheeling, IL	2007
#16 Lone Tree, CO	1995	#41 Avondale, AZ	2006
#17 Long Beach, CA	1995	#42 Clackamas, OR	2007
#18 Torrance, CA	1997	(still operating)	
#19 Concord, CA	1996	#43 Tualatin, OR	2007
#20 Valencia, CA	1997	(still operating)	
#21 Mission Viejo, CA	1998	#44 Vegas Town Center, NV	2007
#22 Redmond, WA	1998	#45 Palmdale, CA	2008
#23 Northridge, CA	1998	(still operating)	
#24 Phoenix, AZ	1999	#46 Brookfield, WI	2008

Each location was decorated with antiques (Claim Jumper had a massive warehouse in Tustin full of relics to outfit new places), such as old scales, milk bottles, animal heads, jugs, quilts, trunks, tureens, folk art, and more. They carried the theme throughout, with the bar area referred to as the Saloon and the hostesses dressed in denim skirts, white ruffled blouses, and of course sheriff badges. Once you gave the hostess your name and how many were in your party, you would receive a cardboard badge with the name of someone or something from the Old West. This is what they would call when your table was ready. Sometimes the wait could be up to two hours on the weekends. To pass the time, you could play a game of checkers or another game they had close by in the waiting area.

Claim Jumper catered to the family with the "Little Jumper" menu, where kids were weighed and charged five cents per pound (taken from the Big Yellow House [page 61]). The menu featured rotisserie barbeque chicken (which you could see in the kitchen from the hostess stand), ribs that fell off the bone, fish dishes including the fresh catch of the day, sandwiches, and pasta. The salad bar put others in the industry to shame with fresh fruits, sliced avocados, crab salads, salami and ham, cottage cheese, and hot bacon dressing. Fresh-baked mega muffins were included in the a la carte salad bar. The baked potatoes were the largest in the industry. They are referred to as #35's, which means 35 potatoes to a 50-pound box.

After one visit to Claim Jumper, you learned that you should fill up at the salad bar and take your entrée home for two meals. Each table had a bottle of Claim Jumper Barbeque sauce for you and plenty of stock at the register in case you wanted to take some home.

Desserts were featured in the front of the restaurant when you walked in, so that they would tempt your tastebuds and you could plan ahead. The ever-popular Motherlode Cake had to be served lying down on the plate, as it was six layers of chocolate cake with fudge frosting sprinkled with walnuts. In 2003, the Food Network counted down the top five "Ultimate Food Indulgences"; Claim Jumper's Chocolate Motherlode Cake was number two, with only caviar beating it out. Sales of the cake skyrocketed after the prestigious award. The Ideclair was a nine-inch éclair filled with vanilla ice cream, whipped cream, and hot fudge.

Every menu item was made with the freshest quality ingredients, tasted perfect, and came in large servings. The only way to leave without a to-go bag is if you were starving when you arrived. Each Claim Jumper location made soups, dressings, and other items for the diner. Every place had the same menu without any deviation. Keeping the food taste and quality throughout the chain was essential to the company's success.

In 1984, the California Alligator Farm roadside attraction attendance was lacking, and the Cottage Pottery Shop lost its lease; a new center replaced them on the corner of La Palma and Beach boulevards across from the Knott's Berry Farm amusement park in Buena Park. The new center would be a perfect spot for a new Claim Jumper. The restaurant would feel like a continuation of the customers' day, as it was themed like the park. Today, this is the longest continuously functioning Claim Jumper since 1989.

Torrance store #18 was the most controversial. The restaurant was built from the ground up in the newly

Owner Time Line

1977–2005:	Nickoloff Family	46 locations in 8 states
2005–2010:	Leonard Green & Partners	45 locations in 9 states
2010–Present:	Landry's Inc.	23 locations in 7 states

The Nickoloff Family of Restaurants		
Nicholas Nickoloff:	Pullman Lunch, Pontiac, Michigan	1920s
Nicholas and Carl Nickoloff:	Nick's Patio Restaurant, Los Angeles	1940s
	Lookout Drive-in Norwalk	1940s
	Nik's Café & Viking Room Long Beach	1957–1980
Carl and Craig Nickoloff:	Claim Jumper Restaurants	1977–2005
Craig and Amy Nickoloff:	Connie and Ted's, West Hollywood	2011
Nick Nickoloff:	Nick's Laguna	2008
	Nick's San Clemente	
	Nick's on 2nd	
	Nick's Manhattan Beach	
	Nick's South Lake Avenue	
	Nick's Del Mar	
	South of Nick's Mexican Kitchen	
	Laguna and San Clemente	
	Nick's on State, Carlsbad	
Nicole (Nickoloff) and Tim Humphry:		
	Humphry's Sandwich Shop	2010–2020

developed Crossroads Center on Crenshaw Blvd.; on one side of the street was the City of Lomita. From the beginning, the mayor of Lomita, Dave Albert, fought with the City of Torrance over building the trendy restaurant. He even claimed that his city would have to spend more on police patrols because "the restaurant will spit out drunk drivers into the streets." Albert always loved to boast that his tiny city had more churches than liquor licenses. Claim Jumper did not take this allegation lightly, as Claim Jumper is a family restaurant with a designated-driver program supported by Mothers Against Drunk Drivers (MADD). In their 18 years of operation, Claim Jumper had not had one violation. The location opened on time. In 1999, MADD received one dollar from the restaurant per non-drinking driver of a group, and provided soft drinks and a button. If the group did not have a designated driver, MADD would call and pay for a cab.

After opening over a dozen locations, the original Los Alamitos closed because the landlord and the Nickoloffs could not agree on a new lease. Long Beach opened five miles from the original spot in 1995. Craig took the threshold of the original site and installed it in the new Long Beach location. Long Beach closed in the summer of 2020.

In June 1996, the Nickoloffs created a frozen-food and packaged division to sell some of their top-selling products in supermarkets coast to coast. They held on to the division for four years before selling it to American Pie Inc. Many food items had a higher price tag than other frozen foods, but the products were comparable to the restaurants; in some taste-test panels, the panelists could not tell the difference.

Over the years, Craig has been awarded many accolades, including the prestigious 1999 California Restaurateur-of-the-Year Award and the Golden Chain Award. In 2003, the Spirit of Life was awarded by the City of Hope Medical Center. In addition, the Nickoloffs have always been a provider for fundraising community events. The Good Shepherd Lutheran Home of the West Housing for adults with disabilities, Joswick Therapeutic riding center (equine therapy for people with disabilities), and Saddleback vocational vision job training for those with disabilities were just a few.

Nick Nickoloff, Craig's son, worked in every job at Claim Jumpers as a dishwasher, busboy, pantry cook, and host before he moved to corporate headquarters, eventually leading the marketing department. Today, Nick owns a large conglomerate of restaurants along the Pacific Coast from Los Angeles to San Diego.

C.J. Meats was created and worked directly for Claim Jumper out of Rogers Poultry in Huntington Park. It was designed to maintain the standards of the Nickoloff family for Claim Jumper locations. However, when Landry's bought Claim Jumper out of bankruptcy in 2009, they had no interest in using C.J. Meats; Craig and Amy Nickoloff acquired the company's rights, renamed it West Coast Prime Meats, and launched their own company in 2010. Currently, the company supplies award-winning meats to many restaurants in the Western United States.

In October 2001, a month after the 9/11 terrorist attacks on the nation, Claim Jumper, with over 4,000 restaurants nationwide, donated all the profits of one day to the American Red Cross, raising millions for the effort.

Over the years, all the Claim Jumper locations created and participated in local non-profit fundraising events. For example, high school scholarship fundraising efforts found teachers, school administrators, and coaches working alongside the restaurant staff, earning tips for the scholarship fund. Tip-A-Cop nights were also popular, as local law enforcement agencies in uniform would work alongside the team, with the proceeds going to the Special Olympics and the Law Enforcement Torch Run.

Fourth-grade students in California would study our country's history as part of their curriculum. With the theme of the restaurants being the California Gold Rush of 1849, the Claim Jumper began the Gold Discovery Project for kids. Entries of the classroom's art projects, maps, journals, and such that were based on the Gold Rush were judged, and winning classrooms were invited to lunch and a tour of their nearest Claim Jumper.

In 2002, the 25th Silver Anniversary was a year packed with events, from car giveaways to 25,000 bottles of the signature barbeque sauce to all diners on September 27, the same day as the original location's opening.

The Nickoloffs franchised one location called C.J. Diggings in Park City, Utah. Unfortunately, the name Claim Jumper was already taken by a rancher, so they had to use the initials. Also unfortunately, it lasted only one year, as the quality standards did not meet the Nickoloffs', so the franchise agreement was terminated.

2005 was the end of an era for the Nickoloff family; Claim Jumper was sold to Leonard Green and Partners. Claim Jumper lost sales, quality, and locations in the five years of new ownership.

In 2010, after the downturn in casual dining, Claim Jumper Restaurants were up for auction through bankruptcy. Craig Nickoloff had made two offers to buy back Claim Jumper since 2009; Landry's Restaurants out of Houston made the winning bid.

Today, Landry's Inc. owns the Claim Jumper chain. The portfolio is half what it was when Nickoloff's owned the company. Landry's has re-branded the restaurants with new logos and new menu items. Today, you cannot enjoy the remarkable roasted chicken or ribs that helped make the Claim Jumper so popular, but you can have a pizza and a slice of Motherlode Cake. ✖

Mrs. Fields' Chocolate Chippery

SLOGANS: "Some people take flour and add chocolate chips; we take chocolate chips and add flour." • "Good Enough Never Is"

NAME TODAY: Mrs. Fields Cookies

ORIGINAL LOCATION: Liddicoat's Restaurant Mall, 322 University Ave., Palo Alto

OPENED: August 18, 1977

FOUNDER: Debbi Fields

CURRENT OWNERSHIP: Famous Brands International

CURRENTLY AT THE FIRST LOCATION: Maum Restaurant

There are 125 locations in twenty-five states and many countries worldwide.

MrsFields.com

"I ALWAYS SAY 'FOOD TALKS.' Give a freshly baked item; it will open doors." Debbi Fields would bake cookies for her husband's clients like a dutiful wife when she accompanied him on business trips and meetings for several years. Many times, people would ask what she did for a living. "Housewife," she would answer, with a feeling of being belittled—until they tasted the cookies. It soon became "Will Debbi have some cookies for our meeting?"

Knowing the cookies were a favorite, Debbi thought about opening a cookie store. All the people she told the idea to thought it was impossible. "It won't work." "You are going to lose everything!" "Who would loan you money?" There were only negative responses. Even her husband, Randy, thought the idea was a little dicey. One loan officer told Randy that if she did this, the good part would be that he would always know where she was and it would keep her busy: she would learn a valuable lesson; and her failure would be a terrific tax shelter for Randy's business.

After obtaining a loan from Bank of America at 21 percent interest, Debbi started looking for a space. She ended up with a tiny 300-square-foot store that was part of the Liddicoat's Restaurant Mall on the busy University Avenue in Menlo Park. She outfitted the shop with used equipment that would do the job. But she was very smart to spend money on what the customer would notice and experience—the ingredients. She surrounded herself with the best people to help her purchase equipment and quality ingredients. Many ingredient suppliers tried to get Debbi to try different products, such as dates instead of the high-priced raisins when the weather destroyed the California crop. She was also pitched a blend of 50 percent butter and 50 percent margarine. All of these products were inferior. She wanted the highest

Opposite: Debbi holding tray of cookies, (top): Valentine's Day cookie tin, (bottom): Mrs. Fields mall location

quality for the final product. Debbi never put preservatives or chemicals in her cookies or the dough.

On Thursday morning, August 18, 1977, Debbi Fields opened her first store, Mrs. Fields' Chocolate Chippery. She felt the words Mrs. Fields' displayed the feeling of someone in the kitchen: older, matriarchal, and of quality. Debbi, only 20 years old, bet her husband Randy that she could make over $50 in sales on the first day. She sat all morning waiting for customers, and none came in. She was determined not to lose the bet, so she got out in front of the store, took samples of the fresh cookies, and walked up and down the street. She ended up selling $75 in cookies. After this, she created hourly sales goals. "Good Is Never Enough" became her catchphrase. She spoke of it often.

She set things up the way she liked to be treated, and her new store employees were trained to treat their customers that way. While making cookies for her husband's clients, she saw people enjoy the delicious cookies right out of the oven without even being cooled before eating. This resulted in her cookies being sold within two hours of her taking them out of the oven. If cookies were not sold

First location in Palo Alto, CA

in the allotted timeframe, they would be given to local charitable groups, mainly focusing on children. These cookies were called "Cookie Orphans." The Mrs. Fields Children's Health Foundation was formed shortly after creating her company. "Children are our greatest asset," she says; Mrs. Fields allocates donation dollars to Cystic Fibrosis and the Starlight Foundation.

Randy created a motto on the first store's wall: "Some people take flour and add chocolate chips; we take chocolate chips and add flour." Debbi stated that she could not put one more chip into her cookies or they could fall apart.

Debbi wanted a family atmosphere at the shop. Employees had to love the product and the job. She never put together a manual on how to work, as each applicant was different. She did have a three-part method for the interview process. First, the candidate was given a cookie to eat; they were judged on their reaction to consuming it. Second, you would be given a tray of cookie samples and sent to the front of the store to see your interaction with potential consumers. Third, you would be given the lyrics to Debbi's Happy Birthday song and told to sing as if someone had just come in and it was their birthday. Creating a fun and exciting atmosphere in the store, Debbi made a song for the employees to sing to the tune of Zip-a-Dee-Doo-Dah.

Chippity doo-dah
Chippity-ay
My, oh my, what a wonderful day!

In 1979, Warren Simmons, a developer of the new shopping area Pier 39 in San Francisco, approached her to open a second store on the Pier. It was slated to be a tourist destination. Simmons kept the spot open for a year before Debbi finally said yes. The Pier 39 spot was so popular that the line of customers would wrap in front of the other stores, thus creating a problem with the other tenants. Today this location is still open.

Debbi knew she could hire the type of employee who she felt would work well with the company at each location. She and Randy created many software programs to manage the sites from a central location. The objective of the technology was to achieve two things. First, store managers were preoccupied with the paperwork, planning, forecasting, and all the processing stuff; so, instead, she automated all the administrative work. This enabled the managers to focus on the quality of their product and, more importantly, on their customers. The objective of the technology was to leverage Debbi into every store in real time with best-practice advice. Randy called this "Retail Operations Intelligence" or ROI. This artificial intelligence based on technology would analyze information in real time, allowing the store manager to receive suggestions regarding staff scheduling, production, and purchases on a local store level. It would help every store have the correct product amount without overbaking or overpurchasing.

Once the Pier 39 location manager arrived at work, they would call up the Day Planner program created by Randy, with sales projections based on the prior year. Adjusting for weather, day of the week, holiday, or a regular day, the Day Planner would determine how to bake for the day, hour by hour, and calculate how many customers were needed each hour to reach the day's goals. The program would also tell the manager how many batches of which cookie flavor were required for the daily production. Keep in mind that having a computer in your workplace was very innovative for the early 1980s. Each hour, the manager kept the computer informed of the progress as the day elapsed.

> **Top Items sold**
> Milk Chocolate Chip Cookies
> Milk Chocolate Chip Cookies with Walnuts
> Semi-Sweet Chocolate Chip Cookies
> Semi-Sweet Chocolate Chip Cookies with Walnuts
> Semi-Sweet Chocolate Chip Cookies with Macadamia Nuts
> Debra's Special (Oatmeal, Raisin, Nut)
> Coco-Mac (Fresh Coconut and Macadamia)
> Peanut Butter Dreams (Peanut Butter and White Chocolate Chips)
> Royal Pecan (Semi-Sweet with Pecan)
> Triple Chocolate (Cocoa, Semi-Sweet, and White Chocolate)

In 1981, 14 stores were in operation. Debbi was the only person who had the recipes, and those were in her head. If something happened to her, Debbi needed to have the ingredients prepackaged from their suppliers. Also, prepackaging was a way to expand the ever-growing need for cookies in places that Debbi could not be. They still mixed the cookie dough at the store level. The dry mixture would be shipped to the stores with the packages listed as "Mrs. Fields dry cookie mix" on the bags.

The following year, Debbi and Randy moved their family and business to the famous mountain resort of Park City, Utah, known for the clean air and living. They built and owned many buildings in the famous skiing town. Cookie College, a training school for management, was also placed in downtown Park City.

In three short years, from 1985 to 1988, the company opened 225 new stores. Debbi overruled the idea of franchising, as she knew the cookies and methods could be duplicated but that the warmth of the bakeries and the employees' character could not. In 1987, the menu included 14 varieties of cookies and five types of brownies, ice cream, candy, and muffins.

In the mid-1980s, an urban myth/hoax started, as many have. Someone asked for a product's recipe while in a shop purchasing cookies. She supposedly was told it would be "two-fifty." Her charge card was charged, and she got home and saw on the receipt that she had been charged $250. She supposedly called to complain, and they would not offer a refund. So, the lady in question made copies of the recipe and the story, and told everyone to send out the information to all they knew. Remember that this was before email and the Internet, so people took time and money to send this out. In response to the chain letter, Debbi Fields posted a sign in all her stores:

"Mrs. Fields' recipe has *never* been sold. A rumor is circulating that the Mrs. Fields Cookie recipe was sold to a woman for $250. A chocolate-chip cookie recipe was attached to the story. I want to tell all my customers that this story is *not valid*, this is not my recipe, and I have not sold the recipe to anyone. Mrs. Fields' recipe is a delicious trade secret."
—Debbi Fields

Before placing the laminated letter on the counters of the stores, the general office received hundreds of calls. So, Debbi sent everyone cookie cards for a free dozen.

This myth also happened with a cookie recipe from the Dallas-based department store Neiman Marcus's Zodiac Cafes. These cafes didn't even serve cookies; the formula was identical to Mrs. Fields's fake recipe. The New York Waldorf-Astoria was a target with a similar hoax involving a red velvet cake.

In the first quarter of 1983 and before expansion in the New York City area, Debbi and Mrs. Fields were highlighted with a story and announcement in the *New York Times* business section. It was a "warning" to the top-rated local David's Cookie Company that Mrs. Fields was heading east.

What makes the cookies unique? First, the company says, it prepares all its products on location. Moreover, the company refuses to package its cookies for department-store sales and has spurned repeated

Debbi baking cookies in the first location

requests to sell franchises. Mrs. Fields's employees mixed fresh ingredients, pure creamery butter, pure chocolate chips, natural vanilla extracts, and nuts into large batches that they hand-shaped into large rounds to bake into fresh cookies.

Mrs. Fields Cookies planned to open its Miami and New York stores on April 1, 1983, then follow with Boston outlets. In 1983, with the cookie shops having so many locations, the Marshall Field's department store in Chicago that opened in 1853 went head-to-head on naming rights to the name "Field's" and filed a claim against Mrs. Fields Cookies with the United States Patent and Infringement Office claiming the name Fields was first used by them in 1853 and that Mrs. Fields used a similar font in all their logos. Mrs. Fields won the claim and continued to use the name.

In 1987, the company was doing very well and earning a significant profit. Looking at their growth, a frozen facility was needed, so they purchased La Petite Boulangerie, a chain of 119 French bakery/sandwich shops in the western United States. In the purchase, they obtained a frozen facility just outside Los Angeles, in Carson. A few years after the purchase, they set up a system of mixing the dough in Carson, shaping it into "dough balls," and flash-freezing it into boxes so they could be delivered directly to the stores. Still, Mrs. Fields used the same high-quality ingredients. Now the new locations would only need a freezer, not a mixer or area to make the recipes. This would also help in creating perfect cookies with less room for error.

In 1990, Debbi entered into an agreement with the Marriott Corporation to produce and sell Mrs. Fields' products in stores owned and operated by Marriott. Under the agreement, Marriott financed and built 60 Mrs. Fields cookie stores in the following five years. These stores were built in travel plazas, airports, and hotels, paying five percent of the gross sales. Marriott, the world's largest hotel and contract food management group, used brand names throughout their retail food outlets worldwide.

Publicity photo of Debbi Fields Rose

Many other products and company partnerships happened. For example, you could fly 45,000 feet in the air on a United Airlines Flight and, after your meal, receive a hot Chocolate Chip or Oatmeal (Debra's Special) on a white dish with a Mrs. Fields napkin, but only for those in first class. Prepackaged items included refrigerated cookie dough, ice cream cookie sandwiches, ice cream with the Mrs. Fields cookies or brownies mixed in, and Mrs. Fields chocolate chips with a cookie recipe on the bag. Debbi also wrote many cookie and dessert books and was the first on the new Food Network to teach how to make desserts, sometimes showcasing her daughters.

In 2000, Mrs. Fields had over 500 locations and over 5,000 workers in 10 countries. Then Debbi sold Mrs. Fields to an investment firm. After a few purchases and company sales, Mrs. Fields is currently owned by Famous Brands International (FBI), headquartered in Broomfield, Colorado. FBI also owns TCBY Yogurt Shops®. Today, you may find the two of them packaged together in one store. Dustin Lyman, the former Chicago Bears tight end, was the CEO of the parent company of Mrs. Fields Cookies for several years.

Since the sale, many things have changed. The cookies more than two hours out of the oven are not donated to any charity. Instead, they are kept for sale in the stores. No longer are they sold hot from the range. Today, if you taste a Mrs. Fields cookie at one of the stores, it does not resemble the cookies offered at Mrs. Fields' Chocolate Chippery or Mrs. Fields's many stores. Once this happened, Debbi could no longer associate her persona with the organization.

Today, Debbi is a motivational speaker and philanthropist for health and children's issues. 🍪

Mimi's Café

SLOGAN: "Celebrate Food, Friends, and Family"

NAME TODAY: Mimi's Bistro + Bakery

ORIGINAL LOCATION: 1240 N. Euclid Ave., Anaheim

OPENED: 1978

FOUNDERS: Arthur J. Simms and Tom Simms

CURRENT OWNERSHIP: Le Duff America, Inc. Groupe

CURRENTLY AT THE FIRST LOCATION: Googie Car Wash

Today there are forty-six restaurants in twelve states.

mimiscafe.com

THE SIMMSES ARE A restaurant family woven into the fabric of their beginnings in Southern California, starting with first-generation Arthur J. Simms working at the MGM Commissary and bringing that experience into his restaurants. One of the notables was the French Market Place restaurant in West Hollywood (1973–2015), opening in the large retail two-story building at Laurel Avenue and Santa Monica Boulevard. The French-inspired restaurant was open until very late and housed on the ground floor and outside the large building. This was the starting point of Mimi's Café. From the food on the first menus of Mimi's, you can see the influence of the French Market Place.

Arthur had been stationed in France during World War II, so he and son Tom took trips over there. In brainstorming for names for their new venture, they came up with Mimi. Mimi was a woman Arthur had met at a party for American soldiers back in the day. The name Mimi stuck with them both.

The father-and-son team, with investors Brian Taylor and Paul Kurt, formed the SWH Corporation. Mimi's would fill a new niche in the family-friendly casual dining concept—a French-inspired New Orleans French Quarter experience. Tablecloths, linen napkins, and the warm bistro look of a fine dinner house with the value of a coffee shop would create the upscale casual restaurant Mimi's.

The first Mimi's opened near the Disneyland Theme Park area of Anaheim in 1978 with a whimsical look. Within a year, an outdoor patio was added for additional seating and dining. The success of Mimi's SWH led to the opening of a

Opposite: First location in Anaheim, CA, (top): Matchbook cover

Ownership	
1978–1996:	SWH Corporation
1996–2004:	SWH Corporation and Saunders Karp & Megrue (SKM)
2004–2013:	Bob Evans Farms
2013–Present:	Le Duff America, Inc. Groupe

Dining booth at Anaheim location

second location in the neighboring city of Garden Grove three years later. After Garden Grove, the expansion was fast, with one place every eight months for the next few years, with eleven locations opened by 1989. The Simmses felt no need to franchise, as the concept would be difficult to execute while keeping the quality of service and food at the standard they demanded. Decreasing the staff turnover rate was very important for SWH. In 1990, a five-day learning program for front-of-the-house team members detailed how each dish was prepared and created for the locations. It was called Mimi University.

Mimi's was open from breakfast to late-night dinners, emphasizing American fares such as hearty soups, pot pies, pot roast, pork chops, steaks, and arrays of kinds of pasta, as well as some French/Creole inspired dishes; over 100 items made up the menu. Mimi's also had a lengthy unheard-of (for the time) children's menu. When you were seated, a basket of mini-muffins and slices of bread with rich whipped butter would be placed on your table. This basket was almost a meal in itself.

In the early years of the 1990s, SWH opened additional units; research showed that women influenced where to dine when not eating at home, so Mimi's featured pastel color themes in the new locations. When the chain started to expand into suburban and rural markets, the décor changed to earth tones.

In 1995, growth was on the mind of the Simmses, but help was needed; Saunders Karp & Megrue (SKM) stepped in, a private merchant bank known for their supportive hands-off approach. SKM purchased 65 percent of SWH, allowing Arthur and the two other investors to cash out, with Tom Simms retaining 35 percent ownership and continuing to run the company. With the help of SKM, over the next five years Mimi's doubled their size with 49 locations, also opening in three additional states.

October 20, 2000, was a sad day for the Simms family as Arthur J. Simms, in the business for more than 50 years, passed away. At that time, Tom Simms too was reaching his limit for managing a chain of over 50 units with national expansion. So, when Mimi's opened four restaurants in Texas in a little over a year, Tom knew he had to hire Russ Bendell (CEO of Habit Restaurants) to serve as president and CEO while he became the chairman of the board to grow Mimi's.

Unit Numbers	
1978:	1 unit
1981:	2 units
1989:	11 units
1993:	16 units
1998:	21 units
2001:	53 units
2004:	80 units
2007:	115 units
2010:	146 units
2013:	145 units
2014:	119 units
2019:	77 units
2022:	46 units

During Bendell's almost eight-year tenure at Mimi's, he opened additional locations and expanded eastward into nine states. Then, out of New Albany, Ohio, Bob Evans Farms purchased Mimi's Cafés, hoping to expand their presence into the West Coast from the Midwest. Bendell stayed with Bob Evans Farms to help with additional expansion of the Mimi's brand for another three years before moving to the Cheesecake Factory as president (page 105).

Bob Evans Farms saw that same-store sales were down for their Mimi's brand, so a remodel from top to bottom was tested at the Valencia location. They started with the front area, creating a larger space for take-out for their signature bakery and bread items and a coffee bistro bar serving a branded French roast coffee and whole beans to enjoy at home.

After nine years and frequently closing locations, Bob Evans Farms sold Mimi's division at a loss to the Le Duff America, Inc. Groupe, a French restaurant conglomerate with over 1,310 restaurant locations in the United States and Europe.

Le Duff in 2019 brought significant changes to Mimi's brand like never before. A remodeled take-out counter when you first walk in, a new name from Mimi's Café to Mimi's Bistro + Bakery, and a new updated font. There are over 30 new dishes featuring the French-influenced "Bites & Beverages" shareable menu; Mimi's branded wines from the Bordeaux region in France are served; and new artwork and photography from French artists adorn the walls of the locations. The overall menu has been scaled down from 149 to 76 menu items.

Today, Mimi's has shrunk to the size it was 25 years ago. Tom Simms opened his new Lazy Dog concept (page 203), growing eastward with all the knowledge and background from his grandfather and father. ✖

1990 menu cover

Souplantation

AKA: Sweet Tomatoes (1990)

ORIGINAL LOCATION: 6171 Mission Gorge Rd., San Diego

OPENED: Fall 1978

FOUNDERS: Ron Demery, Steve Hohe, and Dennis Jay

LAST PARENT COMPANY: Garden Fresh Restaurant Group

CURRENTLY AT THE FIRST LOCATION: Mission Square Center

At one point, there were 110 locations in fifteen states. Since the closings of Souplantations/ Sweet Tomatoes, there have been many attempts of reopening and energizing the brand; we shall wait and see.

THREE FRIENDS AND WORK BUDDIES developed a self-service restaurant concept in the Mission Gorge area of San Diego. Dennis Jay (a former bartender), Steve Hohe—both from Springfield Wagon Works, a cowboy chuckwagon-themed restaurant and bar—and Ron Demery (a bail bondsman) worked four and a half months building their restaurant. Steve designed the entire interior of pine and cedar, skylights, and hanging plants to make a park-like atmosphere. Stained-glass windows and copper hoods over the soup kitchen completed the look.

The first Souplantation was born. Two 30-foot-long self-serving tables with large bowls and containers sat parallel to the workspace for the employee to refill the ingredients and clean the spillage. The first location stocked over 20 salad items and four soups, including homestyle chili, with New England Clam Chowder as the staple. The bread station had freshly baked corn muffins, two types of bread, pumpernickel, and sourdough. Seafood selections were the highlight of the weekend choices with Alaskan King crab and fresh shrimp.

Sandwiches were also part of the opening menu, with roast beef and ham served open-face style au jus on a hearty roll. However, these were deleted from the menu after only a few weeks, as they didn't quite relate to the more salad-focused concept of the restaurant.

To open with outstanding soups and baked goods, the founders collected family recipes from past generations and tested the favorites they felt would also become their family favorites.

They tested their concept, added salad items, and expanded the soup choices, mini-loaves of bread, and muffins. Two additional restaurants were opened in San Diego County, which proved a success.

After five years, the three founders sold their interest to Tony Brooke and Michael Mack. After Brooke's father had

> **Company Values**
> + Accountability for results
> + Success through relentless improvement
> + Passion for serving
> + Integrity in all actions
> + Respect for each individual
> + Embracing change

Opposite (top): West Palm Beach, Florida Fresh Tomatoes exterior, (bottom): Souplantation exterior

Inside West Palm Beach, Florida location

lunch in the original location and told the two about how it was a great food concept to invest in, they formed the Garden Fresh Restaurant Group.

The restaurants were very popular with the healthy beach lifestyle of the area customers, but would the concept work outside of California? In the 1980s, the company maintained rapid growth in the Southern California area and began eastward expansion. At one point, the San Diego area had five salad-soup restaurant concepts competing for the same diner. The other four competitors started adding everything from meat and potatoes to carving stations. But Souplantation kept its prices stable, and the menu was original to the mission: soup and salads. The massive array of over 60 salad items, pasta, and premade salads, such as Asian Chicken Salad and Cobb Salad, kept the diners returning. In addition, a complete dessert bar was created with healthful to sinfully delicious—from fresh fruit cobblers and frozen yogurt to warm cookies served hot out of the oven—for diners to enjoy. And they did.

A regional kitchen serviced each restaurant to ensure food consistency and freshness. There were 20 regional kitchens. To ensure product consistency, these kitchens prepared all the soups and mixes for the baked goods for daily delivery to the locations. Salad ingredients and perishables were delivered to the restaurants directly for on-site preparation. The test kitchen was located at the general offices in San Diego. That is where innovative culinary ideas, new-recipe development, nutritional analysis, and focus groups would meet.

Often, the recipes would be highlighted on the website so you could make them at home. For example, the chicken noodle soup recipe was from the founder Ron Demery's grandmother's recipe. In addition, recipe and idea cards were created monthly to help the guests make the best choices for themselves.

Brooke and Mack started expanding outside of Southern California in 1990, using the name Sweet Tomatoes for the new Arizona and Florida locations. They felt the name would positively reflect the product they were selling instead of Souplantation; Southern Californians had already known the brand for 20 years, so changing the name there would have been a marketing blunder.

The Garden Fresh Restaurant Group became a vibrant contributive part of each community they did business in. Garden Fresh offered a "Fun-Raiser" program through which non-profits or charities could host in-store events. Each local restaurant would market their events with in-store flyers and banners. The company would give a percentage of the sales to the group. Grand openings were always part of a non-profit event for the new community.

One of the best publicity campaigns of the company was its new motto: "24 hours after being in the ground, from truck to the restaurant, that's how our product gets to us!" Customer complaints, suggestions, and correspondence that came through the main office were all handled very personally, with handwritten letters.

In 1990, Palm Harbor, Florida, was the first location outside of Southern California and the first location to use the new name, Sweet Tomatoes. Not long after, the Garden Fresh Restaurant group opened 110 locations in 15 states, all company-owned. Over the years, the location count hovered around the 100 mark.

Club Veg®, a guest education and involvement club, kept members updated on the latest openings with newsletters and promotions. Out of the club, in 2007, the Kitchen Cabinet® was formed. Twelve ladies made up the cabinet and agreed to travel to San Diego to taste new and conceptual menu items twice a year for three years. This market research group came from all over the country where the restaurant had current locations or planned to open new ones. After a few groups, the number was increased to 16 ladies with only one-year "terms."

> **2004 Fun Facts**
> 28,921,028 Guests Served
> 12,576,936 Blueberry Muffins Served
> 7,717,256 Cornbread Muffins Served
> 706,568 Gallons of Chicken Noodle Soup Served
> 102,082 Cases of Romaine Lettuce
> 3,521,000 Freshly Tossed Salads
> $267,172 Donated to Charities Through the
>   "Fun-Raiser" Program

In 2010, "crEATe a Recipe" contest was created to interact with customers. The first contest rules were to make a dish using the restaurant's fresh ingredients. The first winner, Liz Turk-Setton of Los Angeles, created the Egg' N Cheese' N Veggie Biscuit. Turk-Setton's recipe was featured on table cards, and she received meal passes for an entire year as her winning prize.

The last promotion was the 700 Club. The menus focused on only consuming 700 calories in a meal at the restaurant. Each menu included at least three of the five major food groups, less than 10 percent calories from saturated fats, zero trans fats, and five grams of fiber. The ten menu cards ranged from vegan to plant-powered protein to Southwestern choices. The menus were not just the salad bar but included pasta dishes, soups, and desserts. Some recipes were inventive, such as a baked potato with low-fat herb dressing instead of butter.

In March 2020, due to the COVID-19 pandemic health risk and emergency, all 97 locations coast-to-coast closed, and 4,000 employees were unemployed; two months later, the parent company, Garden Fresh Restaurant Group, filed for Chapter 7.

Since that closing, four years later at this writing, there are rumors that a new Souplantation will be opening in the San Diego area. 🍲

The Cheesecake Factory

ORIGINAL LOCATION: 364 N. Beverly Blvd., Beverly Hills

OPENED: February 25, 1978

FOUNDER: David Overton, CEO

CURRENT OWNERSHIP: The Cheesecake Factory Incorporated, publicly traded

CURRENTLY AT THE FIRST LOCATION: The first location is still in operation.

Today, there are 214 Cheesecake Factory Restaurants in the United States, one in Canada, and thirty-two international locations in nine countries operating under licensing agreements.

thecheesecakefactory.com
thecheesecakefactoryathome.com

THE STORY OF THE FAMED Cheesecake Factory starts almost 30 years before its opening and 2,300 miles away in a suburb of Detroit, Michigan. Then-28-year-old Evelyn Overton, a homemaker with two small children, was reading the newspaper's food section and came across a cheesecake recipe. After she gave one to her husband Oscar's employer, the boss quickly ordered additional cheesecakes for client gifts. Evelyn was now in business; she opened a bakery called Lyndee's. Famous for the cheesecakes, she employed her two children, David and Renee, to fold boxes after school. She later continued to bake cheesecakes in the family's home basement.

In the mid-1960s, son David Overton was accepted at Hastings College of Law, only lasting a year before he started playing the drums in the Billy Roberts Blues Band. A few years later, in 1971, David persuaded his parents to leave Michigan's cold, bitter winters for sunny Southern California and to open a commercial bakery. The Overtons found a 700-square-foot storefront in North Hollywood. Evelyn baked the cakes and Oscar sold them to the area's restaurants. David would come down from the Bay area and help at times until the bakery outgrew the location and moved to a larger facility in Woodland Hills in 1975. After that, David moved to Southern California full-time to help with the growing bakery.

Evelyn had an extensive menu of cheesecake flavors for

Menu Items from Opening That Are Still Offered

Original Cheesecake
Fresh Strawberry Cheesecake
Carrot Cake
Hot Fudge Sundae

Opposite: The Grove Los Angeles location, (top): Oscar and Evelyn Overton, (bottom): Oscar Overton showing catered platter

wholesale restaurants and accounts to choose from, but the plain cheesecake was the flavor most requested. David grew tired of hearing that many restaurant owners would say "No one needs more than one flavor of cheesecake," as his father Oscar attempted to sell Evelyn's selection of cakes, or they would sometimes switch to an inferior product to save a nickel a slice. Out of frustration and to show other restaurants that their guests would enjoy a large selection of high-quality desserts, David Overton decided to open a restaurant to showcase his mother's cakes. Knowing the town's resident appreciation for quality, he chose Beverly Hills. He couldn't think of a name, so he would call the restaurant "The Cheesecake Factory," just like his parent's bakery.

So, in February 1978, David opened the first Cheesecake Factory Restaurant on Beverly Drive, only one block from the famous Rodeo Drive. It

Top 5 Cheesecakes
1. Fresh Strawberry
2. Oreo Dream Extreme Cheesecake
3. Ultimate Red Velvet Cake Cheesecake
4. Original
5. Lemon Raspberry Cream Cheesecake

(top): Fresh Strawberry Slice, (left): Fried Mac and Cheese Balls, (middle): Lemon Raspberry Cream Cheesecake, (right): Miso Salmon Platter

was a small restaurant, able to serve 100 diners, serving breakfast, lunch, and dinner—and don't forget the cheesecake! David also promoted the sale of wedding cakes and catering. Soon after opening, they expanded when the shoe store next door became available. In 1983, the Marina del Rey location opened; that was much larger and sat 250 guests at 10,500 square feet with an expanded menu. The Woodland Hills bakery was outgrowing its space, with adding the additional restaurant; this stretched the facility.

For the expansion of the restaurants, the bakery production had to expand. So, in 1986, they moved the cheesecake and bakery production into a new 16,400-square-foot plant in Calabasas. With a new bakery production facility, Restaurant #3 opened in the former Tiki Beach Bum Burt's in Redondo Beach; on the harbor, it became the most extensive place to eat at 20,000 square feet and seating 450 patrons. The views of King Harbor at sunset on the balcony made this location special. In addition, the kitchen was bigger than either of the other two locations.

The chefs prepare the menu items early in the morning for the day of service. The first menu had about 60 items, whereas today's menu has over 250 dishes made from scratch, over 700 different

(top): Hostess Linda Candioty at the Beverly Hills location, (bottom): Group staff of Beverly Hills

ingredients, and more than 160 sauces and dressings to make up the offerings. Many exclaim that the menu is like a book; reading and figuring out what you will order takes a while. The menus are up to 21 pages, with a secondary "Skinnylicious" menu. David still approves the seasonal menus, in which some items are retired and some are new selections.

Many dishes are quite time-consuming to make, yet they are some of the most popular. Since the Avocado Egg Rolls with Tamarind Cashew Dipping Sauce was introduced in 2000, it has been at the top of the popular appetizer list yearly. The dish takes over four hours to make, with 18 ingredients to make the sauce alone. Chicken Madeira with mashed potatoes, one of the most popular entrees, is butchered fresh in-house; a cook pounds the raw meat by hand every day, which takes two to four hours.

Twenty-plus years ago, if you went to your local market, you would be hard pressed to find fresh herbs

First Unit Numbers

1. 1978: Beverly Hills, CA
2. 1983: Marina del Rey, CA
3. 1988: Redondo Beach, CA
4. 1989: Woodland Hills, CA
5. 1991: Washington, D.C.
6. 1993: Newport Beach, CA
7. 1993: Brentwood, CA
8. 1993: Atlanta, GA
9. 1994: North Bethesda, MD
10. 1994: Coconut Grove, FL
11. 1995: Boca Raton, FL
12. 1995: Chicago, IL
13. 1995: Houston, TX
14. 1995: Chestnut Hill, MA
15. 1996: Skokie, IL
16. 1996: Baltimore, MD
17. 1996: Kansas City, MO

International Locations
UAE
Kuwait
Saudi Arabia
Qatar
Bahrain
Mexico
China Mainland
Hong Kong
Macau

(top): David Overton, CEO, in Dubai Mall serving cheesecake,
(bottom): 2010 menu cover

outside of Los Angeles. This was the dilemma with opening Cheesecake Factory Restaurants in other locations. Finishing a few pasta dishes required sprinkling fresh herbs such as basil or chives. How the company handled this was the "herb" employee. The herb employee would order enough herbs for the entire chain. Then FedEx packages to each location would go overnight so they would have fresh herbs. Even in the dead of winter in Chicago, the pasta dish would have fresh herbs topping the plate.

Today, you can find fresh herbs at your local market, and the produce buyers for the Cheesecake Factory also can obtain fresh herbs year-round worldwide. The Cheesecake Factory's Fresh Strawberry Cheesecake is served year-round. Many ask how they have fresh strawberries every month. Driscoll Berries guarantees a perfectly ripe strawberry with their three growing regions from Central Coastal California growers to Florida to Central Mexico. Within hours of picking, the berries can be shipped to the restaurants ready to top that perfect slice of cheesecake.

The first location outside Southern California was Washington, D.C., in 1991. Learning that the East Coast loved the Cheesecake Factory, expansion started eastward. The Cheesecake Factory was incorporated in 1992 and went public in the following year, with a three-dollar-per-share listing under the Nasdaq CAKE.

Again, the production bakery outgrew its facility. So, in 1995, the company purchased a 3.3-acre site and built a 60,000-square-foot headquarters that houses a 45,000-square-foot production bakery, the training center for management, the culinary center (test kitchen), and general offices.

From 1993 to 1996, ten Cheesecake Factory restaurants opened in the Midwest and East Coast. The Calabasas plant provided all the cheesecakes and baked goods to all the locations, again being stretched; in 2006, an East Coast plant in Rocky Mount, North Carolina, opened—a 115,000-square-foot bakery operation. The East and West Coast bakeries produce 40,000 cheesecakes daily, besides layer cakes, tiramisu, brownies,

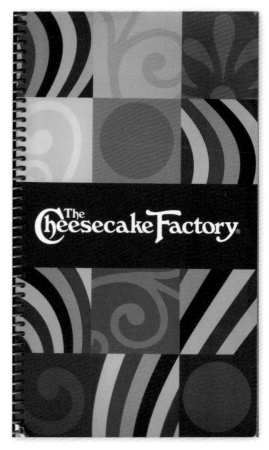

(left): Bacon Bacon Burger, (middle): Oreo Dream Extreme Cheesecake, (right): Avocado Egg Rolls

apple crisps, and cupcakes.

After the passing of Oscar in 1987 and Evelyn in 1996, the Cheesecake Factory Oscar and Evelyn Overton Charitable Foundation was created. Today the foundation is still granting money and changing communities where Cheesecake Factory restaurants are located. For example, the City of Hope Comprehensive Center and the Salvation Army at Thanksgiving donate meals to thousands of families to provide support to local employee choices of nonprofit organizations. Renee Overton, sister of David, was on the foundation's board of directors until her passing.

In 2003, the 25th anniversary of opening Beverly Hills, the company celebrated by opening 14 locations and the first in Hawaii. That same year, the Founder and CEO David Overton was named the "Executive of the Year" by *Restaurants and Institutions* magazine.

In 2011, the international expansion of the restaurants started in Dubai, located at the bottom of the indoor ski slope at the Mall of the Emirates. In Middle Eastern countries, the only difference is that the menu does not contain pork or alcohol. In addition, all the cheesecakes and baked goods for the international locations are baked at one of the two American bakeries.

Besides going to one of the restaurants, you could also enjoy Cheesecake Factory cakes with the 2013 partnership with Harry and David; this partnership brought the famous cheesecakes directly to your home. After that, large membership stores started carrying sliced whole cheesecakes with 16 slices in four flavors. Finally, in 2018, you could get Cheesecake Factory products through grocery store bakeries, including their famous brown bread that the server brings to your table when you visit a restaurant. Also offered are the Cheesecake Factory at Home ice creams, puddings, and more.

Many employees and management personnel have made the Cheesecake Factory their career. For nine consecutive years, the Cheesecake Factory has been named one of the top 100 Fortune Best Companies to work for. In addition, every year, on National Cheesecake Day (July 30), you can purchase a slice of one of the 36 varieties for a fifty percent discount when dining at one of their restaurants. 🍰

Grand Luxe Cafe, The Other Concept of The Cheesecake Factory

The sister brand of Cheesecake Factory opened in Las Vegas at the Venetian Resort in 1999. Grand Luxe Cafes are more extensive and opulent, and have higher-priced menu items than the Cheesecake Factory. They also serve Cheesecake Factory desserts. Their menus are like visiting European markets, with French, Italian, and Greek dishes.

La Salsa: Fresh Mexican Grill

SLOGAN: "Air. Water. Food. Salsa."

ORIGINAL LOCATION: 11077 W. Pico Blvd., Los Angeles

OPENED: 1979

FOUNDER: Howdy Kabrins

CURRENT OWNERSHIP: Kahala Brands

CURRENTLY AT THE FIRST LOCATION: Strip-mall businesses

There are currently six restaurants in two states.

lasalsa.com

AS A COLLEGE ANTHROPOLOGY STUDENT, Howdy Kabrins lived with a family in the heart of Mexico, studying the cuisine and culture. Observing the locals, he saw that each day the wealthy and working class would stand around the same tall tables and counters eating tacos and salsa at the corner taqueria. Kabrin immersed himself in the culture of Mexican heritage. His grandfather was born in Mexico and was a produce merchant; his father, a seafood importer, influenced his interest in the food trade.

Howdy decided that his restaurant would be different: a new Tex-Mex fast-food restaurant. Unlike any others, he was the first to offer a fresh salsa bar. Howdy found a strip mall at the busy intersection of Pico and Sepulveda boulevards. Wanting his customers to have the same authentic experience as the taquerias of Mexico, Howdy encouraged his employees to speak Spanish to the guests and give them a "Spanish lesson for the day" when they order. He had all the menu boards written in Spanish with the words "sales tax not included" as the only English words printed. He even had tall tables for everyone to eat Mexica style. This only lasted for the first few locations, until he started putting in tables and standardizing the menu in English.

A primary difference between La Salsa and other Mexican fast-food restaurants is that they serve traditional margaritas, fresh fruits, blended margaritas, beer, or wine. The entrees and salsa are low in fat and salt and made without preservatives; after trimming the fat, they charbroil the meats such as chicken, beef skirt steak, and pork. Tortilla chips are fried in cholesterol-free oil and sprinkled with sea salt, and the black beans are cooked without shortening or lard.

In 1984, in Pasadena, Jerry Anne diVecchio, formerly of *Sunset Magazine*, put together an array of the top chefs in

Locations	
1984:	5 locations
1986:	6 locations
1992:	30 locations
1993:	34 locations
1994:	40 locations
1999:	98 locations
2016:	23 locations
2022:	6 locations in two states

Opposite: La Salsa bar, West Los Angeles location

Los Angeles for the Olympic Arts Festival. The area's top chefs, Ken Frank, Michael Roberts, Mary Sue Milliken, Susan Feniger, and Wolfgang Puck, were joined by the only fast-food maven, Howdy Kabrins, to supply an array of salads for the benefit. Many asked diVecchio why La Salsa. She felt that his food was excellent and wanted to highlight a salad that everyday customers would buy and had the flavors of Los Angeles.

By 1992, Howdy employed a taquero at each location. A taquero is the Mexican version of a sushi chef. They slice the meats and vegetables in front of the guests to create handmade tacos and burritos.

For San Diego expansion, Howdy purchased the small chain of seven Baja Broiler restaurants to convert into La Salsas in the first four months of 1993. He was reluctant to put a drive-through in a location because he did not think someone ordering from their car would get the same experience as when they walked in. But the former Baja Broiler in Escondido had a drive-through, so Howdy decided to test it out. The drive-through customers were greeted warmly, as if they had walked into the restaurant. Customers loved it.

Managers in the locations are encouraged to be in the dining room as much as they can, delivering the food to the tables and conversing with the guests. Emphasis is heavy on warm service and fresh food. All employees are encouraged to go overboard, serve the customers, and speak Spanish to teach them phrases and words for a more authentic experience.

(top): Soda cup advertisement, (bottom): West Los Angeles dining room

La Salsa bar

In July 1993, Howdy realized that he could not take the chain any further without venture capitalists, so he raised money with six investor groups; La Salsa would expand faster, so Howdy stepped down from ownership to board member. Seven months later, Howdy purchased a number of the San Diego and Los Angeles locations from the parent company to become the largest franchisee of La Salsa, because he missed the day-to-day operations at the store level.

At an awards dinner in 1994, prestigious restaurateurs of Southern California named Howdy Kabrins Man of the Year for contributing to the positive image of Latinos by bringing the tastes and foods from the ranches of Mexico for millions to enjoy.

With almost 100 locations, La Salsa was sold to the Santa Barbara Restaurant Group, which owned the Green Burrito (page 115) chain at the time.

Howdy Kabrins would never have moss growing under his feet, so he opened a Latin seafood restaurant in Culver City called Pacifico's, planning on franchise expansion at one point. Instead, Pacifico's remained in business for only six years.

Howdy then opened Howdy's Sonrisa Café in Malibu in 1995, a small taco stand like those he'd visited in Mexico as a child. In the fall of 2014, he announced he would close for good, which lasted only six years before he returned to the beachside community. He brought the iconic dishes he'd introduced over 25 years before back to Pico Boulevard, now with a better beach view. 🌮

Ownership

1979–1993:	Howdy Kabrins and Vicky Tanner
1993–1999:	Sienna Holdings and InterWest Partners
1999–2007:	Santa Barbara Restaurant Group
2007-Present:	MTY Food Group (Kahala Brands Division)

The Green Burrito

ORIGINAL LOCATION: 12006 E. Carson St., Hawaiian Gardens

OPENED: 1980

FOUNDER: Rubin Rodriguez

CURRENT OWNERSHIP: CKE Restaurant Holdings

CURRENTLY AT THE FIRST LOCATION: Don Ruben Mexican Grill

Today there are over 300 co-branded Green Burritos and Carl's Jr. Restaurants.

carlsjr.com

RUBIN RODRIGUEZ PURCHASED a small stand in Hawaiian Gardens in 1980. Unfortunately, the building only had an outside patio for dining and no drive-through, as the building was not big enough. As a result, many mistook the building for a former Taco Bell.

The Green Burrito is Mexican cuisine based on Puerto Rican recipes with huge portions, low prices, and less spice. The signature Green Burrito meal was served with a fork, as it was so big and topped with sauce. The Big Ed Burrito was a trademark menu item, a two-pound double tortilla burrito. If you could eat three in a row in under 40 minutes, you would be awarded $1,000 ($3,600 in 2024 dollars). Those who lost would have their picture on the "Wall of Shame."

In 1986, Superior Ventures Corp, a venture-capital group in Downey, outside of Los Angeles, paid for a 40-percent interest in the Green Burrito for expansion in Southern California.

In May 1990, they raised $3.9 million with an initial offering of public stock under the Boston Stock Exchange symbol GBFC to help expand the Mexican food chain, relocate and expand the central commissary, and reduce debts.

Many new communities like LaVerne and Temecula started building homes for commuters. Rubin decided to start placing Green Burritos in these areas before the larger chains came to win the consumers over. This worked, as these "far-off" cities became high-sales locations. Rubin opened a central commissary in Anaheim, California, which was important for all 44 sites.

In 1992, a new burrito chain opened two locations in Columbus, Ohio, naming themselves the Red Burrito. Everything from the décor, menu items, and look copied the Green Burrito. They even copied the Big Ed Burrito and the Green Burrito, the company's trademark burritos. That same year, the Green Burrito partnered with Arby's, a fast-food roast-beef restaurant in Long Beach, California, to see if partnering with a non-Mexican food location would boost

Opposite: La Habra, CA sign

Ownership	
1986–1998:	GM Foods
1998–2002:	Santa Barbara Restaurant Group
2002–Present:	CKE Restaurants

sales for both. Sales doubled in a short time. Five additional Arby's were also converted for a test.

William M. Theisen, the founder of the Midwest pizza chain Godfather, expanded the pizza brand to 900 locations in ten years; he had sold his interest in 1983 and had been looking for a Mexican fast-food brand to turn around and expand like Godfather. He took 60 percent control of Green Burrito, moved his team in, and trimmed the existing staff. The stock went up five-fold with Theisen at the helm. Theisen also felt that by co-branding with other fast-food companies, you would not have to build another location but add additional kitchen equipment and signage. Theisen was unsure if something like the Arby's experiment would only work in Southern California or if it would work nationwide.

In 1994, the Anaheim-based chain Carl's Jr. agreed to test a co-marketing branding with the Green Burrito in six locations. They set up a mini-food court that was popular in shopping malls. Carl's Jr.'s menu was primarily hamburgers and fries, so the Mexican menu would bring additional choices for the diner. In addition, Carl's Jr. added the items to their value-menu concept, which promoted good food and lower prices. They shared the profits of the Green Burrito menu items between the two companies during the test without having to remodel any Carl's Jr.'s. After a two-year trial and 30 percent added sales from the year prior, the Green Burrito and Carl's Jr. decided to co-brand 140 Carl's

Location Numbers

1990: 41

1991: 44 (35 franchised and 9 company-owned)

1992: 64 (53 franchised and 11 company-owned)

1993: 61 (50 franchised and 11 company-owned)

1994: 67

1995: 66 locations, with 140 Carl's Jr. locations being converted to dual restaurants.

1999: 194 dual locations, Carl's Jr. and The Green Burrito

2008: 300 dual locations, Carl's Jr./The Green Burrito and Hardee's/Red Burrito

Jr. locations. Lunch sales of Carl's Jr. and dinner sales of the Green Burrito skyrocketed in the two-year test.

After opening the first Green Burrito and 66 additional locations around Southern California, Rubin Rodriguez resigned in 1994 to pursue other interests. He owns several locations and decided that would be his main focus.

In 1997, Carl Karcher Enterprises (CKE) Restaurant's chairman William Foley acquired controlling interest, thus converting and incorporating Green Burrito's into Carl's Jr. restaurants. Theisen sold most of his stock and resigned. This was the same year that CKE Restaurants purchased and merged with the Hardee's restaurant burger chain. The restaurants keep separate names, but both adopt the yellow star logo.

After two years, in 1999, La Salsa (page 111), a chain of 58 new Mexican restaurants, was acquired. For a short time, Kevin Osborn became president of the La Salsa and Green Burrito brands, both part of the Santa Barbara Restaurant Group.

CKE acquired the Santa Barbara Restaurant Group in 2002, moving their corporate headquarters from Anaheim to Goleta, California, in a swap for company stock. The two companies shared

Burritos

+ The Big Ed: Filled with carnitas, refried beans, rice, beef, cheese, guacamole, lettuce, and tomatoes. Over two pounds.
+ The Green Burrito: Your choice of steak or chicken, house-made tomato salsa, cilantro-lime rice, refried beans, four different cheeses, hot sauce, all in a grilled tortilla smothered with a house-made tomatillo green sauce, sour cream, and Mexican cotija cheese.

First location in Hawaiian Gardens, CA of The Green Burrito.

board members, and the Santa Barbara Restaurant Group and CKE Restaurants at the time felt it was easier for CKE expansion, as they had the most significant number of dual restaurants.

The La Salsa (see page 111) brand was sold off to Baja Fresh (page 171) as CKE Restaurants did not successfully expand the newer brand.

Eighteen years after the Red Burrito lawsuit, CKE Restaurants co-branded all of Hardee's brands with Red Burrito east of the Rockies, while all the Carl's Jr. locations were co-branded with Green Burrito.

Today, a few standalone Green Burritos restaurants are scattered around Southern California, while the Green and Red Burritos co-branded with the CKE Restaurants are the same. Sadly, the Big Ed Burrito is gone, and so are the corporate headquarters of CKE Restaurants, which moved to Franklin, Tennessee. 🌮

Farmer Boys

SLOGANS: "Breakfast, Burgers and More" • "Fast Food So Good, It Tastes Like Slow Food"

ORIGINAL LOCATION: 18510 Highway 395, Perris, CA

OPENED: August 25, 1981

FOUNDERS: Five Havadjias brothers

CURRENT OWNERSHIP: Farmer Boys Food Inc.

CURRENTLY AT THE FIRST LOCATION: An empty lot

There are currently 103 locations in three states.

farmerboys.com

Farmer Boys - Perris, CA Opened 1981

FROM AN EARLY AGE on the Mediterranean island of Cyprus, five brothers (Chris, Demetris, George, Harry, and Makis) Havadjias learned what hard work was and how to work together. They grew up on the family farm. They used the harvest in their family's local restaurant. Besides the farm producing vegetables and fruits for the restaurant, it also fed the locals. So, at an early age, the Havadjias boys knew how vital fresh farm produce was.

Makis emigrated to the Los Angeles area in 1973, and the other four brothers soon followed. They opened an Astro Burger stand in Torrance, south of downtown Los Angeles, to try a business venture that used fresh ingredients and nothing frozen. They kept it open for two years before opening a restaurant in Hawthorne named Theodore's.

In August 1981, the five brothers bought McCoy's Greatest Hamburger Stand off Highway 395 outside Perris, California. The location had a huge parking lot that could accommodate large trucks traveling from Arizona to the Southland. Changing the restaurant's name to the Farmer Boys was a nod to what they were known as on their home island of Cyprus.

With their knowledge of running a hamburger stand and a coffee shop, they used the best elements and styles to create the Farmer Boys restaurant. They took the coffee shop menu and narrowed it down to items that could be made in five to seven minutes or less. They called it the "fastaurant" concept. The menu had 75 different items.

The Farmer Boys created excitement. Everything was made fresh and from scratch: hand-battered French toast and freshly cracked free-range eggs for omelets, hand-chopped

Five Brothers and Titles

Chris Havadjias (Founder)
Demetris Havadjias (CEO)
George Havadjias (Founder)
Harry Havadjias (Founder)

Opposite: Farmer Boys truck delivery, (top): Perris CA first location

Ingredients

Lettuce	Duda Family Farms	Salinas, CA
Hamburger Buns	Galasso Bakery	Mira Loma, CA
Milk Products	Alta Dena Farms	City of Industry, CA
Ice Cream	Thrifty Ice Cream	El Monte, CA
Juices	Perricone Farms	Beaumont, CA
Apples	Farmington Fresh Farms	Stockton, CA

salads, sliced tomatoes, sliced onions that are hand-battered for rings, and specialty zucchini grown to king-size at each location for cutting into deep-fried richness. Each site sources local ingredients whenever possible. Farmer-fresh sides of onion rings, zucchini sticks, and fried pickles are hand-cut and breaded daily in each restaurant. Lettuce, cabbage, and tomatoes arrive whole within days of the local harvest. The mission and goal of the boys are to keep local farmers working, and, as a result, the best ingredients are purchased. Over 17 million cage-free eggs are cracked yearly. Some menu items, such as soups and salads, are only offered in season.

The raw goods such as the vegetables and ingredients for Farmer Boys menu items come directly from the source to the locations with as few middlemen as possible. All the dairy products are free of hormones and artificial ingredients.

Many of the menu items have received numerous awards. For example, the ⅓-pound Farmer's Burger, a hand-formed patty with 100 percent USDA fresh beef (never frozen), is grilled to order over an open flame to create the signature char-grilled taste. Farmer Boys was the first fast-casual chain to launch a third of a pound natural burger made with fresh, never frozen, hormone-free, antibiotic-free beef. In addition, the company tests new products and rolls out seasonal items, sometimes for only a limited-time offering.

In 2008, KCBS-TV Los Angeles,

Farmer Bob with a huge cheeseburger

Menu Items	
May 2010:	California Chicken Sourdough Sandwich
November 2011:	⅓-pound Farmer Burger
October 2014:	X-Treme ½-pound Bacon Boy Burger
October 2014:	California Omelet
November 2014:	Partnering with LaBrea Bread Soup Bowls for the winter season.
May 2015:	The Southwest Chicken Salad & The Harvest Salad
July 2015:	Barn Burner Burger (spicy patty of pepper jack cheese)
October 2015:	CinnaTreats Dessert
May 2016:	SmokeHouse BBQ Line of Foods
September 2017:	Double Chili Burger, Chili Fries
May 2018:	Chicken Caesar Salad
November 2018:	Always "Crispy" French Fries
November 2021:	Loaded Chicken Sandwiches
March 2022:	Parmesan Crusted Sourdough Cheese Burger

Inland Empire magazine, and MyFOXLa awarded Farmer Boys burgers the best in the Los Angeles area.

The year 2010 marked the beginning of the thirtieth anniversary year of the first location in Perris. A thirty-pound burger was unveiled, to the excitement of the crowd.

The year 2017 marked a milestone for the company by opening a location on the famed star-studded Hollywood Boulevard.

Onion Lady with huge onion rings

In 2020, in honor of Women's Month, they renamed their locations Farmer Girls for the month.

Today, the Farmer Boys donate thousands to Loma Linda Children's Hospital, Feed America, and Las Vegas Children's Hospital charities with yearly fundraising efforts. The fundraising has surpassed one million dollars collected to support children's health since first launching in 2000. When a new location opens, fundraising starts on opening day for the community it serves.

Since day one at Farmer Boys, fresh ingredients, delicious food, and hearty portions have never gone out of style. 🍔

Islands Restaurants

SLOGAN: "Live, Love, Aloha."

NAME TODAY: Islands Fine Burgers and Drinks

ORIGINAL LOCATION: 10948 Pico Blvd., Los Angeles

OPENED: July 25, 1982

FOUNDER: Tony DeGrazier

CURRENT OWNERSHIP: Privately owned

CURRENTLY AT THE FIRST LOCATION: Vacant (closed in 2018)

There are currently forty-four restaurants in two states.

islandsrestaurants.com

WALK INTO AN ISLANDS RESTAURANT, and you are transported to the beaches of Oahu, Hawaii. That is precisely how founder and surfer Tony DeGrazier wanted you to feel when you walked in, just as he had in the 1960s on the Islands after surfing with his friends. The first Islands Restaurant was a former DL BBQ Restaurant on Pico Boulevard in West Los Angeles. Pico Boulevard runs from the Pacific Ocean to Downtown LA, 16 miles away.

The restaurant had a bar in the center a few steps up from the dining area, which wrapped around the bar to the sides. The staff members all wear Hawaiian shirts and smiles. When you sit down, you notice the tables are made of beautiful woods and the menus are already on the table so you can choose what you want without waiting.

In the early 1980s, you rarely found a full restaurant devoted to hamburgers; hamburger chains that served fast food with ready-made meals were everywhere. Islands Restaurant's opening menu was straightforward: one page, packed with burgers, chili bowls, soft tacos, and frozen margaritas. Half-pound burgers with island-inspired toppings such as pineapple and teriyaki sauce became the most popular. Baskets of French fries, to this day, are still cut by hand daily from fresh potatoes, cooked to order, and seasoned with a unique salt. Diners would drive as far as 40 miles to eat at the Islands. Some promotions have included all-you-can-eat French fries when you order a burger.

Drinks were served in large mugs, so the waitstaff could carry several drinks easier than on a tray. The mugs could hold soft drinks, beer, and frozen adult drinks. Big-screen TVs at first showed mostly surfing movies and videos, until many customers asked for a popular sporting event such as the Super Bowl or the Olympics. Islands then

Owners

1982–1993:	Tony DeGrazier
1993–1996:	Chart House Enterprises
1996–2020:	Tony DeGrazier
2020–Present:	Private Investors

Opposite: Menu cover from 2022, (top): Coaster

(top): First location, Pico Blvd., West Los Angeles,
(bottom): Print ad from 1983

became more of a "sports bar," although the sound is down when a sporting event is shown.

Tony opened a second location in Marina del Rey, only three blocks from the beach and closer to his home. It was very successful for 37 years, until it was closed. Tony continued to open locations in Southern California, Arizona, and Florida. In 1993, Tony decided to retire and sell the concept and name to Chart House Enterprises Inc., an upscale steak-and-fish restaurant chain in iconic buildings mainly on the shores of the Pacific, also with an island theme and the staff wearing khaki shorts and Hawaiian print shirts. Chart House kept the menu the same but added little touches, such as glass mugs instead of the plastic used prior. Islands were only under the Chart House Enterprise umbrella for a few years before Tony re-purchased it. Today Islands is still privately owned.

A very bold move for the company in 1997 was

Burgers Still Available Since Opening Day

+ Big Wave: lettuce, tomato, onion, pickles, and mustard
+ Big Wave with Cheese: lettuce, tomatoes, onion, pickles, mustard, and cheese
+ Hawaiian: fresh pineapple, teriyaki sauce, lettuce, tomatoes, onion, Swiss, and mayo
+ Pipeline: chili, cheddar cheese, lettuce, tomato, onion, pickles, and mustard

to create a safe working space for the employees and patrons by going completely smoke-free in all their restaurants; this was a year before the State of California enacted laws about this and the other states that had Islands locations did not even have the rules yet. Of course, many patrons voiced an opinion, but this was the wave of the country, and Islands wanted to be at the forefront.

Islands offered more than burgers. Rotisserie platters of roasted chicken had not become as famous as it was thought they would. Instead, with all that chicken, Islands started serving chicken tortilla soup, which became a cult favorite. The early 2000s brought the need for healthier options; fish rice bowls with pineapple and teriyaki sauces and wraps of chicken and tuna became popular.

Unfortunately, during the pandemic in 2020, Islands closed eight underperforming locations and, like most establishments, switched to delivery under unpredictable circumstances.

Today, Islands is a fine-tuned restaurant chain with great food that a family can afford in a welcoming tropical setting. 🍔

(top): Menu insert of history, (bottom): Carlsbad, CA location

Ruby's Diner

SLOGANS: "Only the Best for Our Guests" ✦ "Shooby Dooby Down to . . . Where the Food Is Great!"

ORIGINAL LOCATION: 1 Balboa Pier, Newport Beach

OPENED: December 7, 1982

FOUNDERS: Doug Cavanaugh and Ralph Kosmides

ARCHITECT: Ian J. N. Harrison

CURRENT OWNERSHIP: Ruby's Restaurant Group

CURRENTLY AT THE FIRST LOCATION: The first location is still in operation.

PRIOR AT THE FIRST LOCATION: Originally a live bait and sandwich shop

There are fifteen locations in two states.

rubys.com

DOUG CAVANAUGH ENJOYED early-morning jogs around the Newport coast. Passing the 1906 fishing pier daily, he noticed a dilapidated building on the end of the pier that was in disarray: a live-bait-and-sandwich concession. The city of Newport Beach owns the pier and the building; Doug went to the council, wanting to take over the concession and turn it into a restaurant. However, the city council felt he lacked the knowledge to run a restaurant and turned down his offer.

Doug moved to the East Coast and opened and managed the Summer House, a restaurant and inn in Sconset on Nantucket Island, Massachusetts, for two years. The restaurant was very successful, but Doug wanted to be on the West Coast, close to his family.

Doug now felt he had gained the hospitality know-how he had lacked; he returned to the Newport city council ready to negotiate and was granted the lease for 15 years. Then, knowing he needed funds and partners, Doug invited a group of his high school friends to dinner to sell them on the idea. Unfortunately, only one took the bait: Ralph Kosmides. They both were from the class of 1974, Foothill High, in the nearby city of Tustin. So, Ralph and Doug got busy remodeling the former bait shop into a diner and setting their sights on a spring 1982 opening.

Doug wanted to take the guests back to a time after the War that he heard his parents talk about with fond memories. The late 1940s created the theme. First, the name. He initially thought the Balboa Diner would work until he and Ralph felt the title would be difficult for a multi-location restaurant. He asked his mom Ruby what she thought of naming the restaurant after her; she said "Absolutely not." But Doug felt the name invoked a simpler time of the country and great homage to his mom. His mom had graduated in 1940 from Fremont High in Los Angeles and had been on the drill team. Finding a picture of her in uniform, Doug commissioned an artist couple that would stop past while he was renovating, asking to do some work for him. Doug told them to work up a drawing based on his mom, highlighting her holding a tray

Opposite: Ruby Cavanaugh, the founder's mother who the company was based on.

Opening Day Prices	
RubyBurger:	$2.15
Fries:	$1.00
Milkshake:	$1.60

Top Burgers
1. Basic Burger
2. Cheeseburger
3. Bacon Burger
4. Super Burger (Melted Double Swiss, Lettuce, Tomato, Ruby Sauce, Avocado, on a toasted Parmesan Sourdough Bun.)

Newport Beach Pier, first location

with a burger and coke. They returned a few weeks later with several different sketches; Doug loved the one still used today.

Ruby Cavanaugh got over the restaurant being named after herself when she first saw the sign illuminated with red letters spelling out her name. In many openings, Ruby would be at the ribbon-cutting, signing autographs for the fans.

The vision for the restaurant would be red and white to reflect the name "Ruby's." The interior had photos reminiscent of the 1940s. Every table would have a single fresh red carnation in a white vase. Female servers were outfitted with red and white striped dresses with a white apron on top and a matching headpiece, and the male waiters wore black pants, a crisp white button-down short-sleeve shirt, and a red bow tie with an apron. A retro cash register and gumball machine completed the look. A thick red heavy paper napkin is placed on the table when your order has been taken. The menu was small so that the kitchen could handle the cooking: just hamburgers, hot dogs, fries, shakes, and a few desserts. After six months, breakfast was introduced and available at all hours Ruby's is open. Doug learned how to cook from his grandmother, as cooking skipped his mother's generation.

The opening was not without obstacles; weather on the pier and beach created havoc, thus pushing the opening day back. Doug and Ralph kept thinking, what were they doing opening a restaurant on a pier in the middle of winter? Finally, opening day, Tuesday, December 7, 1982, with three employees, brought a brisk crowd; Doug and Ralph's register receipts amounted to $63.43 ($187.39 in 2024). News traveled fast, though, and within days the line to dine in the 45-seat restaurant went down the pier.

Six months after opening, Ruby's was granted two awards, the California Historic Presentation Award for remodeling and the Art Deco Building and Rehabilitation of a Commercial Project. With the awards, Doug's vision of rehabbing the old bait shop into a new diner became reality.

A year after opening, the high school friends opened a 70-seat location in Mission Viejo. In the following four years, three additional Ruby's opened: Ruby's Jewel Diner on Seal Beach Pier; Fullerton MetroCenter; and the Crystal Court of South Coast Plaza in Santa Ana. Each location's menu, décor, service, and restaurant size evolved. This helped the two set the stage for more aggressive expansion in the 1990s.

Doug and Ralph set goals for the staff when seating and serving the guests. For example, after being seated, the guest should be greeted within 60 seconds, menus should already be on the table, a beverage order should be taken, and, within three minutes, the beverages should be brought to the table (except for shakes and malts). If the guest sits at the counter, they should be greeted within fifteen seconds.

1987 brought on a pier fight with HEG Enterprises, who wanted to open a high-end steak house on the Seal Beach pier where Doug wanted to place a Ruby's. Many retirees from the community of Leisure World testified at the city council meetings that most wanted affordable pier food and that a steak restaurant would out-price them. Ruby's won and named it Ruby's Jewel Diner.

An out-of-the-ordinary Ruby's opened in July of 1990 at the base of the Newport Import Jaguar Dealership in Newport Beach. To keep the theme of the British imports, Ruby's offered an English Breakfast; Bangers and Mash; and Fish and Chips—and they also stocked English beers. For about a year, the diner was open 24 hours before complaints started from the neighbors over noise and traffic. The coastal planning commission denied the request for a 24-hour operation. Ruby's Jaguar Diner closed only after two years as the dealership foreclosed.

1992 was a busy year for Ruby's, with opening the first international location at the new Euro-Disney (currently named Paris Disney) outside of Paris. Doug and a dozen staff members flew to Paris to work on the project. Doug didn't want the Walt Disney Company to have the full rights of Ruby's for Europe; the restaurant was named after everyone's favorite Musketeer, Annette. Today Annette's is still going strong as a famous American Diner in Disney Village.

With the knowledge of how to open outside California, Ruby's submitted a bid for the concessions at the new National Bowling Stadium in Reno, Nevada. They won to be the concessionaire for five years. The new stadium would house the restaurant with entrances outside the building, so non-visitors of the stadium could enjoy Ruby's experience without attending a bowling event. Ruby's vacated the bowling stadium in Reno after only three years.

December 1992 became a celebration for the tenth anniversary of Ruby's Balboa Pier. The pier turned into a midway of carnival games, clowns, magicians, mimes, and face-painting for kids. In addition, prices were rolled back to the original pricing of 1982.

From 1996 to 1998, Ruby's employees and staff decorated and competed in the annual Rose Bowl Parade in Pasadena with winning entries every year. The parade was viewed by millions worldwide, and, as a result, the

1996 Rose Parade float

Ruby's brand was front and center in everyone's home as they watched.

The great storm of January 1988 saw death and devastation. About 100 feet of the end of the Huntington Beach pier crashed into the Pacific Ocean, which had housed the iconic End Café. Nine years later, Ruby's Surfside Diner opened in the enlarged two-story octagonal 6,510-square-foot building on Huntington Beach pier. In 2018, the top floor was redecorated as Jan and Dean's Tiki Lounge. You could order anything from Ruby's menu, specialty island foods, and tropical drinks. Sadly, in 2021, after 25 years, Ruby's closed, to be replaced by a seafood restaurant.

(top): 1997 Rose Parade float, (middle): 1998 Rose Parade float

Many locations with large parking lots (e.g., Whittier and Redondo Beach) would host a monthly Classic Car Show. Hundreds of automobiles and motorcycles from the 1940s to the 1960s would be displayed for all to admire. After the car show, a burger and shake would be on the menu. For example, Ruby's AutoDiner in Laguna Beach opened in 1990, and you could see a collection of 1950s cars in the front. These were part of Doug Cavanaugh's car collection; after about five years, Doug would sell the cars and pick up new ones.

1990 to 1999 saw the most extensive growth in company and franchise units, with the opening of 21 diners in California and three in Pennsylvania. The new diners all had the basic décor of 1940s poster art with red and white booths and white Formica tables. Still, many were themed for the local area, such as the Ruby's Aerodiner in Laguna Hills, which was near the El Toro Marine Base and featured a collection of miniature aircraft that "flew" on a ceiling track; the Ruby's Streamliner Diner in Old Orange housed in the former 1888 Santa Fe train depot had model trains on tracks above your head; and Ruby's Redondo Beach and Huntington Beach had beach/surf themes.

In 2010, the historic Five Points area of Anaheim had recently moved a 1926 two-story commercial building to expand Lincoln Boulevard and was looking for a restaurant to occupy the landmark structure; Ruby's was the answer. This location could have carhop service, as the parking lot was only large enough for a dozen cars. A call

Pier/Ocean Locations	
1982–Present	Ruby's Balboa Pier, Newport Beach
1987–2021	Ruby's Jewel Diner, Seal Beach Pier
1990–Present	Ruby's AutoDiner, Laguna Beach
1996–2021	Ruby's Surf City Diner, Huntington Beach
2018–2021	Jan and Dean's Tiki Lounge
1996–2021	Ruby's Oceanside Pier
2006–2022	Ruby's Shake Shack, Crystal Cove
2010–2013	Ruby's Shake Shack, Malibu

went out for 100 roller-skaters to be servers. The Five Points location interior broke from tradition and installed booths of tan and brown with rich wood accents to harmonize with the historical look of the building.

For the 55-and-older crowd of diners, Ruby's started the "Jitterbug Club." The deal was a ten percent discount on entrees for you and up to three guests during happy hour. An email would be sent monthly with news and offers to entice you to dine at the restaurants. When people saw Cavanaugh around town, they would get into their wallets and show their Jitterbug Card.

On July 29, 2015, her ninety-third birthday, Ruby Cavanaugh attended her birthday celebration at the Corona Del Mar location; this would be her last celebration, as she passed away the following December. The Ruby Dooby Foundation was started, to help the children of Orange County. On every birthday of Ruby Cavanaugh's, one dollar for each burger sold is given to the foundation, besides other fundraising events throughout the year.

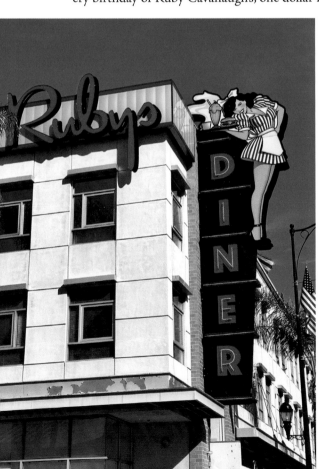

In 2015, starting with the Costa Mesa location, Ruby's interior changed from the 1940s to the 1950s with a "Googie" look, even updating the logo. Unfortunately, the new look and logo did not have a positive result, so this idea was scrapped. The three eatery concepts are full-service restaurants, an airport concept with dual full-service and take-out, and a take-out window walk-up concept.

2020 devastated the food industry worldwide, and Ruby's was not immune; COVID-19 forced the closure of over a dozen locations. This same year, Doug sold his interest in Ruby's to focus on his three areas outside of Ruby's (The Beachcomber Café, The Lighthouse Café, and the Crystal Cove Shake Shack).

The Ruby's Restaurant Group is focusing on the current franchisees and looking for new ones. 🍔

Brea, CA location

Wings & Things

NAME TODAY: Epic Wings & Things

ORIGINAL LOCATION: 1404 Garnet Ave., Pacific Beach

OPENED: 1982

FOUNDERS: Frank and Michelina Sacco

CURRENT OWNERSHIP: The Sacco Children: Sam, Greg, Joe, Cathy, Cierra, and Mike Sacco

CURRENTLY AT THE FIRST LOCATION: Poke Chop Restaurant

There are currently thirty-nine locations in six states.

epicwingsnthings.com

FRANK SAVERIO SACCO WAS BORN in central Italy in the village of Staletti; at age 15 in 1947, he emigrated to New York City and moved mid-state to Rome, New York. Frank became an expert barber, barbering for over 35 years and having his picture often in the local newspaper. In 1956, Frank married Michelina Grillone; after 26 years and six children, they packed everything into their Oldsmobile for a new adventure in Southern California.

Frank and Michelina had no experience in the restaurant business. However, Frank was an optimist and a risk-taker. Leaving New York and starting a new business in a new occupation would not be easy, but Frank felt you could be successful with hard work, determination, and persistence.

In 1982, Frank and Michelina opened Wings N' Things in the Pacific Beach area of San Diego, a quiet beach neighborhood. Chicken wings were made famous by the Anchor Bar of Buffalo, New York, but had not yet made the trip out West. Likewise, wings as a food item had not been served on the West Coast yet—the Saccos created flavorful wings with nine different sauces to choose from.

These wings were all about the bright orange sauce that covered them. In addition, the Saccos' wings were created with flavor in the wing's meat instead of tossed in dressing as original Buffalo wings were.

Slow sales in the beginning did not deter the new family venture. On the contrary, when customers were reluctant to try the latest product, the family would stand outside the restaurant and offer free samples. Once tasted, the customer would be hooked. But it still proved difficult to sell chicken wings that nobody had heard of, so the family added sandwiches, hamburgers, hot dogs, and rice balls.

Still today, the locations do not have freezers; everything is made from scratch with family house-made recipes—the promise to serve the best meal possible with the freshest ingredients.

After a few years, the Saccos had to move out of their first location, as parking and accessibility for the onslaught of customers became difficult. The family moved to a more prominent area with

Opposite: Founder Frank Sacco in the kitchen of the first location

(top): First location of Wings & Things, Pacific Beach, CA, (bottom left): Epic Chicken Salad, (bottom middle): Bone-in Wing Platter, (bottom right): Pizza Sticks

parking and a larger kitchen.

Epic Wings started franchising in 2018 with the first location outside of San Diego County in Mission Viejo; within a short time, ten additional franchise locations opened as far away as Glendale, Arizona. The plans are to open over 100 locations throughout the Southwest, Midwest, and Florida in the next few years.

Currently, all six Sacco children work in the company. ✎

Sauces

Buffalo Sauces
Extra Hot
Hot
Medium
Mild
Garlic Parmesan
Honey BBQ
Lemon Pepper
Original BBQ
Sweet Chili

(top): Sam Sacco, Cathy Sacco, Michellina Sacco, Frank Sacco Sr., Frank Sacco, (bottom): Greg Sacco, Mike Sacco, (center) (left side): Angela Sacco, Alicia Sacco, Joe Sacco, (right side): Frank Sacco, Michellina Sacco, Kristina Sacco, (bottom row) (all three pictures): All employees.

Panda Express

ORIGINAL LOCATION: Glendale Galleria, 3214 Galleria Way, Glendale

OPENED: October 1983

FOUNDERS: Andrew and Peggy Cherng

CURRENT OWNERSHIP: Panda Restaurant Group Inc.

CURRENTLY AT THE FIRST LOCATION: The first location is still in operation.

Today, there are over 2,300 locations in twelve countries, all company-owned.

pandaexpress.com

ANDREW CHERNG WAS BORN in Northern Shanghai, China. He came to the United States for school, studying mathematics at Baker, a Methodist university outside of Kansas City.

After graduating, he fell in love with his soon-to-be wife, Peggy, and they moved to Los Angeles in 1970.

Andrew's cousin owned a Hunan restaurant and needed a manager. Andrew started working while Peggy worked as a computer programmer. Shortly after, Andrew's father Ming-Tsai Cherng and other relatives came from China to live the American dream. Andrew wanted to learn every aspect of the restaurant business while saving as much money as possible; with the help of family and friends, the Cherngs saved $60,000 to open a restaurant.

Andrew hired his father, a master chef, to create the menu and manage the kitchen of his new endeavor. The Panda Inn opened in 1973; a timeless Mandarin and Sichuan cuisine sit-down restaurant with modernized cooking styles made the restaurant famous.

After five years as a successful restaurateur, the Cherngs were approached by Patrick Donahue, the developer of the Glendale Galleria, to alter and modify the menu for a new food-court installation. In 1983, the first Panda Express was born. Cherng used the Panda Inn recipes as a starting point for the new fast-casual, convenient, and on-the-go menu items for the new venture. The food would sit on steam tables after being prepared but had to taste fresh while still being ready to eat. The Cherngs had never served their kung pao chicken

Opposite: Andrew Cherng sitting in Panda Inn Restaurant, (top): Logo, (bottom): Orange Chicken

New Product Releases by Year	
1987:	Orange Chicken®
2010:	Honey Walnut Shrimp
2013:	Honey Sesame Chicken
	Sriracha Shrimp
2014:	Shitake Kale Chicken Breast
2015:	Chinese Spareribs
2017:	Five Flavor Shrimp
2019:	Wok-Fired Shrimp
	Sichuan Hot Chicken
2021:	Crispy Almond Chicken Breast
	Orange Chicken Sandwich

and chow mein off steam tables. A great deal of food testing took place before the menu items were as tasty and fresh as right out of the kitchen. Thirteen additional locations opened in the next five years.

In 1987, Corporate Chef Andy Kao created the best-selling and iconic Original Orange Chicken®. Years later, Orange Chicken is still the number-one item ordered at Panda Express. Using bold flavors and quality ingredients, Chef Kao has created new and exciting menu items for the company.

All the locations are company-owned, not franchised, from the first location in Glendale to the most significant Asian dining concept in the United States and the world.

Panda programs like the University of Panda and the award-winning Store Leadership Training System focus on holistic growth opportunities for all associates and provide them with the skills and resources needed to run a great restaurant.

The University of Panda was built on the founders' success in achieving their American dream. Panda prides itself on its people-first culture and whole-person approach regarding its associates' physical, mental, and emotional learning.

Andrew meditates and hikes regularly. In addition, he conducts monthly Saturday-morning personal wellness seminars for his employees to hear about self-improvement, nutrition, and self-awareness. About 100 employees attend each month. In addition, all associates have access to Panda's benefits, including medical benefits that cover associates' physical, mental, and emotional well-being.

Panda Cares® was launched in 1999. Its philanthropic endeavors have raised more than $300 million and garnered thousands

Andrew cooking at Panda Express

Milestone Numbers

1993: 100th restaurant opening

1997: 1st drive-thru restaurant opening (Hesperia, CA)

2001: 1st freestanding location (Bethesda, MD)

2002: 500th restaurant opening (San Diego, CA)

2005: 100th drive-thru restaurant opening

2006: 500th freestanding restaurant location (Tampa, FL)
888th restaurant opening (Sacramento, CA)

2007: 1,000th restaurant opening (Pasadena, CA)

2010: 1st international location opens (Mexico City, Mexico)
1,450th restaurant location opened.

2012: 1,500th restaurant opening (Cordova, TN)

2013: 2 locations open in Canada
Guam opens first of 6 locations

2014: International locations in Dubai and Korea open
1,750 locations open

2015: 1st restaurant in Mumbai, India
1st New York City location opening

2017: 2,000th location opening (New York City, NY)

of volunteer hours, focusing on education and health for over 12 million youth worldwide. In addition, since the 2022 Russian/Ukraine war, Panda Express pledged up to $2 million to relief efforts for Ukrainian refugees and suspended corporate support and business development in Russia.

2019 became a turning point for Panda Express and its menu offerings. First, they launched half a dozen vegan-friendly entrees company-wide. Prior, Panda Express flavored all its dishes (except plain rice) with a chicken-based seasoning; going forward, Panda Express eliminated the practice.

Most food businesses have a test kitchen and research and development center at their corporate headquarters. Panda Express has theirs as a functioning restaurant for guests to eat in. This is the Innovation Kitchen for Panda in Pasadena.

Panda's menu innovation strategy expanded to include hand-held items like the Original Orange Chicken® Sandwich. The brand continues to offer easy-to-go options with the flavor that guests love and the quality that guests expect. One of the food and consumer trends that came out of the pandemic of 2020 is guests' increasing preference for quality ingredients and nutrition-forward options. Panda has been doing much behind-the-scenes work to elevate Chinese American recipes, like reducing sodium and sugar and rolling out chicken raised without antibiotics and cage-free eggs. The brand is also working on removing all artificial colors and flavors as part of its Panda Promise™ initiative. In addition, Panda recently launched Panda Cub Meal sets created based on USDA dietary recommendations for children. These meals are nutrition-forward, with Treetop® Apple Crisps and a beverage. Having options and variety is what Panda Express innovation is known for. In 2021, Panda Express created a plant-based protein Original Orange Chicken® to great acclaim.

Panda Express has been at the forefront of the dining experience with new innovative menu items for community and social endeavors. 🥡

Panda Express Sauces on the Retail Market

1. Beijing Sauce
2. King Pao Stir-Fry Sauce
3. Mandarin Teriyaki Sauce
4. Orange Sauce
5. Sweet Chili Sauce

Awards and Accolades

+ *Forbes Magazine* named them one of America's Best Employers and one of the Best Employers for Diversity
+ Included in the *Los Angeles Business Journal*
+ Asia Society of Southern California
+ Honorary Doctor of Humane Letters by California State Polytechnic University, Pomona
+ Member of the International Advisory Board for the William F. Harrah College of Hospitality at the University of Nevada Las Vegas
+ Inducted into the National Restaurant Association's Hall of Fame
+ California Restaurant Association Hall of Fame
+ Carnegie Corporation's Great Immigrants

Corona, CA location

Rubio's Coastal Grill (Rubio's)

SLOGAN: "One Bite and You're Hooked"

ORIGINAL LOCATION: 4504 Mission Bay Dr., San Diego

OPENED: January 25, 1983

FOUNDER: Ralph Rubio

CURRENT OWNERSHIP: Mill Road Capital

CURRENTLY AT THE FIRST LOCATION: The first location is still in operation.

There are currently 151 locations in three states.

rubios.com

RALPH RUBIO TOOK HIS FIRST spring-break trip in 1974 with college mates to the seaside town of San Felipe, Mexico, a historical fishing town on the coast in the Gulf of California. The area lacks chain hotels, so the college kids camped on the beach for the week. They would eat local from little stands selling beer-battered fried fish stuffed into corn tortillas topped with cabbage, crema, salsa, and fresh lime juice. Of course, Ralph would top it off with ice-cold Corona beer. Every spring break, Ralph returned to the fishing village, meeting with Carlos, the cook from his favorite taco stand.

Ralph attended San Diego State University to teach, going into education like many of his relatives. But after many spring breaks in San Felipe, eating his meals off the taco stands, he thought it was a shame there were no stands in San Diego. He knew that the beer-battered tacos feasted on by the college kids would be popular in San Diego too. So, on one of his final spring-break trips, he asked Carlos to come to San Diego and help him with the venture. Carlos declined but did give him his recipe for the fish. The batter was the key, and Ralph knew he needed the recipe.

Ralph wrote the recipe down on notebook paper: flour, dry mustard, garlic, oregano, pepper, water, and a good-quality lager beer. He put it in his wallet and kept it for eight years. During those years, Ralph worked in many aspects of the restaurant industry in many chains, learning as many facets as possible of the food business.

Opposite: Rubio's first location, Mission Bay in San Diego,
(top): Ralph Rubio enjoying the beach in San Felipe, Mexico

The Many Names of Rubio's	
1983:	Rubio's Home of the Fish Taco
	Rubio's Baja Grill
	Rubio's Fresh Mexican Grill
Present:	Rubio's Coastal Grill

(top): Ralph Rubio's "Rhonda Honda," his car he would drive down to Mexico, (bottom): Ralph Rubio

Years later, Ralph still felt that his fish-taco idea was feasible. Ralph's father, Ray Rubio, offered him $70,000 to help with his adventure. He was looking through newspaper ads and wanted a location close to the beach and not far from a college campus. A former Orange Julius stand that was converted into Mickey's Burgers was for sale. Sadly, Mickey wanted $80,000 for the business. Ralph, knowing that he needed to keep some operating capital and to make many improvements on the building, wondered if this location had enough traffic flow and was busy enough for his venture—plus the price was higher than he wanted to pay. Ralph sat across the street and watched the walking and vehicle traffic under his father's direction and saw that the customer flow was lacking.

Knowing that Mickey's Burgers lacked enough business, Ray, under his father's advice, offered Mickey $15,000 cash. Mickey hung up on him, then called him back a few hours later and accepted the offer. Ralph's parents and four siblings painted the former burger stand with bright festive colors. Opening day was a disaster, as they did not do a soft opening; they just opened the doors with a line down the street. Ralph said half of the orders had to be refunded for the mistakes. They had never made food to scale. The idea of fish in a taco was bizarre for the day, unlike today, where you find it on many menus. After the calm from opening and testing, they had a hit. The buzz around town about fish tacos at the little shack grew sales. He opened a second location near SDSU a few years later.

Soon, people from Los Angeles and Orange County started driving to eat the fish tacos. At Rubio's, Californians could be transported by their taste buds to San Felipe, Mexico, without leaving the country. If the Internet had existed in the 1980s, a fish taco stand would have been opened before Rubio's.

Tacos

The Original Fish Taco®
Salsa Verde Grilled Shrimp Taco
Classic Chicken Taco
Wild Caught Mahi-Mahi Taco
Fish Taco Especial
Grilled Gourmet Shrimp Taco
Classic Steak Taco
Grilled Gourmet™ Chicken Taco
Grilled Gourmet™ USDA Choice Steak Taco
Mexican Street Corn Shrimp Taco
Mango-Wild Caught Mahi Mahi Taco
Street Taco®
Atlantic Salmon Taco
Grilled Gourmet™ Veggie Taco

(top): Fish Taco Plate, (bottom): Guacamole and Chips

Over the first four years, Rubio's expanded to 63 locations. Fish tacos became the official food of San Diego. Rubio's went public in 1999, allowing it to grow to 204 sites.

Rubio's performance was underestimated only a few years after going public, and locations closed with over 100 employees being let go. In addition, opening Rubio's in non-beach cities, growing too fast, and markets that would not understand the product resulted in a lack of sales.

Ralph Rubio stepped down as CEO, became chairman and co-founder, and Rubio's became private again. Ralph is still a minority owner and works mainly with the culinary department and customer/employee service areas daily.

The fish tacos are still the number-one best-seller menu item, and they are prepared fresh at each location, battered and fried. On April 5, 2016, San Diego proclaimed it Ralph Rubio Day. Besides working in the culinary department, Ralph and Ray work with many ocean-driven non-profit groups. Ralph is regarded as an expert on fish tacos, and it shows. 🌮

Juan Pollo Rotisserie

SLOGANS: "The Best Flavor" ♦ "The Best Tasting Chicken"

NAME TODAY: Juan Pollo

ORIGINAL LOCATION: 1702 S. Euclid, Ontario

OPENED: January 18, 1984

FOUNDER: Albert Okura, CEO, "The Chicken Man"

CURRENT OWNERSHIP: The Okura Family

CURRENTLY AT THE FIRST LOCATION: Tijuana Tacos

There are currently twenty-five locations in Southern California.

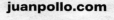
juanpollo.com

ALBERT OKURA WAS BORN to Japanese immigrants in Wilmington, California, in 1951. A compulsive personality drove him to be the best in all he did. At 11, his first job was delivering the *San Pedro News Pilot* newspaper from his shiny new bike, making 30 dollars a month.

Albert's next job changed his life and his sense of business. While attending Los Angeles Junior College, he applied for a position at Burger King to help pay for his day-to-day expenses. Albert made $30–40 per week, at one dollar and fifteen cents per hour. Learning every position in the restaurant, he knew, would mean job security, and he could be called to help at a moment's notice if a worker failed to show up for their shift. In a short time, Albert became an assistant manager and catapulted himself to becoming an area supervisor.

At 26, Albert purchased his first piece of property, a two-bedroom house, with his savings from working at Burger King. He only owned it for one year and learned from many mistakes, such as renting to friends and letting friends live rent-free. Finally, he sold it for a profit that covered his expenses and losses. It was a learning experience about what not to do the next time.

In 1977, Albert was approached by the Azusa Greens Country Club's owner to be his golf course's general manager. Mr. Johnson, the owner, persuaded Albert to join his team by explaining that Albert was just a number at Burger King and that he would be a team member with fewer rules and regulations at the country club. After one year, Albert felt he had learned everything he could and decided to change direction and take his real estate license. After passing the test, Albert worked with his father flipping low-income apartment buildings for two years.

In 1981, at 29, Albert knew that dealing with tenants and all the problems that entailed was not the direction he wanted to go in his career path. Knowing he loved the food industry, Albert started investigating other chains besides the large ones, such as Taco Bell and McDonald's (his two favorites). Finally, he came across a smaller chain that was a mix of both: Del Taco from San Bernardino, California.

Opposite: Miss Juan Pollo and Albert Okura, (top): Full chicken dinner with sides

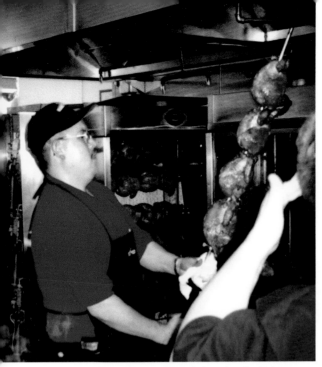
Albert Okura cooking whole rotisserie chickens

One of the qualities that Del Taco possessed was a sense of family, unlike making employees just a number at Burger King. Albert was soon promoted to supervisor at the Carson #67 location. In the three years that Albert worked for Del Taco, he took his restaurant from being the worst store in the district to the top store in the entire company. He didn't fire one employee in those three years, and they would win every store incentive program, such as suggestive selling contests.

In 1981, while working at the Carson Del Taco restaurant, Albert noticed construction on a new fast-food location across the street; six months later was the grand opening for El Pollo Loco. At first, with that name, Albert thought it was a Mexican restaurant. He was surprised to find that it was all about marinated open-flame grilled chicken. He walked in to see the grill packed with whole chickens butterflied leg by leg to feed the long line of consumers. At this point, most chicken sold in fast-food restaurants was fried; never had he seen a fresher grilled chicken. Over the years, the chain has been sold and the menu has changed from just chicken to an array of products that include chicken.

After leaving Del Taco in 1983, Albert started looking toward his next career move. Talking with his cousin Glen Komatsu about opening a charbroiled chicken restaurant, he contacted the friend he called Uncle George, who owned a shopping center in Ontario with a vacant restaurant space. Euclid Avenue was initially designed to have a large park in the middle of the north and southbound sides of the street as a promotion for the city. The park is a fifty-foot green landscape with trees and roses, one of the most beautiful streets in the county. Albert loved the location and started planning on a chicken restaurant.

When Armando Parra immigrated to California from Chihuahua, Mexico, his sister-in-law was working at the Del Taco with Albert. The two men met and became fast friends. One day when Armando was still at Del Taco, he and Albert started talking about the new chicken restaurant. Armando said he had had an idea for charbroiled chicken before El Pollo Loco opened, and they had copied it.

Recalling this conversation with Armando, Albert called to work with him to start their own venture. The first thing was the space in Uncle George's mall; the location was great, but the space had too small a kitchen to cook the chickens on a grill. So he and Armando changed the concept to a rotisserie, because rotisserie ovens took up less room. After submitting blueprints to the city and the health departments, they had an opening date of the first week of January 1984. The goal was to enhance the chicken's natural flavor with citrus and spices. The recipe has not changed since day one.

At first, they decided to name the restaurant Don Pollo; they knew they wanted Pollo, as it was the Hispanic word for chicken. After printing business cards and flyers, though, it was brought to their attention that there was already a restaurant named Don Pollo. So Juan Pollo became their name. It had the Hispanic theme they wanted and Pollo in the name of what they served. Like other restaurants, they wanted a mascot—not a natural person, but a character that could be anywhere they needed. Armando's brother Fernando was a graphic designer and created the chicken character that wore a cowboy hat and matching vest.

On January 18, 1984, Juan Pollo opened without fanfare. Albert and Armando decided to have a soft opening. The grand opening would take place the following month with a radio station and giveaways. Armando trained the employees on the flow of the jobs and how to cook the chicken. For the grand opening, Albert wanted to offer that with every chicken sold, you got half a chicken for free; but Uncle George thought "buy one, get one free" was a better incentive, so that was the deal. The morning of the grand opening, the crew got in early to marinate all the chickens and start the rotisseries. The lines were long, and the market in the same parking lot was upset as their customers could not find parking places. Armando ran out of chicken by noon, but the lines kept growing. The customers waited until another batch of chickens had cooked, and those, too, sold out. By 7:00 p.m., they stopped taking orders, as all the chickens had been sold.

Armando stayed on for three additional months to train more help. Salad, potato salad, rice, and beans were all made from scratch. Armando's employees unfortunately started taking liberties with the recipes and adding their own spin. This did not set well with Albert, as he knew everything had to be consistent. After nine months of slow sales, Albert called Armando to see what he could do; after evaluating, he told Albert that his prices were too low and they needed to be raised. He also advised focusing only on chicken and not the new items he had added to the menu such as French fries, Jell-O, and hot dogs. Sales increased, food preparations refined, and consistency improved tenfold.

In 1986, Juan Pollo #2 opened in San Bernardino. It was a deal that Albert could not pass up. The owner of the shopping center had previously had two other chicken restaurants. However, when the owner tried to open his own restaurant, it had failed. Albert was given the deal of just paying for the equipment. Albert decided not to have a grand opening, but to offer the "buy one, get one chicken free" deal.

Location after location opened. Most of the managers and owners were former hourly employees, and many from the first locations opened. Many landlords of strip malls came to Albert, having him write his lease without much negotiation as the sites had been idle from former tenants.

In 1998, Albert picked up a copy of the *San Bernardino Sun* newspaper and read about the site of the original McDonald's that still had part of the signage and a refurbished 4,000-square-foot commercial building. After buying it, Albert was not sure at first what to do with the location. Then someone suggested that he open a McDonald's Museum. Calling local franchisees of McDonald's, Albert asked if they had any memorabilia; none would help, as they didn't want to ruffle the corporate feathers. Albert placed the corporate offices of Juan Pollo into a fourth of the building, and the remainder he turned into the Unofficial McDonald's Museum. The grand opening coincided with the 50th anniversary of the beginning of McDonald's, December 12, 1998. It is still open daily with free admission.

In 2005, Albert purchased the entire town of Amboy, which sits on historic Route 66 between Barstow and Needles. In the deal, Albert took possession of the gas station, café, motel, and the larger-than-life thirty-five-foot Roy's Café sign. Today the gas station is open and hosts visitors from around the globe who drive the route from Santa Monica, California, to Chicago. Plans are to remodel the motel for guests. In addition, many films and video shoots take place weekly in the town.

Sadly, on January 27, 2023, Albert Okura passed away. Many tributes poured in from across all fast-food restaurants and dignitaries around Southern California. His son Kyle and right-hand man are now fulfilling Albert's dream with 25 locations open, primarily in the Inland Empire. They are also keeping the McDonald's museum open and plan to be a global brand with the best-tasting chicken on the market. ✎

California Pizza Kitchen

SLOGAN: "We Are Passionate Individuals Committed to Inspiring Others by Bringing California Creativity to Every Meal"

ORIGINAL LOCATION: 207 S. Beverly Blvd., Beverly Hills

OPENED: March 27, 1985

FOUNDERS: Rick Rosenfield and Larry Flax

CURRENT OWNERSHIP: Golden State Capital

CURRENTLY AT THE FIRST LOCATION: The first location is still in operation. *There are currently 140 locations in ten states.*

cpk.com

IN 1982, WOLFGANG PUCK OPENED the famed Spago's on the Sunset Strip in West Hollywood. He hired pizza maker Ed LaDou to create the best pizza in Los Angeles. LaDou worked at Spago's open kitchen for two years before opening his own restaurant, Caioti, in the San Fernando Valley. While working in his kitchen, LaDou used his pizza-making skills from Spago's to teach pizza-making in local cooking schools around Los Angeles. In October 1984, LaDou taught a class at Ma Cuisine Cooking School that Rick Rosenfield and Larry Flax attended. They were impressed and hired him to create a namesake pizza as he had done for Wolfgang.

Rick and Larry, federal prosecutors and then defense lawyers in Los Angeles, gave up the courtroom for cooking. They opened the California Pizza Kitchen (CPK) in the heart of Beverly Hills Little Restaurant Row on Beverly Blvd., at the site of many failed restaurant attempts and down the street from the original Cheesecake Factory (page 105).

Rick and Larry were hands-on in the business, from hiring staff to creating the menu items. Their beginning guiding principle was ROCK, which stood for Respect, Opportunity, Communication, and Kindness. Every team member is equal, from the dishwasher to the server to the manager and chefs. They were convinced that a restaurant would fail if you didn't have each job working together. Everyone is on a first-name basis. CPK did not have a corporate office, but a restaurant support office. Open, friendlier terminology would successfully open the business with the ROCK principles.

CPK had an open-air kitchen like Spago's, with clean white, bright yellow, and black polished tiles. The pizza oven is the heart of the restaurant; the black, red, and yellow tiles symbolize the California sun. Servers wore white pants, shirts, ties, and tennis shoes under a long black apron. The servers would polish their tennis shoes with Hollywood Sani-white® shoe polish to bright white.

Top Five Pizza Flavors
Original BBQ Chicken
Thai Chicken with Spicy Peanut Sauce
Margherita
California Club
Wild Mushroom

Opposite: Inside the pizza oven, (inset): Stretching pizza dough, (top): Logo

In the early years, CPK commissioned California artists of every age to create one-of-a-kind pizza box art showcasing CPK's fresh ingredients. The painted boxes were displayed like museum art pieces in the dining rooms.

The opening menu was eclectic and very California. They blended fresh ingredients that would not be featured together, such as barbeque sauce and chicken, and freshly picked herbs and vegetables with spices would top the pizzas, pasta, and salads. Even though the restaurant had "pizza" in its name, they also offered pasta, salads, cocktails, and desserts to round out the menu for a whole-restaurant experience.

At the time, *Los Angeles Times* restaurant critic Ruth Reichl said that the pizza kitchen was not warm but had a calm modern environment with its open kitchen. But she could not imagine any Italian sitting down to a pizza topped with barbeque chicken. She also felt that the place was born to be cloned.

Despite this, CPK took Beverly Boulevard by storm. There were lines down the block with guests waiting for tables to enjoy pizza like at Spago's. 1987 was a big year of expansion from a test location in the new Lenox Mall in the Buckhead area of Atlanta to Hawaii; CPK was coast to coast. Both out-of-California locations were selected because they were not "known" cities for having a regional pizza, such as New York or Chicago. Testing a pizza with California flavors in Georgia and Hawaii was instrumental to the success of franchises and additional locations for CPK. Both locations took to the innovative flavors of the pizzas and pasta.

Travel & Leisure magazine quoted the following year: "If designer pizza was born at Wolfgang Puck's Spago's, it was perfected at California Pizza Kitchen." *USA Today* called CPK "one of the Top Ten Pizzas in the United States." These are just a couple of the accolades that CPK has received over the years.

The Atlanta Lenox Square location was concentrated in businesses, hotels, and offices. Most pizza deliveries were of bland pizzas like cheese and pepperoni. CPK started delivery in a 1.5-mile radius, which was well received.

Nick was a Chicagoan who was transplanted to California and knew he wanted the next location to be in the Windy City. His brother Neal still lived in the Chicago area and became a partner in CPK Illinois Inc., opening the first location on a snowy winter evening in the River North area of the city. Over 100 city dignitaries dined on thin-crusted California pizzas with "strange" toppings such as Peking duck, bamboo shoots,

Founders Rick Rosenfield and Larry Flax

and barbeque chicken. A few of the guests commented on how "gross" the pizzas sounded until they hit their tastebuds; they were hooked. Chicago was location number eight.

Every location opened with the "open kitchen" concept, the same color scheme, and the same menus. Since the menu was not regional like other restaurants, it was challenging for the kitchens and chefs to execute the menu without adding regional or seasonal items.

Red carpets for movie premieres in Los Angeles happen weekly, with caterers looking for new and exciting ways to highlight their movies. In 1991, CPK created 575 children's pizzas for the new movie premiere *Teenage Mutant Ninja Turtles II: The Secret of the Ooze*. Unfortunately, the pizzas were filled with peanut butter and chocolate—only for the premiere party and never again.

In 1992, Rick and Larry decided to bring in PepsiCo as an investor at 66 percent ownership. The only change the customers noticed was that the fountain drinks switched from Coke® to Pepsi®. There was also an expansion of additional locations.

In the middle of the "Trial of the Century" of O.J. Simpson, in April 1995, Flax contacted Judge Lance Ito, inviting the entire jury to dine at the restaurant. A strange circumstance that was not revealed was that Ron Goldman, who was murdered the same night as Simpson's former wife Nicole, had worked at a California Pizza Kitchen. The following week, most of the jurors wore matching black T-shirts from CPK in the jury box with the saying "Fourteen ethnically diverse cultures peacefully coexisting on a thin delicious crust." The press had a field day trying to understand the motive behind the shirts.

December 1995, a few weeks before the holiday season, CPK released the CPK Cookbook, filled with recipes from their menu offerings. The book was one of the first in the industry of restaurant cookbooks. It was an instant success, packed with 35 recipes, including step-by-step instructions on how to make the perfect crust by letting your dough rise three times. The photography was done by Brian Leatart, who did the pictures for all the menus. All the proceeds went to children's charities.

Locations	
1985:	Beverly Hills
1987:	Atlanta, Georgia (Lenox Square)
	Hawaii
	Brentwood
	Chicago
	Newport Beach
1988:	Beverly Center, Los Angeles
1989:	Chicago River North
	Topanga Plaza
	Downtown Los Angeles
1990:	Studio City, CA
2000:	83 full-service restaurants and 24 CPK ASAP in airports
2001:	The Gateway, Utah
2004:	Orem, Utah
2004:	146 restaurants open, nine in Asia
2008:	210 restaurants, 29 states, and seven countries
2020:	146 restaurants, ten countries
2023:	140 locations in 10 states

A new concept was launched at the United Airlines Terminal 8 at Los Angeles International Airport, CPK ASAP. This was a quick version of CPK with menu items that could be ordered and boxed for travel. Since an airport is open earlier than a traditional CPK, an entire breakfast menu, including brunch choices of smoked salmon and eggs benedict pizzas, was explicitly designed for the airport. Most of the CPK ASAP locations were licensed to Host Marriott, with a few in high-traffic shopping malls.

With Very Best Wishes –

Nancy & Ronald Reagan

Beverly Hills staff with President Ronald Reagan and First Lady Nancy Reagan

The two founders became instant commercial stars for American Express in 1997, touting "Don't Leave Home Without It." A print ad was also launched with American Express.

Four years after the PepsiCo® purchase, Rick and Larry, with New York investment firm Bruckmann, Rosser, and Sherrill & Co., bought back the shares of CPK.

Rick and Larry decided to release the second cookbook in the summer of 1999; this book focused on the pasta, salads, soups, and sides that were not included in the first book. Again, a detailed questionnaire went out to all the company employees to see what recipes they wanted in the book, and the book included anecdotes from them. Furthermore, proceeds were donated to children's charities.

In September 1999, Rick and Larry again became television commercial stars, but this time for their product. New frozen pizzas arrived in the grocery-store aisle. Kraft Foods Inc. made the pizza under a licensing deal with CPK, which would get a percentage of the sales. Other frozen items added to the line were single-serve pizzas and flatbreads.

The year 2000 brought the first IPO to raise an estimated $70 million, using $40 million to pay down bank debt and buy back preferred stock. The bank debt was caused by over-expansion when PepsiCo controlled the company. For example, they opened 60 restaurants in five years and then closed 16 of them. The company sold 5.3 million shares on the Nasdaq under the symbol CPKI. Rick and Larry remained on the board without day-to-day control.

After a veteran restaurant executive was fired, the board installed Rick and Larry as co-CEO and co-chairs. They held these positions for eight years until 2011, when Golden Gate Capital acquired CPK.

Former Restaurants at 207 S. Beverly

1979: La Cascade ~ French Restaurant
1980: Raphael's Hideaway ~ Italian
1980: Monti's ~ Italian
1982: Peking Garden ~ Mandarin
1982: B Minor ~ Jazz Club and Restaurant
1984: Zen Japanese Restaurant
1985: California Pizza Kitchen

Beverly Hills first location exterior

In the summer of 2013, the CPK at the Westfield Topanga mall location became the prototype for the new look. The interior changed from white, black, and yellow polished tile to rustic and organic. The tabletops were made from reclaimed barn doors. The host stand had a sizable see-through bookcase wall behind it that housed an herb-growing area and a large chalkboard for messages of specials. There was also an updated menu and wine/drink offerings. The servers' outfits were also more relaxed, with the former matching uniforms discarded with the bright shiny surfaces. The wait staff no longer recites a long script and can be more spontaneous. The menu was also trimmed down, with an under-600-calorie menu item section, and local produce is used in the kitchen for freshness. You could see everything happening because of the open-air look.

In the fall of 2013, CPK had one of the largest rollouts of a product since opening in 1984 with 100 percent gluten-free pizza. The online Gluten Intolerance Group highlighted CPK's efforts to create pizzas and pasta dishes for gluten-intolerant diners. Additional crust offerings were cauliflower and chickpea.

Rick and Larry teamed up one last time after departing CPK with a seafood restaurant venture called Bottlefish in the Brentwood area of Los Angeles. Bottlefish was named one of the top ten seafood restaurants in America. Unfortunately, Bottlefish only lasted four years and closed during the 2020 pandemic. Bottlefish's menu could not be revamped for takeout, as the dishes would not have the same quality when they arrived home with the customer. Incidentally, the location is now a CPK. Bottlefish was just one of the many restaurants that closed in 2020.

Rick Rosenfield learned a lot from the opening of Bottlefish and closing in the pandemic and his many years at CPK. Rick and his wife Esther recalled their great pizza in Rome, a pizza sold in squares and by weight, filled with fresh vegetables and cheeses. Rick tested the idea in a pop-up shop first, calling it ROCA (RO for Rome and CA for California). The location would focus more on takeout instead of wait service. The restaurants would be about a fifth of the size of one of the CPKs. The pizzas are served in squares, half-sheet, and full-sheet sizes. Again, they focused on the fresh ingredients of California. The crusts tasted tremendous, and they warmed up as if the food had been delivered. Today, Rick and Esther have two locations open and more are coming in the future.

CPK filed for Chapter 11 in July 2020 and emerged four months later. Today, CPK is looking to sell or for an IPO. 🍕

Chevys Mexican Restaurant

SLOGAN: "Good Food. Good Times."

NAME TODAY: Chevys Fresh Mex

ORIGINAL LOCATION: 2400 Mariner Square, Alameda

OPENED: June 21, 1986

FOUNDERS: Warren L. Simmons Sr. and Warren "Scooter" Simmons Jr.

CURRENT OWNERSHIP: Xperience Restaurant Group

CURRENTLY AT THE FIRST LOCATION: A retirement building

There are currently twenty-two locations in nine states, seven of which are franchised.

chevys.com

IN THE 1970s, WARREN SIMMONS SR. founded and managed the Tia Maria Mexican restaurant chain, spanning almost a dozen locations. In 1975, Warren started working with a developer to build a recreational pier area in San Francisco with a dozen restaurants and shopping like no mall in any suburbs. Each business would be unique, as they would not be chains but stores and restaurants run and owned by the shopkeeper. Over time, many turned into a chain (see page 91, Mrs. Fields Cookies) after opening their first location on the pier. Pier 39 is still going strong, more than 45 years after opening.

At a young age, Warren "Scooter" Simmons Jr. started grating cheese in his father's restaurants before he could walk. Scooter loved the restaurant business and the ports. So he and his father partnered in 1986 to open Chevys in the port area of Alameda, over the Bay Bridge from San Francisco. Scooter went to Mexico to research and learned more about Mexican foods. Collecting recipes from Mexican border towns and décor for his new venture filled his suitcases.

Most restaurants at the port were seafood-based, with Chevys focused on Mexican with some seafood dishes. Unlike any other restaurant of the day, Chevys would not have a can opener in their kitchen, or a freezer. Everything would be fresh. Produce would come from the market in season. Meats would never come frozen, and dairy would be fresh from the farm. The chefs would prepare everything from scratch, like the *mamacitas* in Mexico.

Before the grand opening and to create buzz, Scooter used stationery from the El Camino Hotel (Room 303) in Tijuana, Mexico, to announce

Opposite: Tableside Guacamole, (top): Founder Mr. Simmons

Ownership	
1986–1993:	Simmons Family
1993–1997:	PepsiCo/Taco Bell
1997–2005:	J.W. Childs Equity Partners
2005–2018:	Real Mex Restaurants, Inc.
2018–Present:	Xperience Restaurant Group (XRG)

the beginning of the new restaurant; he sent them to all the newspapers and columnists as the press release. In addition, he used foreign stamps and mailed them from one of his trips to Mexico. This ensured that the letters would be opened and the media would pay attention.

Besides the fresh ingredients, Scooter tasted the hand-made tortillas made from fresh masa, pressed, and cooked over an open flame. However, he knew that hiring someone to make the tortillas would be very time-consuming, and purchasing a machine that could manufacture tortillas would be costly but also a focal point if placed in the dining room. Today, the La Machino tortilla machine can produce a six-inch tortilla every four seconds (900 per hour). Tortillas are served hot with butter on each table, besides being fried for chips and salsa.

Scooter placed the cantina on the second floor, overlooking Oakland Bay and Jack London Square. At night, the lights of the city and port were incredible. Happy Hour specials and festive south-of-the-border drinks were celebrated. The female wait staff wore skirts with vibrant ruffled shirts that fell off the shoulders, while the males wore black pants and button-down shirts.

In 1989, General Motors of Detroit forced Chevy's Café in Portage, Michigan, to change its name to Flip's for trademark infringement, as they had lots of Chevrolet décor. Mothers Against Drunk Drivers (MADD) and GM shareholders felt the company should not be associated with establishments that served alcohol; the GM lawyers did not approach Chevys Mexican Food, as they never had any décor that would associate them with Chevrolet even though the restaurant was named after Scooter's first car, which was a Chevrolet.

With over two dozen locations open in the Western states, Scooter felt it was time to spend dollars on advertising. The Goodby, Berlin & Silverstein ad agency was given an unheard-of task by Chevys: making a commercial in the morning and broadcasting it that afternoon. They were called "fresh TV spots." These ads were the first of their kind in the ad industry. Each commercial is broadcast for one day and never seen again. Sales jumped, and so did the openings of additional Chevys locations.

In 1992, Simmons ran into a shortage of U.S.-grown cranberries for the signature margaritas. They went down to Santiago, Chile, and bought 750 acres, hoping to harvest cranberries a few years later against everyone's prediction. The CranChile farm became the world's largest grower and producer of cranberries.

A fun item in the lobby for a while was the Excuse Booth; it was a phone booth with 16 different background noises, from airport to police-station sounds. You could tell someone that you were at

Years and Unit Numbers

1993: 37 locations
1997: 70 locations
2006: 104 locations
2021: 22 locations in 9 states, 7 franchised

Other Simco Family Restaurants

Pier 39 (San Francisco)
Fog Harbor Fish House
Pier Market Seafood
WipeOut Bar & Grill
Eagle Café
Crab House

First location in Alameda, CA

the airport catching a flight or had been arrested.

On August 13, 1993, PepsiCo®/Taco Bell® purchased the 37-unit chain from the Simmons family. PepsiCo planned to open several hundred locations within a few years, and they currently had 4,000 Taco Bell locations in their portfolio. The Simmonses focused on other restaurants in their collection, mainly on Pier 39, which the senior Simmons had created.

In four years, PepsiCo® doubled the number of units open of Chevys, but this growth was too slow for them: hoping to have hundreds soon after purchasing the chain, selling the 70-unit chain was next. Then, in May 1997, J.W. Childs Equity Partners purchased Chevys, hoping to continue the coast-to-coast openings.

Xperience Restaurant Group Brands
El Torito
Chevys Fresh Mex
Sol Mexican Cocina
Las Brisas
Solita
Sinigual
Acapulco
El Torito Grill
Who Song & Larrys

In 1999, Applebee's International Inc., owners of 66 Rio Bravo Cantinas mainly in the Southwest and Midwest, sold them to Chevys. Chevys planned to rebrand the Rio Bravo Cantinas to have over 130 locations open.

With many underperforming locations, Chevys closed a few dozen restaurants and sold the chain to Real Mex Restaurants. Real Mex Restaurants in 2018 rebranded its name after a bankruptcy sale and changed it to Xperience Restaurant Group (XRG). Today Xperience has ten Mexican brands. Each brand is unique, with different atmospheres, menus, programs, and flavors; some are casual and others are upscale, some are California-based and some are national.

In 2006, Warren Simmons Sr., the founder of Chevys, passed away at the age of 79 in Napa; that same year, the original Alameda location closed after 30 years.

Chevys brand still uses fresh ingredients today, and you still will not find a can opener in their kitchens. Nine locations are in California, seven are franchised, and the rest are east of the Rockies.

Grand opening ribbon cutting at Fairfield, CA location

Johnny Rockets

SLOGAN: "The Original Hamburger"

ORIGINAL LOCATION: 7507 Melrose Ave., Los Angeles

OPENED: June 6, 1986

FOUNDER: Ronn Teitelbaum

CURRENT OWNERSHIP: FAT Brands

CURRENTLY AT THE FIRST LOCATION: Vegan burger restaurant

Today, there are 283 sites, with 276 franchised and seven company-owned in twenty-four countries.

johnnyrockets.com

RONN TEITELBAUM GREW UP with a father as a famous furrier for the studios and private collections of the elite in Beverly Hills. Ronn began in real estate rental before opening his high-end men's clothing store in Beverly Hills. In 1982, while searching for a source of a garment in a rural town outside Milan, he noticed that a contract buyer from Macy's was also at the sweater maker's. At that point, Ronn realized that the big-box department stores had found his specialty sources in Europe. It was time to sell his company, Eric Ross & Co. Clothing.

After selling in 1984, Ronn focused on his next venture. He had always had a dream of owning a restaurant. He recalled a diner he saw as a kid called Sweet Sixteen Fountain Grill on Montana and 16th in Santa Monica. Ronn wanted to recreate his childhood diner.

In the 1980s, Melrose Avenue was one of the chicest shopping, dining, and entertaining streets in Los Angeles. The trends of California started on Melrose. Along the two-mile stretch from La Brea Avenue to Kings Road, you would find next year's trends in clothing and fashion from vintage to independent clothiers. This was the street where Ronn Teitelbaum would open his exciting burger joint.

Property on the famed Melrose Avenue was pricey; he found a small beer bar of 840 square feet that he could transform into a 1940s diner with a minimal menu. Large plate-glass windows faced the street; looking inside, even with only the staff, the place would look packed. So Ronn placed metal facing on the outside of the building to make it look like an East Coast 1940s diner. The inside had an open grill in the center with twenty red vinyl stools surrounding the white Formica® counters and chrome with high-gloss white walls.

Ronn wanted his burger joint to be a unique

Opposite (top): Original Melrose Avenue, Los Angeles location with motorcycle rally, (bottom): Ronn Teitelbaum, founder and an avid Harley-Davidson rider inside the Melrose location, (top): Logo

Ownership	
1986–1995:	Ronn Teitelbaum
1995–2007:	Carpenter Investment & Development Corp.
2007–2013:	RedZone Capital
2013–2020:	Sun Capital
2020–Present:	FAT Brands

destination, not just a place to get a meal. So, he named it Johnny Rockets; the first name came from Johnny Appleseed, and Rocket came from the Oldsmobile Rocket 88 automobile. The wall art was that of 1940s gals and military men. Ronn found 30-year-old spindle mixers to make malts and shakes, also tabletop vintage Seeburg Wall-O-Matic® jukeboxes that could belt out a hit from a former decade for a nickel. Every employee would be outfitted in a tapered crisp white shirt topped with a black bow tie to match the black pants and penny loafers, all covered with a clean white apron. The wait staff would also do their own "bank," which Ronn thought would eliminate the need for a cashier. This lasted three days, until Ronn brought his daughter Jill in to help.

Johnny Rocket's ketchup smile

Soon after opening, the staff on Melrose started adapting song-and-dance routines to entertain the guests, using ketchup bottles as makeshift microphones. For example, Johnny Rockets would run through bottles and bottles of Heinz® ketchup, not just for their musical performances but also for when a guest ordered fresh French fries. The waiter would draw a smiley face in ketchup on a secondary plate next to the hot fries. Seeing the smile on the plate would also put one on the customers' faces.

The opening menu was mainly hamburgers and homemade sandwiches. Tuna and chicken salad were made fresh in the little kitchen with homemade apple pies, the shakes made with rich ice cream and whole milk. Weeks before the opening, Ronn's daughter Jill would canvass the street and give coupons to all the other shop employees for one free hamburger, fries, and a coke. In the front of the restaurant was a countdown sign as to how many more days until they opened. A few times, with setbacks, they had to change the number of days. Those free meals were for opening week, so the other employees kept tabs on the countdown.

The small Melrose location fed between 600 and 700 guests per day from their 20 stools; many weekends, they stayed open until five in the morning. The lines of hungry guests would go down Melrose until the wee hours. Many, over the years, have stated that Johnny Rockets was a knockoff of the Apple Pan on Pico Boulevard on the Westside, or Ruby's Diner (page 127), which it was not. It was a 1940s diner, and all restaurants of that time had burgers, fries, and shakes.

Venues for Johnny Rockets	
Theme Parks:	28
Airport Locations:	22
Casinos:	17
Cruise Ships:	14
Sports Stadiums:	8

Seeing the popularity of Johnny Rockets, Ronn opened reproductions in Westwood, Beverly Hills, and Sherman Oaks. Finding that franchising was an option, he sold franchises for Atlanta, Chicago, Minneapolis, and San Francisco. Only three years after the

Ronn Teitelbaum at the Melrose Avenue location

Melrose opening, Johnny Rockets went international in Tokyo and, in 1990, opened in London. Ronn's daughter Jill had been working in Chicago as a waitress while in school. She decided to relocate to Japan for three months to help open the location.

The growth of the company was fast and furious. Then, in 1992, Ronn brought in a former executive with a large fast-food company to become president, limiting his responsibility as chairman and chief executive.

In 1995, Ronn sold Johnny Rockets to the Carpenter Investment & Development Corp., remaining a minority stockholder and creative consultant. Sadly, in September of 2000, Ronn passed away at 61 from brain cancer.

Johnny Rockets skyrocketed to continued global growth with the new ownership. Opening 49 restaurants would place a Johnny Rockets on every continent except Antarctica.

Ronn created a legacy, not a chain of restaurants. His passion for excellence in every location was apparent. When not working or visiting his sites, Ronn's passion was leathered-up, riding his Harley-Davidson on the back roads of America. He even had a publicity shot with one of his Harleys in the restaurant.

In 1999, Johnny Rockets partnered with Royal Caribbean Cruise Lines to put the iconic diner on board fourteen of their ships. A flat fee is charged for an all-you-can-eat meal, with added charges for drinks.

Johnny Rockets started testing plant-based burgers for vegan customers and rolled them out worldwide in 2021. Since 2020, FAT Brands, a conglomerate of food franchises from steak houses to hot dog companies, has owned Johnny Rockets.

The original Johnny Rockets sold its last plate of fresh fries on October 26, 2015. Unfortunately, the owner of the building and Johnny Rockets could not agree on a lease upon the expiration of the old one. The Melrose location had a long run of 29 years. For six weeks, the place was turned into a pop-up restaurant called the Peach Pit to replicate the restaurant featured on the hit show 90210. Today, the location serves vegan non-animal burgers and drinks. 🍔

Top Five Burgers

+ The Original: Lettuce, tomato, chopped onion, relish, pickles, mustard, and mayo.
+ The Bacon Cheddar Burger: Applewood smoked bacon, cheddar cheese, lettuce, tomato, sliced onion, and Special Sauce.
+ The Rocket: Cheddar cheese, lettuce, tomato, sliced onion, and Special Sauce.
+ Smokehouse: Applewood smoked bacon, crispy sourdough onion rings, cheddar cheese, and Smoke House BBQ Ranch.
+ Route 66: Swiss cheese, grilled mushrooms, caramelized onions, and mayonnaise.

Noah's New York Bagels

SLOGAN: "A Neighborhood Gathering Place for Good Conversation and Great Food"

NAME TODAY: Noah's

ORIGINAL LOCATION: 3170 College Ave., Berkeley

OPENED: August 4, 1989

FOUNDER: Noah Alper

CURRENT OWNERSHIP: Panera Brands

CURRENTLY AT THE FIRST LOCATION: Boichik Bagels

There are fifty-five locations in California.

noahs.com

IT WAS THE WEEKEND of the annual Berkeley area Jewish Film Festival downtown. Noah Alper and his staff were getting the new bagel shop ready to open. With the aroma of the fresh bagels coming out of the oven, a blind man walked into the unlocked, unlit shop. He commented on how great it smelled. Alper looked at the staff and said "I guess we are open!" The gentleman was the first customer—Alper gave him a sesame bagel right out of the oven in the house. Also, by providing bagels over Jewish Film Festival weekend, word spread fast, and the shop was jammed almost immediately. Honest-to-goodness New York bagels—like no one had tasted outside New York.

Noah's would be a different place, a unique bagel shop. First, it was going to be kosher. Obtaining kosher certification was not an easy task, but Noah's would be not only kosher but also open on Shabbat. Second was Jewish pride: creating a place where all kinds of Jews and others would feel comfortable. All from ultra-Orthodox, reformed, straight, and secular to gay Jews could enjoy kosher foods. Besides Noah's products being certified kosher, Noah's was a gathering place.

Noah Alper believed eating a bagel should be an event to remember. Bagels should be tasty, crisp, and large, crusty outside and chewy on the inside. On a trip to Brooklyn in 1986, Alper had discovered the ideal New York-style bagel that helped inspire him to begin his own company and spread his love of bagels in the Bay area. Noah's bagels were lighter and larger than most other bagels, with a great crunchy crust on the outside. He used all-natural ingredients, and the bagels were steamed, not boiled. Bagels were made fresh throughout the day, with day-olds given to local charities.

Noah was also one of the first to toast bagels. Most places sold only untoasted and room-temperature

Opposite: Bagels for breakfast, (top): Noah Alper, founder with large advertising bagel

Ownership	
1989–1996:	Noah Alper
1996–2014:	The Einstein Noah Restaurant Group
2014–2021:	JAB Holdings
2021–Present:	Panera Brands

rounds of bread that they called a bagel. His stores created an atmosphere where you would want to hang out and schmooze. Old black-and-white photos of the Brooklyn Dodgers, New York subways, and other pictures of iconic locations from around New York filled the walls. The iconic logo of Noah's New York Bagels with the city name in tile underneath started with the second shop in North Berkeley in 1991 (which is still in operation today as the most extended operating location).

Location Numbers
1989: 1 location
1991: 2 locations
1993: 8 locations
1995: 38 locations
1996 50 locations
2019: 56 locations
2020: 55 locations

Deli cases ran the wall length, displaying bagels, pickles, and other foods—14 varieties of bagels, bialys, and onion sticks. Knishes were also sold, a hot, flaky pastry filled with a potato-vegetable fruit and cheese mixture. Alper offered house-made cheese "schmears" in different varieties, along with tuna salad, egg salad, rye bread, challah on Fridays, and a wide range of smoked fish. The beverages were endless, with NY Egg Creams, juices, sodas, Peet's® coffee, and espresso drinks rounding out the menu.

Lox Flavors
+ New York Nova (lox schmears)
+ Sliced with Cream Cheese
+ Peppered Lox (spicy coating of coriander, black pepper, and brown sugar)
+ Smoked Salmon Schmear (double whipped)

Alper introduced the word "schmear" into the Bay Area with his array of toppings for his bagels. Garlic herb, walnut raisin, strawberry, hummus, seven-herb, and salmon salad were favorites. Four varieties of lox, the traditional smoked salmon of Jewish culture, could be added to your toasted bagel. Mini bagels for office parties or children's birthdays consisted of plain, chocolate chip, or cinnamon.

He also added non-traditional flavors of bagels, such as oat bran, blueberry, and chocolate chip, into the mix. After testing, Alper felt steaming before baking the bagel improved flavor, as a boiled bagel could be used as a hockey puck by lunchtime.

To expand, Alper opened a central commissary that produced and delivered frozen raw dough bagels daily to the stores. The stores would then thaw the bagels out, age them in a dough retarder (a type of refrigerator that is slightly warmer), dress them with seeds or onion flakes, etc., proof them (using a warming box so they would rise), and then bake them fresh with steam at each store. Wholesale accounts were vital to Noah's, with the production of more than 100,000 per week and 50 employees at the wholesale production facilities. Bagels were sold to delis, grocery markets, and restaurants in the San Francisco area, along with other locations in Candlestick Park, with Northwestern Airlines, and even a New York Style deli in Indonesia. The bagels were entirely produced at the commissary, as were the schmears for the stores.

Employment requests in local newspapers were catchy and exciting, with some of the highlights as:

MAKE YOUR MOTHER PROUD. GET A JOB! AT NOAH'S BAGELS.

We're looking for more good people with character and chutzpah. What do you get?

+ A clean kosher kitchen (no meat or grease)
+ Respectable hours (you'll have enough time off to get a life if you don't have one already)
+ A manager who thinks your opinion counts
+ It's a hip, happenin', hamische place where you will work your butt off and have a great time

Being civic-minded was the number-one priority. Ice cream leader Ben & Jerry's model taught Alper to give back to the community. The Noah's Bagel Foundation was created in 1993 and awarded grants to grassroots organizations to benefit children and community-building. For many years, Noah's sent kids to summer camp. His day-old bagels would be bagged up and given to soup kitchens. Then, in February 1995, Noah's opened a store in a challenging area: the Castro District of San Francisco. Noah paid rent for his shop and the building's other tenant, an HIV resource center, and invested in renovating the 1922 Beau-Arts building, a former branch of Bank of Italy (America) sitting on the busy corner of Market and Castro.

Alper invested in his employees, taking them on cruises and holding corporate events. He tried to teach employees to be *heimish*, which is Yiddish for homey, informal, friendly, and warm. He owned all his stores, without franchising. After about 1½ years, Dan, his brother who gave him the idea of opening a bagel shop, became a partner in the business.

On a visit to the East Bay area in 1994, President Clinton requested a Noah's Cinnamon Raisin bagel, which gained national attention. Now when someone visited the site from outside Noah's locations, a stop for a cinnamon raisin bagel was a must.

Starbucks Coffee Company®, with less than 600 locations in 1995, was looking for a way to expand more rapidly. Starbucks invested in Noah's so they could take advantage of common markets. Starbucks soon appeared next to Noah's. They didn't sell bagels in the coffee shops or coffee in the bagel shops (Noah's used Peet's Coffee) but marketed next to each other. This worked and was implemented for about a dozen locations. Federal Way, a suburb of Washington, D.C., became the first location outside California. The location was chosen as part of an arrangement for additional locations within a Washington supermarket chain's footprint.

With 38 locations in California and Washington, D.C., a large wholesale base, and a commissary, Noah's was sold to Einstein Brothers Bagels in 1996, only seven years after opening the first location. Einstein Brothers Bagels was perfect for purchasing the Noah Brand. Noah's has kept its brand separate; all stores are in California, with Einstein east of the Rockies.

National Bagel Day is February 9, and Noah's gives away a free bagel with schmear. Today 22 regular bagel flavors with seven gourmet varieties make up the offered choices. Sadly, though, Noah's is no longer kosher: they stay open on Passover and sell bacon on their sandwiches. Like Alper has stated: "When you sell someone your house, you cannot expect them to keep the same drapery color."

Today, Noah's is part of the Panera Group, as are Caribou Coffee, Einstein Bagels, and Panera Cafés, with over 110,000 employees in 10 countries.

Noah is connected to his community, with philanthropic work, running a consulting company, and lecturing on his 2009 book *Business Mensch: Timeless Wisdom for Today's Entrepreneur*. He also established the San Francisco Jewish Community High School of the Bay. After selling Noah's, Alper donated his collection of the company's artifacts, from photos to sales records, to the Magnes archives of Berkeley, where it is held for research today. He also feels at home on College Avenue, exactly where he started, as he has been advising Emily Winston of Boichik Bagels opening at the location of Alper's first Noah's Bagels, which closed in 2018. ✸

1991 Bagel Flavors
Plain
Egg
Whole Wheat
Poppy
Sesame
Super Onion
Everything

Pick Up Stix

SLOGAN: "Wok'd Fresh"

ORIGINAL LOCATION: 30461 Avenida de Las Flores #A, Rancho Santa Margarita

OPENED: 1989

FOUNDERS: Xianghua (Charlie) and Ling Zhang

CURRENT OWNERSHIP: Lorne Goldberg Mandarin Holdings

CURRENTLY AT THE FIRST LOCATION: Pei Wei Asian Fast Food

There are currently forty-eight locations in four states.

pickupstix.com

AT AGE TWO, XIANGHUA (CHARLIE) ZHANG watched his father being sent to prison in China for 23 years for not cooperating with the Communist system. When he turned 17, Charlie, with 17 million urban youth, started working in the countryside rice paddies during the Cultural Revolution of the 1960s and '70s.

While working in the countryside, Charlie found his passion for music with his brother's clarinet; he played and practiced when not working long hours in the fields. Music was the perfect distraction from the brutal, backbreaking days. At 26, Charlie was offered a full scholarship from a music academy in Los Angeles; his uncle was living in the States and could sponsor his airfare and passage. He had $20 in his pocket and his brother's clarinet. Realizing that he could not make money as a musician and needed a job as his funds ran out, he applied for over a dozen jobs until he found work as a busboy in a Chinese restaurant; at night he worked as a gas-station attendant. Finally, he realized that music would have to be a hobby instead of a career.

Working in a Chinese restaurant was an education. He learned what diners ate and what came back untouched. He knew every job in the kitchen, so he could step into any position if someone did not show up for their shift. Finding that others in the restaurant could not pronounce his name, he changed it to Charlie at the suggestion of a neighbor. The restaurant staff became his second family. One of the waiters took him to a church gathering where he met Ling, his future wife. Ling was very impressed by how Charlie spoke highly of his mother; soon after, they married.

In 1977, with the help of a business partner, Charlie opened a Chinese restaurant in the beach community of Dana Point; using his adopted name, he named it Shanghai Charlie's. It was a sit-down, full-service restaurant that operated for more than 30 years.

Signature Dishes
House Special Chicken
Orange Peel Chicken
Mongolian Beef
Firecracker Chicken
Beef and Broccoli
Cream Cheese Wontons
Asian Lettuce Wraps
Egg Rolls

Opposite: Pick Up Stix General's Orange Chicken and Broccoli Beef entrees

After about 12 years, Charlie and Ling opened a new Chinese restaurant concept in Rancho Santa Margarita, about 18 miles from Shanghai Charlie's. Realizing that customers wanted a take-out concept, Charlie focused on quick, healthful, and flavorful Asian food. The Zhangs named it Pick Up Stix, af-

Owners

1990–2001:	Zhang Family
2001–2010:	Carlson Companies (Carlson Restaurants Worldwide)
2010–Present:	Lorne Goldberg Mandarin Holdings (Leeann Chin Parent Company)

ter the children's game Pick Up Sticks. Adapting the flavors and spices for the American palate, they opened the kitchen so all could see the chefs with the large woks hot steaming. All the vegetables could be seen in large bins in the refrigerators with see-through doors. All the food was cooked to order over the high-heat burners using traditional woks.

Pick Up Stix became an instant success with the hard work of the Zhangs, opening additional locations throughout the Southern California region. With the other locations, Charlie knew he had to have consistency in the vegetables, meats, and sauces, so he opened a central commissary to streamline the preparation for each item on the menus; this brought uniformity to the locations.

Looking to help those wanting a healthier line of Asian cuisine, Charlie introduced AsiaFit®, a

Pick Up Stix, Torrance Crossings location

Pick Up Stix chef with cart of sauces and fresh produce

full-flavor menu that was under 400 calories per serving. Without changing the recipes, over half of the menu already fell into this category—delicious ingredients with large portions and bold flavors.

In 2001, Charlie sold the chain of 100 locations he had built to Carlson Company, which owned the TGIFriday's chain. Seven years later, in 2008, Carlson Company closed one-fourth of its locations in the West to focus on more healthy markets. Four years later, Pick Up Stix opened in the food court at the Excalibur Hotel and Casino in Las Vegas. In 2022, the original location closed. 🥡

The Many Humanitarian Awards of Charlie Zhang

+ Entrepreneur of the Year (Ernst and Young)
+ Spirit of Life from City of Hope
+ Distinguished Business of Science and Technology
+ Beijing International Entrepreneur of the Year

Baja Fresh Mexican Grill

SLOGAN: "It's About Flavor . . . It's About Fresh . . . It's About Time."

ORIGINAL LOCATION: 3345 W. Kimber Dr., Newbury Park

OPENED: August 1990

FOUNDERS: Jim and Linda Magglos

CURRENT OWNERSHIP: Kahala Brands

CURRENTLY AT THE FIRST LOCATION: Country Harvest Restaurant

There are currently seventy-eight locations.

bajafresh.com

THE TWO-WORD NAME, BAJA FRESH, tells it all. Baja brings the coastal ingredients of the Baja region of Mexico to every city in America. Baja Fresh has no can openers, freezers, microwaves, lard, or chemicals to keep ingredients salable, nor are there any enhancements like MSG.

For 13 years, husband-and-wife team Jim and Linda Magglos had an auto-detailing and window-tinting business in Tarzana called Wax Masters. They were deciding on a career change to open a food business in Newbury Park. Having little restaurant experience, the Maggloses wanted to open a place that served food the way they liked it: fresh Mexican food, quick and easy to order and enjoy. Looking for an affordable location, they found a building on the corner of S. Dewey Avenue and Kimber Drive near Newbury Park. The building had housed several restaurants selling hot dogs and ribs, most recently a Casey's Hamburger stand. If three previous food owners could not make it, they had to think out of the box.

For Baja Fresh, everything would be brought into the restaurant fresh, not out of a can. Tomatoes, onions, and cilantro would come from the produce market to make the salsa, not from the grocery store. Finally, the Maggloses were ready for the grand opening with one of the most progressive menus in fast food. They opened in August 1990.

The restaurant was sparkling clean inside and out; everything from the tables and counters to the bathrooms would shine. It is a food location where the local health department officials had lunch after their inspection. With an open kitchen with nothing hidden, the customers can see the fresh foods being cut, chopped, marinated, and prepared. The walk-in refrigerator had a window in the door so all could see how clean it was inside. The floors

Opposite: Baja Fresh San Bernardino, CA location

Ownership

1990–1998:	Fresh Enterprises Inc. (Jim and Linda Magglos)
1998–2002:	Investor Group headed by Greg Dollarhyde
2002–2006:	Wendy's International
2006–2016:	BF Acquisition Holdings (David Kim)
2016–Present:	Kahlua Brands

had a black-and-white checkerboard pattern with marble tiles. Also, on one wall in the dining area was a salsa bar; six fresh salsas were made daily, from mild to hot, including red and green, chunky, and smooth salsas.

All proteins were grilled, not fried; the only item fried was the tortilla chips, in Canola oil. Chicken breasts were boneless and skinless. Actual chicken tenders were used, not just a breast cut into strips. Each chicken breast has only two tenders—a flap under the breast, sometimes referred to as the filet mignon of the chicken.

The Maggloses opened up two more Baja Fresh locations the following year. The word was getting out that anyone from the East Coast visiting the area had to stop at the fresh grill. In 1993, three additional locations opened, and the Maggloses knew franchising and massive expansion would be next. The Maggloses were very selective about who would be a franchisee; they wanted them to succeed and keep the quality and mission of Baja Fresh as they had when they opened their first location. Baja Fresh franchisees could not just order food from a central commissary, and they had to learn how to use a knife instead of a can opener. Past the California borders, Nevada and Arizona locations opened by 1997; and seven years since the first opening, 34 locations in three states dotted the West. The following year, the East Coast opened 13 restaurants, with four staying company-owned.

In 1998, with 47 locations—and, the following year, 13 openings—Baja Fresh was at a turning point of growth. The Maggloses sold part of their interest to an investment group headed by Greg Dollarhyde but retained a minority interest and seat on the board. Jim Magglos became the CEO and president.

Customers were wary of the new

Location Numbers

1990: 1 location
1991: 2 locations
1994: 6 locations
1997: 34 locations
1998: 47 locations
1999: 60 locations
2002: 157 locations
2004: 300 locations
2010: 1st international location: Dubai, UAE
2010: 255 locations
2012: 1st Asian location: Singapore
2016: 162 locations
2022: 78 locations

Motto in every Baja Fresh: Food this fresh cannot be made @ microwave speed

ownership and felt the chain would change for the worse. In fact, it was just the opposite: Dollarhyde actually implemented food rules and standards for every location that had not been in place with the founders. Food manufacturers such as the spice and marinades premeasured at the factories would keep the quality at each location consistent. At many sites, the employees would not measure the ingredients as precisely as the factory would. Dollarhyde also implemented dating all ingredients when placed into the refrigerator (today, this is a health department standard in most counties). All shredded cheeses should be consumed within 24 hours of shredding. Although many locations would add a little flour or cornstarch to prevent the cheese from sticking after it is refrigerated for a few days, this practice was curtailed. With Dollarhyde at the helm, customers still came to eat there in droves.

In the years following, companies were awarded large metropolitan areas to open Baja Fresh locations. Lettuce Entertain You Group, a group of over a dozen restaurant concepts in the Chicago area that developed and opened 16 locations in the Windy City, and Northern Foods Services in the Maryland area agreed to open 30 in five years.

In 2002, Fresh Enterprises registered with the Securities and Exchange Commission to make an IPO of stock, raising money for future expansion. The Wendy's Company, out of Dublin, Ohio, came knocking, offering to buy the company for the amount they wanted to raise in the stock offering. Weighing the options, the board decided on the deal with Wendy's.

Same-store sales started falling, what with a sluggish economy, mass expansion, and so many items to prepare fresh. Another Mexican fresh food chain was gaining momentum in the markets, even though Baja Fresh had the upper hand; Chipotle Mexican

Chicken Street Tacos at the Culver City, CA location

Grill opened in Denver in 1993, with rapid expansion and funding from McDonald's. Chipotle was set up differently than Baja Fresh, with more of a buffet style of ordering and the customers lining up and making choices with a minimal menu, unlike Baja Fresh's "order and wait for the kitchen to make your meal." By 2005, Chipotle outnumbered Baja Fresh locations by 200 units.

In April 2004, William Moreton, formerly with Panara Bread Company, replaced Dollarhyde as chief executive. Moreton halted expansion and worked on delivering the meals to the customer by limiting the menu and offering rotating specials with the items taken off the menu. Also, he used the advertising arm that the company had while under Wendy's ownership.

Today, Baja Fresh is part of the Kahula Brands' portfolio of fast-food concepts of over 28 brands. 🌮

The Juice Club

SLOGAN: "Living a Balanced Lifestyle Incorporating Nutrition, Fitness, and Fun"

NAME TODAY: Jamba Juice

ORIGINAL LOCATION: 17 Chorro St. #C, San Luis Obispo

OPENED: March 31, 1990

FOUNDER: Kirk Perron

CO-FOUNDERS: Joe Vergara (Director of Research and Development), Kevin Peters (Director of Partnership Development), and Linda Ozawa Olds (Head of Marketing)

CURRENT OWNERSHIP: Focus Brands International

CURRENTLY AT THE FIRST LOCATION: The first location is still in operation.

There are currently over 767 locations in thirty-six states and five countries.

jamba.com

KIRK PERRON WORKED VARIOUS JOBS around the San Luis Obispo area for ten years, mainly in grocery stores. Learning from watching and working retail, Perron saved his money and purchased real estate as an investment at a young age. An avid lover of cycling and working out, Perron would stop at the smoothie shop Blazing Blenders on Broad Street in downtown San Luis Obispo about four times a week. He realized that if he was visiting several times a week, others must also be. This became Perron's inspiration for getting into the business.

At 26, Perron founded the Juice Club based on an uncompromising commitment to quality and health. The experience at the Juice Club would not only be healthy but fun. First, search the world for the best possible fruits and vegetables, then blend or squeeze them in front of the customer without any added sugars, preservatives, or artificial flavors, as the natural fruits have enough on their own.

Perron's first hire was Joe Vergara, formerly of Blazing Blenders; he became the Director of Research and Development. The second hire was Kevin Peters as Director of Partnership Development, and the third to join the team was Linda Ozawa Olds as Marketing Manager. During the first weekend, the store was packed, and Perron and his team served over 1,600 customers. After that, many customers returned a few times a week, just like Perron had at Blazing Blenders. Finally, Juice Club turned a substantial profit in the second year. His plan had worked.

Perron decided after the second year that he was ready to expand. Failing to secure an SBA Loan, he chose the franchising route. The first franchise location opened in the fall of 1994 in Irvine. Sixteen franchises were soon operating up and down the state. However, Perron felt growing the company through franchising would impact quality control; plus, the company lacked the funding to make a franchise chain profitable.

Investors came to Perron; he didn't have to search for them. In September 1994, Bob Kagle, a

Opposite: Founder Kirk Perron at The Juice Club, (top): 2022 logo

venture capitalist and general partner in Technology Venture Investors and Benchmark Capital, drove past a newly opened Juice Club in Palo Alto. The line of customers wrapped around the block. He was struck by the line and how people were waiting for a smoothie. He asked a few questions and realized Juice Club could define the category, like Starbucks had for coffee. Kagle phoned Perron and enlisted Howard Schultz, the CEO of Starbucks at the time, for a round of funding for Juice Club. Schultz was invited to join the board of Juice Club; with Schultz's help, Perron used Starbucks's real estate brokers to co-locate some outlets next to or close to Starbucks. Juice Club raised money significantly from several venture groups after Schultz joined the board.

With the added funding, Perron increased his office staff from 17 to 40 and moved his corporate headquarters to San Francisco. Perron felt that the name Juice Club was too generic, with many other smoothie companies opening nationwide with the word "juice" in their names. They created a new name and identity to avoid knock-off brands skirting trademark infringements: Jamba Juice. Jamba Juice became a store that was youthful, trendier, and bright, a store with a more Starbucks-like quality moving away from the bland mono-toned health-store look. The new name Jamba means "to celebrate" in the Swahili language. The décor of the new stores used bright colors: pink, yellow, and lime green. The smoothie names also helped with the branding of the new company.

It took two years to retrofit each store into a Jamba Juice from a Juice Club. Perron had a goal of reaching 1,000 units in a few short years. However, he saw the competition with smaller chains encroaching in markets he knew would be perfect, so he needed to move fast. By July 1996, California topped the 60-store mark, with over half company-owned. With a signed licensing deal with the Austin, Texas, Whole Foods Market, staff was trained by Jamba's personnel using Jamba's logos, name, and smoothie formulas. The goal was to place juice bars in all Whole Foods stores and expand into 17 states. The next area of target for growth was universities and airports.

Training and management retention were factors in finding the best-qualified employees. Store managers were treated as quasi-owners. Jamba Juice created one of the best incentive programs for store managers in the industry: a percentage of the manager's store profits would be paid yearly and another portion of the store's cash flow would be placed into a trust account. After three years, if a manager signed for another three-year term, they would be granted a three-week paid vacation period. Managers also receive stock options. Hourly workers are trained to handle problems and make decisions without consulting upper management. These factors help retain managers and employees for the long term.

While customers were waiting for their smoothies, many sought other options to add to their meal, such as a bagel or donut nearby. Jamba Juice hired the research-and-development group Mattson & Co. from Foster City to produce several new food options. In 1998, the chain introduced the Jambola®, a four-ounce, high-nutrient bread. Jamba used a third party to make their Jambola®, which was delivered frozen to the stores and toasted on site; added to a smoothie, this created a "Power Meal." This also retained freshness from bakery to store to customer. The following year, Souprimos was launched. It was not as big a hit as the Jambola, as it lacked mouth feel and taste. It was re-evaluated, and additional spices and fat were added to the too-bland soups. In 2000, soft salted pretzels were added (Apple Cinnamon and Sourdough Parmesan). Smoothies and soups were combined with slices of bread to create the Jamba Meal.

Jambas are more like a pit stop than a hangout. Unlike Starbucks, people do not linger and treat the place like a second office. Many come in and leave without sitting down. Customer space and public Internet are not required. In the later years, a toaster-type oven was all that was needed, besides the blenders and juicers. The highest overhead is rent, wages, and produce. Having a low buildout for a new franchisee is a huge plus.

In 2001, Jamba Juice acquired Utah-based Zuka Juice to add to its portfolio; Jamba Juice would add almost 100 stores. Opening stores in New York City at the new Warner Center off Central Park, Times Square, and a few other areas of Manhattan made the enterprise a coast-to-coast smoothie company. While still on the Board of Directors, Kirk Perron wrote *Jamba Juice Power*, a book with his 21-day juicing and smoothie plan. Packed with recipes and ideas, it became a best seller.

In 2006, Jamba Inc. became publicly traded (Nasdaq: JMBA) and owned by Florida-based Acquisitions Corp. With becoming publicly traded, Jamba transformed into an active lifestyle brand by adding prepackaged salads, healthy sandwiches, breakfast items, hot beverages, and more to the smoothie line of drinks; this would increase sales and make it more than just a smoothie company. In addition, university campuses were the focus of expanding partnerships with their school lunch programs. 2006 was also the year that Perron left the board of directors.

The Fresh Juice menu was launched with juice blends of fresh beets, kale, and ginger. For a short time in 2016, Jamba-Go®, a self-service juice-blending vending machine, was in operation; later, while many other fast-food companies were looking to lower labor costs with automation, Jamba scrapped the machines, which had mainly been placed and operated in colleges and hospitals.

Today's athletes are always looking for a side business to invest in. Many own fast-food locations, sporting-goods stores, and kids' camps. Jamba Juice is a healthy yet straightforward concept to invest in.

Critical Dates

1990: Opened as Juice Club

1993: The second store opens in Irvine

1994: 16 franchises, making it 17 stores in total

1995: Name change to Jamba Juice

1996: 30 stores opened in California

1997: 60 stores, all opened in California

1997: First stores opened outside of CA in Boulder, Colorado, and Tempe, Arizona

1997: Licensing agreement with Whole Foods Markets to open Jamba Juice bars in CA and other states

1999: Purchased Zuka Juice Stores out of Salt Lake City, adding 98 stores in the merger

2009: Began serving food products

2019: Over 900 locations in 5 countries

Former Forty-Niner tight end Vernon Davis owns a chain of Jamba Juice locations, some in the Santa Clara area, which makes it handy, as they are close to the Forty-Niners' new home, Levi's Stadium. Venus Williams owns several in the Washington, D.C., and Virginia areas. Former NBA star LaPhonso Ellis purchased units close to his alma mater, the University of Notre Dame in South Bend, Indiana.

In the fall of 2018, Atlanta-based Focus Brands purchased all stock and acquired Jamba Juice fully, which they still own today. As a result, the menu has only grown since the days of the Juice Club, with fresh juices, bowls, shots, tasty bites, and traditional smoothies.

Sadly, Kirk Perron passed away in 2020 in his home in Palm Springs. He had been busy with speaking engagements, personal appearances, and corporate events. After several years of being away from Jamba Juice, Linda Ozawa Olds is currently the franchisee with her husband of the original store where it all started, along with a handful of others. Kevin Peters is the CEO of San Francisco's Wiseman Group, an interior design company. 🍹

Wetzel's Pretzels

SLOGAN: "Hand Held Happiness"

ORIGINAL LOCATION: South Bay Galleria, 1815 Hawthorne Blvd. #336, Redondo Beach

OPENED: November 23, 1994

CO-FOUNDERS: Bill Phelps (Co-Founder and Brand Ambassador) and Rick Wetzel (Co-Founder and Board Member)

CURRENT OWNERSHIP: CenterOaks Partners LLC

CURRENTLY AT THE FIRST LOCATION: The first location is still in operation.
There are currently 402 locations in twenty-two states and six countries.

wetzels.com

AS WITH MOST INNOVATIVE PLANS, it all started on a napkin in a bar while on a business trip to Seattle. Bill Phelps and Rick Wetzel created a fresh, low-calorie, hand-rolled, and delicious product idea. From early on, their vision was to be to pretzels what Ben & Jerry is to ice cream. Both former marketing executives for Nestlé continued to work in marketing while launching their idea.

Looking to name their new idea, Phillips could not find a name that had not yet been trademarked. So, Wetzel (who had been taunted in school with "Hey, Wetzel, you pretzel!") figured using his name as the brand was a no-brainer. Not many words rhyme with "pretzel," and with one of the co-founders' names rhyming, it would be a complete waste not to take advantage of this.

The two worked weekends while maintaining their jobs at Nestlé. Needing a $200,000 investment, Rick Wetzel ended up selling his Harley Davidson motorcycle (and never bought another) and used the savings he had hoped to use for a house. After the Nestlé Company announced that their jobs would be moved to Ohio, Wetzel and Phillips both opted for a buyout to stay in the Los Angeles area to work on their new venture. Family members were perplexed at the decision of the two leaving jobs with Nestlé to work at a mall with a bunch of teenagers while wearing T-shirts and baseball caps.

Pretzels became a trending mall snack made with fresh and limited ingredients. Fresh pretzels were made throughout the day so the consumer would have a consistently hot-out-of-the-oven snack. The brand was a solid investment for its franchisees, built on ingredients and operational simplicity. A hot fresh product you can hold in your hand and walk with around the mall makes the pretzel a perfect snack.

Opposite: A Dodger lover loves Wetzel's Pretzels,
(top): Pepperoni Pretzel

Owners	
1994–2007:	Bill Phelps
	Rick Wetzel
2007–2016:	Levine Leichtman
	Capital Partners
2016–Present:	CenterOak Partners

Pretzel Varieties
1. Almond Crunch
2. Cinnamon Glaze
3. Cinnamon Sugar
4. Garlic
5. Jalapeno
6. Pepperoni
7. Wetzel's Original No Butter
8. Wetzel's Original with Butter

Cinnamon Sugar Pretzel, Pretzel Bites, and Salted Pretzel

Training was critical for the franchisee too; a cashier can be trained in less than 2 hours, and time is significant in today's labor market.

In the following year, they opened their next location in Old Pasadena. Pasadena has an extensive shopping and entertainment walking area that was optimal for bringing pretzels to more browsing consumers. The outdoor Century City Westfield Mall became the third location, thus bringing pretzels closer to Hollywood. Many stars would be photographed by paparazzi eating hot pretzels around the outdoor shopping mall. Wetzel's started popping up on the screen, making appearances in sitcoms and late-night talk shows.

In 1996, Wetzel's looked at their product offerings and knew they needed to grow the pretzel line. Wetzel Dogs were created. They were the first pretzel company to launch a pretzel-wrapped hot dog—an innovator for the industry. The same year, a big, bold move was made to bring Wetzel's to the East Coast. "Go Big or Go Home" was Rick's motto. They decided to open at the Garden State Plaza in New Jersey, one of the biggest malls in the country at the time. Today, that mall boasts three Wetzel locations, so no matter where you shop, you are bound to be within the "aroma" range.

The summer of 1997 brought a new location outside the traditional mall: a theme park. Wetzel's opened at Universal Studios Hollywood. A few years later, sporting venues Dodger Stadium and the Los Angeles Staples Center offered hot pretzels, and Wetzel Dogs were a no-brainer for a snack to enjoy during a game or concert. Many other sporting venues sprang up coast to coast: Angel Stadium of Anaheim, Chase Field in Phoenix, US Airways Field, Gila River, Talking Stick Stadium, and many more. The first store outside the continental United States was opened in Puerto Rico in 2003; it also was the hundredth unit.

Downtown Disney is a shopping, entertainment, and eating venue between the original Disneyland and Disney's California Adventure. Disney looked for California-based eateries to fill their new street to enhance the area. Wetzel's fit the bill and became part of the grand opening experience in the new year of 2001. Still today, the Downtown Disney location sells more per square foot than any other location. With the success of the California Disney location, the focus was set on Walt Disney World, which opened a location in 2003; currently, Walt Disney World in Florida has six locations.

When the hundredth unit opened in Puerto Rico, it had been just nine years after opening the first location in Redondo Beach. The following seven years brought unit number 200 in 2008 at the Gurnee, Illinois, outlet mall north of Chicago. Many franchisees that open multi-unit locations in malls receive price breaks for smaller baking and non-baking kiosks. To have a non-baking stall, you must have a baking site in the same immediate locale to provide a freshly baked product.

In 2007, with 167 locations, Bill Phelps and Rick Wetzel sold part of their interest in Wetzel's to Levine Leichtman Capital Partners, which held the company for nine years before selling it to CenterOaks Partners in October 2016.

International openings started with a location in the beautiful coastal city of Villa Velha, Brazil, in 2014 as the first. The same year as international openings, small Dog Bites were introduced, sold in an easy-to-carry bag. With the success of the Dog Bites, a franchisee from the Chino Hills location created the Pizza Bitz and went company-wide. The Jalaroni,® a pretzel topped with jalapeño peppers and pepperoni slices, was launched in 2005. Pairing it with pizza sauce makes it a complete meal—the sweet Cin-a-Bitz® is currently the number one bestseller.

Milestones
1994: 1st store—Redondo Beach, CA
1994: 2nd store—Old Pasadena, CA
2003: 100th store—Puerto Rico
2008: 200th store—Gurnee Mills, IL
2012: First international location in Brazil
2018: 350th store—Denver, CO Premium Outlets

How do you open a store with a product that cannot be written in the native language? Get creative. Opening the first location in Shanghai at the China Reel Mall was full of obstacles. Wetzel paired the company name with "Fresh Baked" since there is no Chinese character for "pretzel" to create the store's signage in the mall's food court. The China market gravitates toward products made with very few ingredients and freshly prepared in front of the customer. Wetzel's was perfect for their tastes. The China market also marketed their beverages toward warm beverages instead of iced; and, with lemonade being too sweet, Lemon Hot Tea is offered.

Every day is a National "something" food day in America; National Pretzel Day is on April 26 of every year. Wetzel's started celebrating the day in 2016, with everyone who entered the store receiving a free pretzel. In 2017, Wetzel's jumped on the social-media bandwagon: "Sign up to follow us, show us at the counter, and get an order of Pizza Bitz®"; thousands signed up.

In recent years, remodeling of the stores has been taking place, with bold, large-style graphics with Southern California pictures and murals, fresh new tile work, an enhanced exhibition counter that showcases the handmade pretzel process, and even custom-made pretzel door handles.

After 25 years, co-founder and CEO Bill Phelps stepped down on January 1, 2018, and became Brand Ambassador, with Jennifer Schuler filling his shoes as CEO.

Phelps always took seriously what Ray Kroc from McDonald's said about business: "Listen to your franchisee; they are the closest to the consumer and know more than you do." Wetzel offers lucrative reward payments for items that become seasonal and ones that stay on their full-time menus.

Rick Wetzel's saying on life: "This is not a dress rehearsal." 🥨

Model crew for Wetzel's

RAW JUICES

Fresh veggies and fruits that are juiced to extract the pure vitamins, minerals and micronutrients.

Small: 6.29 | Medium: 8.29 | Large: 9.99

REJUVENATOR ♡
Carrot, Cucumber, Beet, Apple, Ginger
Cal: 90 / 130 / 220

OPTIMIZER® ♡ ⊕
Carrot, Pineapple, Beet, Cucumber, Red Grapes, Celery Cal: 110 / 160 / 260

ENERGIZER ⚡
Pineapple, Cucumber, Spinach, Red Grapes, Apple, Ginger Cal: 120 / 190 / 320

INVIGORATOR® ⊕
Pineapple, Orange, Kale, Spinach
Cal: 160 / 230 / 380

DETOXIFIER® ⊕
Cucumber, Red Grapes, Pineapple, Spinach, Lemon, Ginger Cal: 100 / 160 / 300

IMMUNIZER® ⊕
Cucumber, Apple, Celery, Kale, Spinach, Lemon Cal: 80 / 120 / 200

Energizer & Rejuvenator

CREATE YOUR OWN
Choose a base:
Apple, Beet, Carrot, Celery, Cucumber, Orange, Pineapple

Choose up to 5 ingredients:
Apple, Beet, Carrot, Celery, Cucumber, Ginger, Kale, Lemon, Orange, Pineapple, Red Grapes, Spinach
Cal: 45-190 / 65-280 / 110-450

SHOTS

Wheatgrass & Ginger

Made To Order 1oz: 2.49 | 2oz: 3.49
GINGER Cal: 15 / 30 ⊕
WHEATGRASS Cal: 5 / 10 ⊕
MIGHTY-C IMMUNITY ⊕
Pineapple, Ginger, Red Grapes & Lemon
Cal: 15 / 30

Bottled 2oz: 3.49
IMMUNITY DEFENSE
with Turmeric & Probiotics Cal: 20

DIGESTION
with Ginger & Apple Cider Vinegar Cal: 20

Juice It Up!

SLOGAN: "Live, Life, Juiced!"

ORIGINAL LOCATION: 955 E. Birch St., Suite G, Brea

OPENED: April 10, 1995

FOUNDERS: Larry Sidoti and Dan York

CURRENT OWNERSHIP: SJB Brands

CURRENTLY AT THE FIRST LOCATION: Great Clips Hair

There are currently eighty-seven locations in five states.

juiceitup.com

IN 1995, CALIFORNIA STATE UNIVERSITY OF FULLERTON alumnus Larry Sidoti and Dan York partnered and opened Juice It Up! in north Orange County. They evolved from the Southern California beach-and-surfing lifestyle to becoming a leading raw-juice-and-smoothie company specializing in fresh-squeezed juices. They started with a dozen fresh juices that they would sell, and a few blends. However, it was a few months until they began adding fruit-based smoothies to the menu.

With the third location opened in Chino, Larry and Dan added an array of freshly baked bagels to the menu; they were well-liked with the lunch crowd but were curtailed after only a few months. Customers were confused about whether it was a juice store or a bagel shop.

Juice It Up! is not just a juice company, but a place to educate customers. Every team member is trained extensively on every ingredient's benefits to help inform the buyer. In addition, they

work with local fruit and vegetable growers and distributors of the finest ingredients to create the best products possible. Besides selling juice products, Juice It Up! is also an advocate of healthy lifestyles.

Opposite: Juice It Up menu from Corona, CA, (top): Logo (bottom): Bagel display case

Owners	
1995–2003:	Juice It Up!
2003–2018:	Balboa Brands
2018–Present:	SJB Brands

The research and development of all of new products offered at Juice It Up! focuses on ingredients and blends to create a healthier world for the future. The handcrafted smoothies are made with fresh fruits and raw juice blends.

Juice It Up! feels that education about a healthy lifestyle and the products that they sell should start at an early age. Juice It Up! goes into elementary schools to educate the minds of the future. The Juice It Up! products help make an impact on those with medical issues. Studies have shown that all-natural ingredients and proper diet structured through raw juices can tremendously enhance health.

By 2000, the chain had 35 units, with many corporate-owned locations, but the brand struggled to stay above water. One of the reasons for their debt problem was owning too many units and having four owners with equal partnerships but no one person in charge.

In 2001, Balboa Brands, Frank N. Easterbrook, a former Nestlé, S.A., and M&M/Mars Inc. executive, took on the CEO role and acquired the brand. His first course of action was to sell the corporate locations to franchisees. The company was in debt, and this would help make it solvent. In addition, competitors

CEOs	
1995–2001:	The Founders
2001–2018:	Frank Easterbrook
2018–2020:	Chris Braum
2020–present:	Susan Taylor

(top) First location in Brea, CA, (bottom): Mall concept kiosk

were getting theme-park and sports-arena contracts. Easterbrook started to look at why, in blind taste tests, Juice It Up! was preferred but the stores were not. One was the look of the stores: all had different appearances. Frank brought on architects from the coffee giant Starbucks to redesign the stores to have consistent looks.

Easterbrook was at the helm of Juice It Up! for nine years and stepped down as CEO when SJB Brands purchased the company. He took the juice company from 35 locations to 87, updating the products to include "superfruit" bowls besides juice and smoothie drinks. Currently, Easterbrook continues to own and operate a few of the locations as a franchisee.

Chris Braum, the president and chief of SJB Brands, became the new leader of Juice It Up!, bringing to the table franchise experience with numerous brands from food and textiles to entertainment venues.

In 2017, the cold-pressed line of products (where no heat is used to extract the juices from fruits and vegetables) came on line. These are more nutritious. The following year, Braum and his staff introduced cold brew into some of their menu items. The company also simplified its menu selections. The menu was laid out into three categories, making it easier for customers to find what they wanted and make their selection, thus creating a faster ordering system. The result is that customers received their items faster.

Braum felt that many explanations on the menu board were no longer needed, as the consumer had been educated since opening in 1995. In addition, tastes had grown with their advanced palates over the years. Therefore, he streamlined the menu boards with new items and made some popular limited-time things permanent.

With 84 units in diverse locations such as travel plazas, college campuses, outdoor malls, and sporting venues, Juice It Up! is here to educate and serve the public for years to come.

Menu Items

Raw Juices (Not heated, cold extracted)

SHOTS:

Ginger Shot

Mighty-C Immunity Shot

Wheatgrass Shot

SMOOTHIES:

Berry Blends

Tropical Blends

Tart Blends

Protein Infused

Superfruit Infused

Plant-Based Infused

BOWLS:

Acai Powered

Superfood Fueled

Smoothie Bowls

Juice It Up menu

Bubba Gump Shrimp Company

ORIGINAL LOCATION: 720 Cannery Row, Monterey

OPENED: 1996

FOUNDER: Anthony Zolezzi/Rusty Pelican Restaurants

CURRENT OWNERSHIP: Landry's Inc.

CURRENTLY AT THE FIRST LOCATION: The first location is still in operation.

There are currently twenty-two locations in nine states that are company-owned, and twelve international locations in seven countries that are franchised.

bubbagump.com

IN THE EARLY 1990S, ANTHONY ZOLEZZI worked as a consultant for the struggling Meridian Frozen Food company. Meridian's focus was mainly frozen seafood products. Anthony had been hired to turn the company around; but after many attempts, he still could not see how. Then, on a Sunday afternoon, Anthony and his wife went to the movies to see a film he knew nothing about: *Forrest Gump.* A light bulb went off halfway through the film about how he would save Meridian— but marketing the frozen shrimp as Bubba Gump would not be easy. He needed the rights to the name and likeness.

The following day, Anthony found himself outside the gates of Paramount Studios on Melrose Avenue in Hollywood. He asked at the guard gate who oversaw Forrest Gump's rights. From eight in the morning to six at night, Anthony waited outside the gates until the guard found Debbie Petrasec, an employee who could finally help him. Debbie said nobody had requested the rights, so he could pay the fees the next day if he wanted them. Ecstatic, Anthony knew he had a winning idea for Meridian. Bubba Gump shrimp was soon packaged and sold coast to coast in every major supermarket.

Anthony also worked with the 31-unit Rusty Pelican Restaurant Group to turn the fledgling restaurants into a profitable organization. In the early 1990s, the 31-unit seafood chain Rusty Pelican Restaurants started seeing a decline in customers and revenue. Most of their locations were high-rent real estate, with one beachfront property with spectacular views. Regrouping with lower prices and expanding the menu slowed the hemorrhaging, and the Rusty Seafood Grotto on Cannery Row in Monterey was only steps from the new aquarium but lacked the customers.

Gordon Miles, then CEO of Rusty Pelican, agreed to turn one location into a Bubba Gump restaurant. At that time, Cannery Row was in disarray with abandoned buildings that once had housed the fledgling sardine industry made famous by John Steinbeck's novels. In October 1984, the area started turning around with the new Monterey Aquarium opening, but dining was still lacking.

The Monterey Bar restaurant was remodeled using the scenery, themes, and props from the

Opposite: George Ernie, Rick Martin and Anthony Zolezzi, displaying the Bubba Gump Shrimp Boat for a publicity shoot, (top): Logo

Paramount warehouses to recreate a place that would look straight out of the motion picture. Using a fishing boat as the center-décor focus in the dining room was the first way to recreate the movie, making the first Bubba Gump restaurant an entertainment location. Theme restaurants like Hard Rock Cafés and the movie-based Planet Hollywood were opening from coast to coast. However, Gump's would be the first restaurant based on just one movie.

Opening in March 1995, a few months before the tourist season, provided the needed time to work out all the snarls. The menu would heavily reflect the movie with over 16 shrimp dishes, plus menu items that reflected the film, such as Jenny's Surf and Surf (Salmon and Shrimp), Mama Blue's Shrimp Gumbo, Lt. Dan's Surf and Turf (Ribs and Shrimp), and of course for dessert a box of chocolates. The menu is much more extensive than the former Rusty Seafood Grotto, with appetizers, soups, seasonal salads, and side dishes from comfort food to international flair, main dishes from seafood to all-American chicken to handheld sandwiches, and an array of desserts. Cajun and Creole dishes also round out the menu.

Some of the Landry's Restaurants

Bubba Gump Shrimp Company
Chart House
Claim Jumper (page 85)
Del Frisco's
Houlihan's
Joe's Crab Shack
Mastro's Restaurants
McCormick & Schmick's
Mitchells Fish Market
Morton's Steak House
Rainforest Café
Saltgrass House
Strip House
The Palm
Vic & Anthony's Steakhouse

After your meal, you can shop in the Bubba Gump store, with unique branded clothes such as T-shirts with Louie the Shrimp from Kenny Lee's Tuff Shirt Company, and sleepwear for the entire family decorated with chocolate candies. In addition, a line of seafood spices allows you to recreate the dishes you enjoyed at Gump's.

With the success of Monterey's opening, Bubba Gump Restaurants started looking to open in touristy seaside locales and high tourist areas such as Hollywood and Times Square. They opened successful restaurants coast to coast at the rate of one every five months for the next 14 years.

Since 1980, friends of high-tech parts and office furniture salesman Steve Weber noticed the similarities between him and Kip Wilson, Tom Hanks's character on NBC's hit show *Bosom Buddies*. Weber didn't think much of it until Halloween 1994, when he decided to go as Forrest Gump. He searched secondhand stores for an off-white suit, dirty tennis shoes, and a suitcase. Weber was a hit with the mannerisms and voice of Forrest. A few years later, Weber heard of a new theme restaurant opening as Bubba Gump; he phoned the restaurant, hoping to get a gig for the opening. He set up an in-person interview; after twenty minutes, Weber got the opening day job. It became a full-time job, posing with pictures at the grand openings on a bench outside the waiting area to sing Happy Birthday to the patrons. Weber portrayed the popular character for over 15 years for the Bubba Gump Restaurants.

In November 2010, Landry's Inc. Restaurants acquired the 32-unit Bubba Gump Restaurants with the original and last remaining Rusty Pelican restaurant in Newport Beach, only a week after the winning bid of the Claim Jumper chain (page 85).

The young soon-to-be actor Chris Pratt dropped out of college and moved to Maui, Hawaii. The second Bubba Gump had just opened, and Pratt, homeless and wanting a job just to cover his minimal living expenses, started serving at Gump. One evening while waiting tables, he met Rae Dawn Chong, an actress, who cast him in a short movie she was directing. Pratt has been busy in films and television for over 22 years. Today, you can see his star on the Hollywood Walk of Fame.

Today, Anthony is no longer involved with the Bubba Gump restaurants but owns a small boutique winery in San Diego County, California. 🦐

Bubba Gump Long Beach location

Lucille's Smokehouse Bar-B-Que

SLOGAN: "Serving the Best Bar-B-Que with the Finest Southern Hospitality"

NAME TODAY: Lucille's

ORIGINAL LOCATION: Long Beach Town Center, 7411 Carson St., Long Beach

OPENED: December 6, 1999

FOUNDER: Craig Hofman

CURRENT OWNERSHIP: Hofman Hospitality Group

CURRENTLY AT THE FIRST LOCATION: The first location is still in operation.

There are currently twenty-one locations in three Western states.

lucillesbbq.com

ALL COMPANIES, INCLUDING RESTAURANTS, need to evolve and know their roots. For example, Hof's Hut (page 13) opened in 1951; with the world of restaurants changing, Craig Hofman, chairman of the board of Hofman Hospitality Group, changed the company's direction by adding an entirely new concept into the family portfolio.

Hofman noticed many "theme" food restaurants opening, from Italian to Mexican and away from the typical American cuisine restaurants. Most companies would revamp a location with a new menu and style, keeping the same name. Instead, Hofman started an entirely new concept. He changed a few of the Hof's Hut locations into Lucille's.

Hofman embarked on a one-year research trip into the Midwest and Southern states to study barbeque cuisine; he noticed that the West lacked great barbeque restaurants. In 1999, he opened Lucille's Smokehouse Bar-B-Que with 10,000 square feet in Long Beach, the city where Hof's Hut had become greatly acclaimed.

The new venture had to be a woman's name with Southern roots. So the fictitious Lucille Buchanan became the story of the new smokehouse. Lucille lived in the fictional town of Greenville, USA, eating at her grandmother's shack off the beaten path on a back road. As

Opposite: Full table of ribs, chicken, sides, and biscuits, (top): Lucille's ribs and watermelon

---

Types of BBQ Style

+ Carolina Style: The meat is mostly pork, brushed with a spice-vinegar sauce while cooking, served with a ketchup sauce on the side.
+ Memphis Style: Slow-cooked, using a dry or wet sauce.
+ Texas Style: Large cuts of meat cooked low and slow, with sauce.

soon as Lucille was older, she started working during the summers and weekends. She learned all of Granny's secrets, from the unique spice rubs to the wet "mops" and sauces. Then Lucille married Joe and followed him to Long Beach, where she started cooking barbeque like her granny used to make.

Craig did not focus on one barbeque style like other areas of the country; he introduced three types he enjoyed on his exploratory trips: Carolina, Memphis, and Texas Style. Most meats are marinated for over twelve hours and smoked with hickory wood. Each restaurant has a smoker that is utilized daily, named "Smokestack Lightning." Southern sides are all made from scratch in restaurants. The West Coast patrons were introduced to some of the Southern sides for the first time, such as Braised Greens, Southern Tomato Pie, and Southern Fried Okra. Freshly made baskets of biscuits with apple butter are set on every table, and homemade Southern dessert tops off the

Sides
BBQ Beans
County Fair Corn Pudding
Creamy Coleslaw
Fresh-Cut Fries
Garlic Mashed Potatoes
Hatch Green Chile Cheese Grits
Loaded Mashed Potatoes
Macaroni & Cheese
Picnic Potato Salad
Roasted Street Corn
Sautéed Seasonal Vegetables
Smoked Jalapeño Cheddar Cornbread
Southern Braised Greens
Southern Fried Okra
Southern Tomato Pie
Watermelon Slices

Long Beach Town Center, first Lucille's location

Long Beach porch room

meal. Full-family feasts are also available for groups of 4 to 12.

Craig saw and implemented many fine Southern barbeque traditions and added hospitality to his locations. In Southern restaurants, you rarely have wait service; some of the places can be found in small walk-up buildings or old gas stations. The food is always served on paper plates with plastic utensils that generally do not hold up to the side dishes, with very thin napkins that you needed a half dozen of to clean your hands from the sauces. Lucille's would have all the great foods of its Southern counterparts but with an entire wait staff of Southern hospitality never seen on the West Coast, cloth napkins, silverware, and porcelain dishes.

You can enjoy one-of-a-kind art throughout all the Lucille's, ranging from Blues Art to Black Folk Art to Southern Folk Art. Most all the art is one of a kind from Southern artists. Lucille's has an entire bar program in their "Flying Pig Bar" with Specialty Southern Punches and Spiked Lemonades.

During the week, small plates and nibbles with drink specials are popular. In addition, the guests enjoy live blues music in many locations during happy hours.

Many guests will buy branded items such as T-shirts and smoking hot sauces to make ribs and meat dishes at home.

Lucille's has been recognized with many awards for its excellent service and barbeque, mainly on the West Coast where the restaurants are located. The Hofman Hospitality Group plans for only additional West Coast expansion.

Together with the three Hof's Huts and Saint and Second, the Hofman Hospitality Group employs over 2,500 staff persons. ✖

Smoking Times	
Chicken	2–3 hours
Pork Chops	2–3 hours
Baby Back Ribs	3–4 hours
St. Louis Ribs	3–4 hours
Turkey Breast	3–4 hours
Beef Ribs	4–5 hours
Tri-Tip	4–6 hours
Ham	6–8 hours
Pork Roast	10–12 hours

Chronic Tacos Mexican Grill

NAME TODAY: Chronic Tacos

ORIGINAL LOCATION: 4533 Pacific Coast Hwy., Newport Beach

OPENED: July 4, 2002

FOUNDERS: Randy Wyner and Dan Beillo

PARENT COMPANY: Chronic Tacos Enterprises

CURRENTLY AT THE FIRST LOCATION: The first location is still in operation.
There are thirty-eight locations in nine states and three countries.

eatchronictacos.com

CHRONIC TACOS' NAME CAME FROM Randy Wyner's former silk-screening T-shirt business Chronic Industries. When he knew that tacos would be a hit, he decided to give the silk-screening business over to his employees so that he could focus on his new fast-casual taco business.

With so many taquerias around the Southern California area, Wyner had eaten at many. He felt the best were the small hole-in-the-wall family-owned places. When on an evening out in Newport Beach with his buddy Daniel Biello, Wyner looked for some quality street tacos but couldn't find any. That's when the idea came: Mexican food that was fast, fresh, and made to order in a fun and great atmosphere. "Taco Life" was born.

Wyner's very close childhood friend Jason Bonilla had always invited him to the family barbecues, which changed his life and taste buds. Wyner was only six but recalled the Bonilla family's events and flavorful Mexican foods. The Bonilla family was from the Fresnillo in the Zacatecas region of Mexico. Wyner recalled the fresh tomatoes and onions being chopped with the great flavors and seasonings of the meats marinating. Wyner made these family traditions part of the Chronic Tacos brand. His concept was to be 100 percent authentic. His most challenging hurdle at first was the recipes. However, when he recalled his first taste of the Bonilla family barbeques, he was blessed with the third-generation Bonilla family recipes to create his taco restaurants.

Chronic Tacos would not be just a taco stand but an entire lifestyle brand, including professional eating contests. Takeru Kobayashi, competitive eater, holds fifteen Guinness World Records and won first-place eater at the Gringo Bandito Taco challenge with Gringo Bandito Hot Sauce and Chronic Tacos for nine years. Randy's silk-screening knowledge brought the restaurant edgy merchandise and T-shirts depicting designs from Day of the Dead drawings to MTV celebrity partnerships.

In 2002, the 26-year-old Wyner opened the first Chronic Taco in Newport Beach with Biello. The dream to make Chronic Tacos a household name had begun. The chain has since gone from one taco stand in Newport Beach to achieving global reach. The Newport Beach location opened a few

Opposite: Chronic Tacos first location in Newport Beach, CA

Founder Randy Wyner, "Taco Life" knuckle tattoos

days before Independence Day weekend to "iron out the kinks" before their big reveal on July 4, 2002. Soon, they had a line around the strip mall with hundreds waiting to try their new tacos; hundreds were served on the first day. They were an instant success. The recipe was to have a flavorful product that you could eat with your hands, and orders had to be fast and close to the beach. The fast-casual taco stand was born.

In 2004, Huntington Beach was the second to open. Now they were on their way to multi-location success. In April 2008, only 25 miles from the original first location, the first franchise was sold and opened in San Clemente. When someone purchases a franchise, they have many weeks of training at one of the corporate-owned locations while building out the store. The trainers go to the new location to help with marketing, staffing, and management until it is up and running.

On March 19, 2009, the Learning Channel (TLC) popular show *Street Customs* by West Coast Customs in Corona, California, created the ultimate taco truck in nine days for the grand opening of the Saugus, California, location. They were catapulting the Chronic Taco brand world-wide. Actor/professional skateboarder/stunt performer Jason "Wee Man" Acuña from the famous MTV's *Jackass* movie franchise became great friends with Wyner. Wee Man was at the grand opening of many of the restaurants. In 2008, he opened his franchise in his nearby Redondo Beach hometown. Acuña has since closed that location, and in January 2017 he focused on revamping the Sterns Street Long Beach location to great success.

In 2010, the four Mohammed Brothers of Calivan Enterprises, Inc. invested in a Chronic Taco restaurant to be the

Takeru Kobayashi's Taco-Eating Records	
2011:	81 in 10 minutes
2012:	106 in 10 minutes
2013:	86 in 10 minutes
2014:	130 in 10 minutes
2015:	144 in 10 minutes
2016:	137 in 10 minutes
2017:	154 in 10 minutes
2018:	159 in 10 minutes
2019:	157 in 10 minutes

first franchisee in Vancouver, British Columbia, Canada. In March 2012, they purchased the entire brand after seeing the potential. Each Mohammed Brother brings their expertise to their company, with Wyner able to focus on sales, locations, and quality.

Mohammed Brothers Roles
Michael: Strategic, Marketing, and Finance endeavors
Dave: Marketing
Dan: Business Development
Joey: Design of Projects

Dan Beillo, co-founder, is the franchisee of the first original location.

For years, Chronic Tacos served the Gringo Banditos hot sauce (they also partnered in the taco-eating competitions). The customers asked for a more sizzling sauce: Ghost Pepper Hot Sauce was born. After several recipes, testing, and the loss of many taste buds, Chronic Tacos took their red sauce and added Ghost Peppers and habaneros, creating a Scoville heat index of over 1 million. The customers could not get enough of the flavorful hot sauce. Once only a limited sauce a few times a year, it turned into being on the tables year-round.

The year 2014 brought a new logo design but the same fresh, home-cooked flavor. Many sporting venues, such as Angel Stadium in Anaheim and T-Mobile Arena in Las Vegas, Nevada, have kiosks of the great tacos to feed fans.

Welcome letter in the first location in Newport Beach, CA

When a store has a grand opening, proceeds go to local charities such as Boys and Girls Clubs, No Kid Hungry, and many other local charities.

Chronic Taco is a complete eating/entertainment experience with sports and TV viewing. If you go to other Mexican fast-food establishments, you take away your food or are rushed to leave.

Chronic is known for bold flavors using fresh, locally sourced ingredients. Each recipe is made from scratch, producing authentic flavors, just like when Wyner first tasted the Bonilla family recipes. The authentic flavor profiles can not come from the food unless each franchisee procures fresh local ingredients.

Chronic Taco kitchens are busy with marinated meats for at least 24 hours, carnitas slow-cooked for three and a half hours, and all the salsas, hot sauces, and guacamole made in-house. Chronic takes pride in cooking the original Bonilla family recipes the way they did.

Catering started at the first location and has become a great asset to the brand. Office parties to wedding events make up the bulk of the catering of each Chronic. They have the World's Greatest Taco Bar and the World's Greatest Nacho Bar as a few menu possibilities. Like at the restaurant, you can create your meals with your desired ingredients. If the location has a beer and wine license, they will source IPAs and local beers to round off their drinks. 🌮

Gateway Market

SLOGANS: "Better People's Day" ◆ "One Cup at a Time"

NAME TODAY: Philz Coffee

ORIGINAL LOCATION: 3101 24th St., San Francisco

OPENED: January 2003

FOUNDER: Phil Jaber

CURRENT OWNERSHIP: Privately owned by Phil Jaber and Jacob Jaber, CEO

CURRENTLY AT THE FIRST LOCATION: Philz Coffee is operating in the original location of the former Gateway Market.

There are currently 68 locations in two states.

philzcoffee.com

IN 1977, PHIL JABER OPENED GATEWAY MARKET on the corner of 24th and Folsom in the Mission District in San Francisco. Besides being a local market for the many residents, Jaber also sold sandwiches, quick market items, coffee, and blends of beans.

Coffee was always Jaber's passion. He and his young son Jacob would hand coffee out at the register of the corner store or to neighbors. In the back room of the market, Jaber created many blends of coffee. The names of the combinations are both personal and reactionary after he has tasted them. Wide varieties are still served 42 years later. Today coffee blends are talked about as would a wine sommelier. All combinations are placed in five categories (darker, medium, lighter blends, decaf, and single origin) and described with aromas such as herbs, citrus, chocolates, floral, tobacco, and more.

As the popularity grew, Jaber decided it was an excellent time to convert the market to a coffee

Opposite: Phil and Jacob Jaber outside first location in San Francisco, (top): Phil Jaber in Gateway Market, (middle): Gateway Market sign

shop. He always wanted the coffee shop to be a gathering place, like Grandma's house, where people would stay all day, work, converse, and meet friends. Food was a natural extension of that. Philz Coffee locally sources pastries, bread, and produce without having a central bakery. So, when you go into a local Philz, you get a local pastry that pertains to the locale you are in, not something mass-produced.

Philz is like no other coffee establishment. Every cup is brewed "One Cup at a Time." Therefore, you will not find coffee pre-brewed or espresso drinks such as cappuccinos or mochas. Instead, you will find 15 to 20 customized blends from high-quality beans sourced worldwide. In addition, several tea blends are also served.

When you visit a Philz shop, you will be greeted by a knowledgeable barista who knows the product inside and out. The barista will help you find the perfect blend for your palate. As a full-service coffee bar, they take care of everything from selecting the beans and blending them to grinding and pouring over the perfect water temperature. They even mix in your cream, sweetener, and a piece of fresh mint if necessary. Philz likes to call drinks "cups of love." If it is your first time at Philz, it is recommended to enjoy your cup "Philz Way," which is medium sweet with cream.

The Philz method differentiates them from others, offering a delicious mocha with sweetness

(top): Chalkboard sign in the first location in San Francisco, (bottom): outside of Philz Coffee, San Francisco

> **A Few of the Blend Names and Origins**
> + Ether—It's made from scratch, coming from nothing.
> + Jacob's Wonderbar—It was so good, he wanted to dedicate it to his best friend/son, Jacob. It means Jacob's Wonderful.
> + Julie's Ultimate—Named for a regular customer at the Mission store.
> + Tesora—This is the first blend Phil ever created. It took over seven years to make and was so special to him that he named it Tesora, which means Treasure in Italian.
> + Silken Splendor—It's like breathing in the fresh air, clean and crisp. It's a feeling of "silken splendor."
> + Dancing Water—Phil likens the feeling of stirring a coffee to watching the ocean waves disappear.

customized to each glass. In addition, a Philz Iced Tea will do the trick to cool yourself down during the hot months.

Jacob Jaber took over as CEO in 2005. Growth and building the company's internal structure were the emphasis. Ever-expanding, Philz roasting plant opened in November 2015 in Oakland, just across the bay from its original location. A blend of beans ranges from two to as many as seven different beans worldwide. Sourcing beans is composed of three areas: quality, price, and sourcing values (commitment to workers' safety and environment for the Earth's health and coffee-bean growers; purchasing only from reliable sources that prove they are protecting and preserving the planet with sound environmental and safety practices).

With every pound of green coffee beans purchased, Philz donates directly to Food Farmers, a non-profit organization with a mission to implement sustainable food-security programs in coffee-farming communities. Philz donates for every green-bean pound purchase.

Moving their coffee and unique drinks outside the Bay area was a bit of a gamble, but it paid off in 2011 with the opening of their Palo Alto Middlefield location. When visiting the Washington, D.C. area, Phil was struck by how reminiscent it was of San Francisco: defined neighborhoods, the intersection of culture, tech, and creativity, and government. Therefore, the Metropolitan D.C. area was the first location outside California. In 2023, after six years, looking at the market, Philz closed all their Washington DC locations to focus on the west coast.

Southern California is a car culture; it is where the drive-thru began. But looking at the personal "One Cup at a Time" ethic, you would think a drive-thru would not work for Philz. The City of Fullerton, not far from Disneyland, ran a test model with limited drinks and food. With Philz's slower approach to making coffee very personally, it can take up to 5 minutes, which is a high average for the industry. Philz is working on making its process more efficient to avoid keeping customers waiting too long.

You will not see many commercials or ads for Philz; the business was built on word-of-mouth "tell a friend" marketing. And that's what they strive for even today. However, people can sign up for their Insider Group to get the latest info on new openings, special events, and other offers.

Three simple words create the Philz mission statement: Better People's Day. We would live in an incredible world if every company had these three simple words as its mission statement. But instead, many know Philz by its motto: One Cup at a Time. ☕

Lazy Dog Restaurant & Bar

SLOGAN: "Makin' Regulars"

ORIGINAL LOCATION: 16310 Beach Blvd., Westminster

OPENED: 2003

FOUNDER: Chris Simms

CURRENT OWNERSHIP: Chris Simms

CURRENTLY AT THE FIRST LOCATION: The first location is still in operation.
There are currently fifty-six locations in eight states, all company-owned.

lazydogrestaurants.com

JUST A HANDFUL OF FAMILIES in the California area have, generation after generation, opened new restaurant concepts and kept at it. The Simms family goes back to the early days of Hollywood. Arthur J. Simms ran the commissary at MGM studios and then opened his first restaurant in 1952: Ben Frank's on Sunset. The family then launched restaurant concept after restaurant concept and generation after generation with their award-winning ideas.

Chris Simms is the third-generation Simms in the restaurant business. His father, Tom Simms, founded Mimi's Café (see page 97) in 1978.

Chris sought a prominent enough location on a busy street to test his concept. A former Tijuana Jones nightclub/restaurant in Huntington Beach had been an eyesore and a policing nightmare. Neighbors had called the police almost a hundred times in their final year of operation; the city council revoked their operating license. So, Chris knew that the city needed to open a family restaurant.

The idea and the name came from the feelings and ideas of the family vacations in the Rocky Mountains. They wanted to share the small-mountain-town ambiance with the enduring love of food and fireside chats. These feelings would be felt from the first day of opening Lazy Dog.

Lazy Dog is the first upscale restaurant/pub

**Opposite: BBQ Bison Meatloaf Platter,
(top): Founder Chris Simms**

Family of Restaurateurs
ARTHUR J. SIMMS: Grandfather
+ Ben Frank's
+ Arthur J's
+ French Market Place
+ The Kettle
TOM SIMMS: Father
+ Mimi's Café
MIKE SIMMS: Brother
+ Tin Roof Bistro
+ Post
+ Simmzy's
+ Fishing with Dynamite
+ The Arthur J's
SCOTT SIMMS: Uncle
+ The Kettle (Manager)
MATTHEW SIMMS: Nephew
+ Sip with Simms (Craft-Beer Business)

place to take "man's best friend." Europeans have been dining with their fur babies for years, and it was now taking hold in America. Europeans can bring their dogs into restaurants, where our health departments only allow dogs on outside patios with a few rules. Lazy Dog has a long-standing tradition of hospitality and is a place for friends and family to gather and spend time together. They know dogs are a big part of the family and are welcome to dine with their family members on the outdoor patio; Lazy Dog even has a dog-friendly menu.

Chris wanted to create a restaurant that offered the same quality as the more excellent, more expensive restaurants but was comfortable and casual at a reasonable level. Helping Chris with his dream was his father, Tom Simms, as an adviser with the concept, menu, and logos. Chris hired an executive sous chef from the Ritz-Carlton hotel chain. Chris wanted the food to be high-quality and creative.

Being a larger chain of locations, the kitchen works differently than other chains. Others have a central commissary or vendors that make recipes, so they are consistent for all sites. Lazy Dog has an intensive training program for its chefs at each location. Every meal is made by hand. All their sauces, salad dressings, and marinades are also made at each location. The produce and ingredients are sourced from local farmers and selected for quality. A test kitchen is located at their Brea location, run by Vice President of Food and Beverage Gabriel Caliendo. Unlike many restaurants, Lazy Dog has a seasonal menu with specials highlighted in each place.

Two unique concepts for Lazy Dog are delivery/pick-up models. In August 2020, TV Dinners were introduced, and Roadtrip™ Bowls in September 2022. TV Dinners are prepared fresh in each location, packaged in a retro foil divided tray, and then frozen for you to take home after your meal or to pick up. The meals are served with an entree, side, and dessert. All can be out of the oven in minutes, from Campfire Pot Roast to Grilled Lemon Chicken. The pricing is about half the price of a meal in a restaurant with about a dozen varieties to choose from. Roadtrip™ Bowls—handcrafted meals in a large bowl—are fresh to be eaten on pickup or delivery. Bowls can be paired with a side dish, a fresh garden salad, or a homemade dessert. Curry Chicken Bowl, filled with peas, carrots, raisins, olives, and yellow rice, topped with crispy chicken and a spicy harissa curry, is just one of the eight rotating selections.

Concord, CA location

(top): Dog Meal, (bottom): Salisbury Steak TV Dinner

An exciting program, the Lazy Dog Beer Club, partners with Melvin Brewing of Wyoming and their team to release craft beers for the club. The Lazy Dog Beer Club is a quarterly subscription-based club for beer lovers, with membership like a wine club. The membership gives its members access to various beers from craft brewers nationwide. The quarterly release is based on a theme from Lazy Dog, and members receive eight beers, two of each variety, to enjoy. You can also try the beer selections with your meal when visiting the restaurants.

Besides Habitat for Humanity, the Lazy Dog company partners with various organizations in their communities. They also create a specialized fundraiser program where a guest can work with any location to support a non-profit for a day and have a percentage of the bill go to the chosen organization.

Every location is a beautiful piece of art from recycled-metal welding artist Terry Jones from Jewett, Texas. The sculptures are created from recycled metal, such as confiscated weapons and found items at the local flea markets. Most of the locations have a dog sitting at attention.

The teammates recognize the motto more than the customers. It is not displayed on their signs like other restaurants, but is more of an "inside" part of their belief system. "Makin' Regulars" aims to make each guest a regular, creating a personalized experience for every guest. In 2021, *Nation's Restaurant News*, the leading magazine for the industry, awarded Lazy Dog the MenuMaster award for culinary innovation during the global pandemic. In addition, for the past five years Lazy Dog has been awarded the prestigious Great Places to Work award through industry studies.

After the first location in Huntington Beach, the company focused on a large 7,500-square-foot building to serve 250 to 300 customers. The kitchen is also more extensive than the typical restaurant, with many more chefs and cooks creating all the foods from scratch.

Today, Chris Simms has opened over 56 restaurants in eight states, and the future is bright for a coast-to-coast takeover. ✖

Pinkberry

SLOGAN: "It Tastes as Good as It Makes You Feel"

ORIGINAL LOCATION: 868 Huntley Dr., West Hollywood

OPENED: January 30, 2005

FOUNDERS: Hyekyung (Shelly) Hwang and Young Lee

CURRENT CEO: Eric Lefebvre

CURRENT OWNERSHIP: Kahala Brands

CURRENTLY AT THE FIRST LOCATION: Wellness Spa

There are currently 260 stores in twenty-two countries.

pinkberry.com

A FEW DOORS FROM SANTA MONICA BLVD. in West Hollywood on a small street sat a tiny 600-square-foot garage space. Hyekyung (Shelly) Hwang and Young Lee wanted to open a small tea house but could not obtain approval from the city. So, Hwang and Lee decided to open a small yogurt shop like those in Asia. Not the sweet, almost-ice-cream frozen yogurt, but tart citrusy flavor.

They started an international chain of frozen yogurt like no other: a citrus tart creamy dessert that, after one bite, hooked over 1,500 customers per day (hence the nickname "CrackBerry").

If you came across the building, it had a security guard and a velvet rope. The guard was put in to police the crowds for the neighbors, informing them that parking on the small street would result in a ticket, cutting the line off 15 minutes before the building closed, and making sure trash was not left around the area. Some thought it was a nightclub in the middle of the day. Sort of. You had to outsmart the meter readers, or a hefty fine would occur. The store was tiny with light green and orange sherbet-hue colors, with white tables, chairs, and lamps. There was seating for less than a handful. Lines would be dozens upon dozens deep, with Suburbans lining the street.

Hwang created the nonfat, 100 percent natural frozen dessert in two flavors (green tea and tart yogurt). You could ask for a topping that consisted of two dozen freshly cut fruits and cereal toppings. Store openings were fast. Two years after opening in West Hollywood, on the funky street Abbott Kinney in the beach town of Venice, Pinkberry opened to controversy. The road was primarily chain-free, and locals felt if they allowed Pinkberry, the next Banana Republic and other chains

Opposite: Pinkberry store in the evening, (top): Logo, (bottom): Original Tart Pinkberry flavor

would make the "artsy" street just like any other. But it still opened on time, with lines down the block like West Hollywood.

When a company is number one, others always want to break them down. In 2007, Pinkberry was in a class-action lawsuit regarding labeling its product as yogurt. California Dairy requirements require frozen yogurt to be mixed off-site, not in stores, as Pinkberry had been doing. This also resulted in Pinkberry giving over their formula for what makes their product different. Although Pinkberry was not allowed to use the word yogurt in their marketing for a short time, it was finally resolved. Pinkberry gave money to two Southern California charities as part of the settlement. There was a lot of misinformation—everything from it isn't yogurt, so there weren't live and active cultures. The product was natural frozen yogurt then, and it still is. The *Los Angeles Times* even conducted their tests and sent samples to a lab, which came back as yogurt.

Pomegranate yogurt using 100 percent California pomegranate juice debuted in 2007, before the holiday season. It is still a favorite and a mainstay in stores today. Just in time for the holidays of 2008, Santana Row in San Jose opened to great fanfare and their first Northern California location. Santana Row was a new outdoor space with hotel rooms on the top of the buildings that housed the shopping experience.

Going international to Kuwait in 2009 was celebrated by the locals with lines 50 deep for hours on end. Peru and Mumbai, India, followed. Then, with international stores and recognition, American Express came knocking. American Express created a new card for start-ups, the American Express Plum Card by American Express Open. Pinkberry was highlighted by the owners in commercial and print ads worldwide. The new Plum card was to help new businesses with deferred payments for up to two months and a return on all purchases—a first for the company. Pinkberry received card number 1,170 out of the initial 10,000 available. Today the Plum card is one of the many cards offered for small businesses by American Express.

With pressure from the city of West Hollywood, Pinkberry's original location closed in 2010;

Frozen Yogurt Flavor Releases

2005: Green Tea
2005: Tart Original
2007: Pomegranate
2009: Coconut
2009: Passionfruit
2012: Chocolate Hazelnut
2012: Strawberry Pinkberry
2013: Butter Pecan
2013: Cherry
2013: Cookies & Cream
2013: Peanut Butter
2013: Salted Caramel
2013: Vanilla
2014: Banana Split
2014: S'mores
2014: Watermelon Cooler
2015: Peppermint
2015: Raspberry White Chocolate
2015: Sea Salt Chocolate
2016: Peach
2016: Peppermint Cookies & Cream
2016: Meyer Lemon
2017: Black Raspberry
2017: Blueberry Muffin
2017: Crème Brulee
2017: Pecan Pie
2017: Power Berry
2017: Strawberry
2018: Banana Bread
2018: Chocolate
2018: Passion Mango
2018: Pineapple Colada
2018: Tiramisu
2019: Cold Brew

Pinkberry felt that with the openings of other places in the immediate area with better parking, it was time. So the building was turned into the Pinkberry Support Center for a short period. Today it is a wellness spa.

May 25, 2012, was a vital day for Pinkberry. A first in the industry, all the toppings became 100 percent free of trans fats, hydrogenated oils, and high fructose corn syrup. Everything you put on your yogurt, from fudge sauces to cereal toppings, would be healthier. The same year, Pinkberry started opening earlier to serve Greek yogurt with toppings from the topping bar for breakfast. An entirely new group of consumers was starting their day with Pinkberry. Celebrating their 200th store opening was the San Francisco Macy's Union Square location with a store-within-a-store concept.

In 2014, Pinkberry partnered with tennis star Maria Sharapova and her candy company Sugarpova to provide toppings for the yogurt. Sugarpova designed a distinctive product line just for Pinkberry. It also marked when Japan became the 20th country to have Pinkberry stores. Also, to-go Pick-Up packs of yogurts were offered. The Middle East expansion in Beirut, Lebanon, opened to crowds in August 2014, soon after Lima, Peru. Additional South America stores opened in Santiago, Chile, and then Istanbul, Turkey, opened in December 2014. Finally, Panama City, Panama, opened in 2015.

Cold Brew Pinkberry flavor

Franchising streamlining is the simplicity of the brand. Pinkberry training is simple and fast to learn, with only a few yogurt flavors to sell and train on. The stores are simplistic, with soft peach, green, and light blue colors—Philippe Starch furniture and lamps by Designs Within Reach. A store location can be up and running within weeks instead of the national average of months.

The PinkCard® loyalty cards and apps were launched in 2013. After purchasing ten yogurts, you are given a free yogurt, also one on your birthday. On its 10th anniversary, January 30, 2015, Pinkberry celebrated worldwide with 10-cent yogurt cups for all; thousands were served for this milestone promotion.

Looking to serve the public and the lactose-intolerant customer better, Tropical Mango, the first dairy-free product, was launched on May 1, 2015. By 2015, Kahala Brands had acquired Pinkberry and moved operations to Scottsdale, Arizona, from Santa Monica. Kahala's brand portfolio comprises 18 quick-service restaurant brands with approximately 3,000 locations in 34 countries.

With other frozen-yogurt companies expanding their brands into frozen soft swirl ice creams, Pinkberry launched Pinkbee's in June 2013 with Vanilla, Strawberry, and Crème Brulee as the essential flavors, with Chocolate coming out a few years later.

To this day, if you taste a flavor or product in a Pinkberry store, you may not be able to a month from now. Almost everything they do is a limited release, thus creating a buzz and getting you to return fast. Oprah Winfrey's favorite flavor was Meyer Lemon, which Pinkberry discontinued in 2017. Oprah even had a party from Pinkberry for her OWN network employees in West Hollywood. This was just in time for the release of *Queen Sugar*, a TV show produced by Oprah.

Pinkberry is still expanding strongly as one of the world's largest yogurt brands. 🧁

UNE FEMME

Sprinkles Cupcakes

ORIGINAL LOCATION: 9635 S. Santa Monica Blvd., Beverly Hills

OPENED: April 13, 2005

FOUNDERS: Charles and Candace Nelson

CURRENT OWNERSHIP: Privately held company

CURRENTLY AT THE FIRST LOCATION: The first location is still in operation.

There are twenty-four bakeries in nine states and forty-three Automatic Treat Machine (ATMs) in seven states.

sprinkles.com

IN 2002, CANDACE NELSON studied at Mary Risley's Cooking School, Tante Marie, in San Francisco for a six-month pastry course. A custom cake business, she realized, would be complicated; creating cupcakes instead would be more lucrative. Cupcakes are singular; you could have one and not feel like you had to buy an entire cake. Cookie shops had been done at so many stores, so cupcakes would still be a novelty.

Testing and creating cupcakes for sale in her home kitchen, Nelson knew she had to use the highest-grade ingredients—not just pure vanilla extract and rich chocolate, but Nielsen-Massey cold-pressed Madagascar Bourbon Vanilla and Belgium Callebaut chocolates. Fresh fruits and vegetables with hand-peeled natural citrus zests were essential.

Now a location needed to be found—a street with walking traffic, parking, central shopping district. A 600-square-foot space on Little Santa Monica Boulevard, in Beverly Hills, was available at the center of the block, with parking in the rear that used to be the tracks of the old passenger red cars.

Candace and her husband Charles knew their new bakery had to have a consistent look from packaging to store design. Kevin Hagen and David Irvin, restaurant branders of Folklor, were hired to design the product's packaging, colors, and overall feel. Andrea Lenardin Madden, an architect from Vienna, was tasked with creating the sleek store designs. When you walk into the bakery, you see a large glass box with slanted wooden "planks" having circular indentations for each cupcake to sit in. There are rows of colorful cupcakes with a signature mound of buttercream,

Cupcake Flavors

Banana
Black & White
Carrot
Chocolate Marshmallow
Dark Chocolate
Lemon Blueberry
Red Velvet
Traditional
Vegan Red Velvet
Sugar-Free Red Velvet
Gluten-Free Red Velvet
Salty Caramel
Sprinkle
Strawberry
Triple Cinnamon
Vanilla
Vanilla Milk Chocolate

Opposite: Six flavor assorted pack, (inset): Cupcake ATM in Newport Beach, CA

which is piled on with a spatula, not piped on like most. This way, the ratio of moist cake to icing is flawless. Each top or crown on the cupcake is decorated with sugar cutouts that are colorful rounds. The rounds are color-coded and continue the theme and look of the bakery.

With a small space and without a place for cupcake lovers to sit, the store arrangement was perfect for customers to file in and out with their purchases. Nelson baked through the night with enough cupcakes for an army, or so she thought. But, opening mid-week on a brisk sunny day, lines formed down the street; shockingly, they were sold out in three hours.

Being in Beverly Hills, you are bound to have a celebrity come through your doors. Barbra Streisand was one of their first customers and sent Oprah Winfrey a box. A few months later, Oprah contacted Sprinkles and highlighted them on her show with Candace and Charles flying to the Windy City with enough cupcakes for the entire studio audience. After the appearance, cupcake sales increased by 50 percent at their Beverly Hills location. Many celebrities of all venues, from movies, TV, and sports, started ordering or sending beautiful handcrafted boxes of cupcakes.

Tray of Mini-Red Velvet Cupcakes with cream cheese frosting

Sprinkles has a core set of flavors that are available daily, limited-time flavors such as fall pumpkin or cinnamon roll, and dozen-box sets. Red Velvet came into the core group at a request from Charles; having Southern roots, he wanted a Red Velvet. Candace hesitated, but it is the best seller of all cupcakes; in fact, it comes in four versions: vegan, sugar-free, gluten-free, and regular.

The first bakery outside the States was in Kuwait in 2013. Then, three years later, in 2016, the Walt Disney Company came knocking, asking them to place a bakery in Downtown Disney in California.

The Nelsons are innovators, from being the first all-cupcake bakery to having a Mercedes Sprinter van customized by West Coast Customs for mobile parties to traveling where a bakery was too far away. Besides cupcakes for humans, they also created a canine line of treats. And they also offer "shots," which are small cups of only the icing.

In fall 2007, the company developed an exclusive cake mix for Williams-Sonoma stores and sold it at their locations. The packaging on the mixes was not the typical square box but that of a cylinder. You add fresh ingredients such as eggs, milk, and vanilla; the package also has a recipe, plus the signature sugar dots are included in the packaging. The mix yields a dozen cupcakes.

On March 6, 2012, next to the original Sprinkles Beverly Hills bakery, the Cupcake Automatic Treat Machine (ATM) was launched. This is a 24-hour machine that dispenses fresh cupcakes one at a time in a beautiful box, perfect for gift-giving. The device can hold up to 600 cupcakes of many flavors, just like the bakery. In September 2013, history was made when Donald Wetzel, the inventor of the cash ATM, made a cupcake purchase at the Dallas location through the cupcake ATM. For a short while, you could see live remotes on the website of cupcake lovers purchasing treats at the ATM.

In summer 2012, the next store to the Beverly Hills location, a La Salsa Mexican restaurant, was closed and turned into Sprinkles Ice Cream, featuring over a dozen high-fat ice cream flavors and toppings.

From the *Today Show* to *Nightline* and the *Oprah Winfrey Show*, Sprinkles has been featured numerous times. Sprinkles has also been featured on reality shows and sitcoms. In addition, Candace has been a featured judge on many Food Network programs, such as *Cupcake Wars* and *Holiday Baking* shows. 2016 was a big year as Candace released her first book, *The Sprinkle's Baking Book: 100 Secret Recipes from Candace's Kitchen*.

The Nelsons ventured into the pizza business in April 2017 with a new start-up called Pizzana with actor Chris O'Donnell and his wife, Caroline. Candice created all the Italian desserts to go with the pizzas.

Today, Sprinkles Cupcakes are going viral with full bakeries to ATMs worldwide. Candice recently released her second book, *Sweet Success*, about her path in growing a business. 🧁

Other Menu Items
Cookies
Red Velvet Cookie
Chocolate Chip Cookie
Traditional
Gluten-Free
Double Chocolate Cookie
Salted Oatmeal Cornflake Cookie
Brownies
Layer Cakes
4-layer 6″ Cake
3-layer 8″ Cake
Chocolates

Crowd outside the first location in Beverly Hills

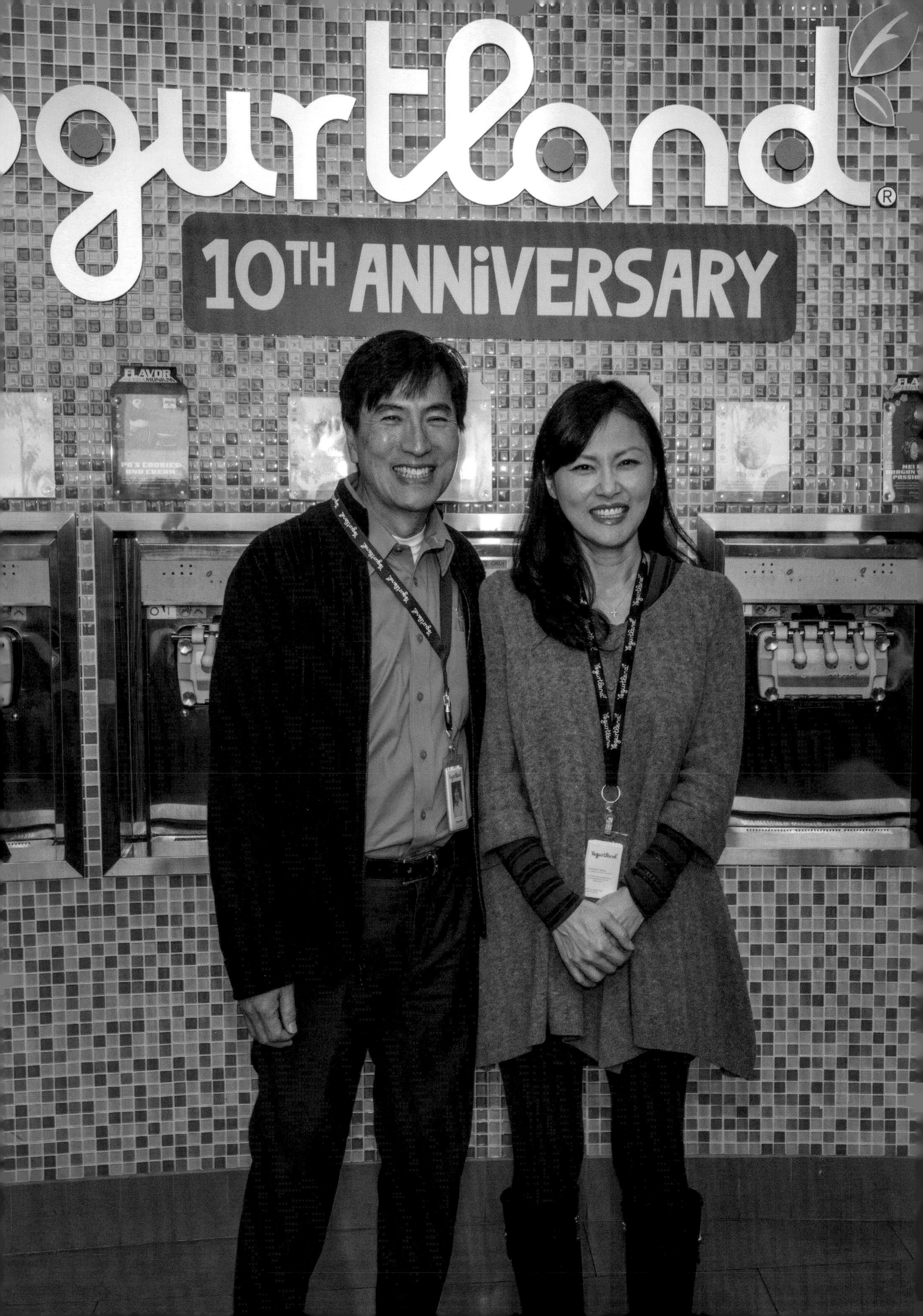
10TH ANNIVERSARY

Yogurtland

SLOGAN: "Serving Others Is a Measure of Our Humanity"

ORIGINAL LOCATION: 501 N. State College Blvd., Fullerton

OPENED: February 2006

FOUNDERS: Phillip Chang, CEO; Michelle Chang, VP

CURRENT OWNERSHIP: Privately held

CURRENTLY AT THE FIRST LOCATION: Nick, the Greek Fast Food

There are currently 230 locations—ten of which are company-owned—in nine countries on five continents.

yogurt-land.com

PHILLIP AND MICHELLE CHANG WERE MARRIED immigrants from South Korea who had grown up in Orange County, California. Looking toward the "American Dream" of owning their own company, the Changs settled on a strip mall a few blocks from Cal State Fullerton to open Boba Tea. Besides the tea, they offered frozen yogurt with a topping bar filled with fresh fruits and toppings. In 2006, a second store in Irvine followed, but this one was just yogurt, cutting out the tea. It was a hit, as the Changs found customers traveling up to 50 miles to enjoy a cup of creamy, smooth, balanced yogurt. Soon after opening about ten stores around Orange County, the Changs knew they had something special. Lines of raving fans waiting to create custom treats were out the door.

Only a year after opening the second location in 2007, franchising started to succeed. Yogurtland was the first self-service "buffet" frozen yogurt operation, with many following. Once inside, you see the clean look of the tiled green wall with eight yogurt machines that crank out the frozen treat. Each frozen-dessert machine produces two flavors with a swirl, which makes 16 flavors. Being self-serve puts the customer in charge. Also, it cuts down on employee labor. You are greeted with a smile and an offer to "sample" cups. You can taste any of the flavors before you fill your large dish.

Each location worldwide has access to the over 200 flavors created with natural ingredients from the Yogurtland team. Each operator can choose their flavor combination based on local preferences. Each location has a plain tart, vanilla, and chocolate ice cream, a sugar-free option, a non-dairy sorbet flavor, and

Opposite: Founders Phillip and Michelle Chang at the first location in Fullerton, CA at the 10th anniversary, (top): Two dishes of yogurt swirls, (middle): Logo, (bottom): Coupon for International Frozen Yogurt Day

Crew from Emirate of Sharjah location

the monthly promotion flavor. They sometimes pair with another well-known company for flavors, such as Hershey® Chocolate and Knott's® Berry Farm for boysenberries, which are great combinations.

Some of the unique flavors are those from lost childhood memories, such as a Rocket Pop in the colors of America (red, white, and blue). Yogurtland has captured the exact flavor in a frozen sorbet of cherry, lime, and raspberry, the same flavors you enjoyed from the ice cream truck as a childhood memory. All the yogurts are smooth and creamy, even the Pecan Praline. You can add your topping for texture. After filling your cup with frozen yogurt, go to the topping bar and finish your dessert with over 60 options, including fresh-cut fruit, candies, cereal, nuts, cookies, and more. And you cannot forget the sauces, from berries to hot fudge to butterscotch.

When friends or family visit, not everyone wants the same thing, such as yogurt; adding ice cream to the menu was a little tricky; but in the summer of 2017, Vanilla and Chocolate soft-serve ice cream was added to the stores. A light Blueberry Lavender ice cream will be next on the horizon. Seasonal flavors are very popular, with Pumpkin Pie as the fall flavor, and other seasons' selections vary. About 15 to 20 new flavors are developed every year. A team of Yogurtland "Flavorologists" creates the flavors, then tests them in the support center before they are selected for in-store. The flavor team uses natural ingredients to make each taste authentic and delicious. Yogurtland owns its dairy and controls the process for the highest-quality yogurt, and it is antibiotic-free.

The locations that seem to do well for Yogurtland are those in centers with a market or drug store, outdoor retail, and strip and lifestyle centers instead of being in a

---

A Sampling of the Flavors

+ Banana Nut Bread: Bananas. Roasted pecans, cinnamon, and caramelized sugars create what tastes like grandmother's flavorful banana bread.
+ Bananas Foster: Caramelized banana, vanilla, cinnamon.
+ Churro: A sweet treat bursting with cinnamon.
+ Cinnamon Graham Crackers: Sweet toasted flavor with cinnamon.
+ Cinnamon Roll: With even the cream cheese icing.
+ Oatmeal Cookies: A creamy frozen dessert just like the fresh oven-baked cookies.
+ Rocket Pop Sorbet: Just like the childhood favorite from the '60s.
+ Yo Frappe: Gooey caramel, rich mocha, and a hint of java.

fully enclosed mall. At the beginning of 2018 in Southern California markets, Yogurtland started testing "Drinkable Creations," a shake that you can top with anything on the topping bar. Sample flavors are Cold Brrrrew Coffee Frappe and the Classic Vanilla Milkshake. In addition, every National Yogurt Day on February 6, Yogurtland celebrates with giveaways; for several years, you could enjoy a free five-ounce frozen yogurt.

Customer enjoying samples at Yogurtland

The original location in Fullerton, California, was sadly closed on October 26, 2020, after fourteen years and four remodels. Unfortunately, the site could not weather the COVID-19 outbreak and simply closed with a note taped to the door to visit other nearby locations.

Unlike many other frozen-food manufacturers, Yogurtland owns its California dairy in the Los Angeles suburb of Paramount. This way, they control everything about the frozen yogurt they serve. Paramount Dairy is Yogurtland's best-kept secret. From start to finish, your cup of frozen yogurt is carefully hand-crafted and scratch made by the flavorologists at the Yogurtland Imagination Studio. Look at your cup and see the seal "Real California Milk." The yogurt starts with milk produced by the happy cows of California. The milk is hormone- and antibiotic-free and pasteurized at Paramount.

Yogurtland has three primary base flavors: sweet, tart, and sorbet. These liquid bases are owned by Yogurtland and processed at the dairy. Thus, the company keeps complete control of the flavor profile from start to finish, ensuring that it is quality-checked every step of the way. Yogurtland makes live and active cultures at the dairy and adds them into their tart and sweet base mixes. For lactose-intolerant customers, sorbet flavors are a perfect choice, as they do not have live or active cultures.

In November 2020, Yogurtland launched a test offshoot of their frozen-yogurt company with Holsom by Yogurtland. Holsom is a complete-meal, healthy, plant-based fast-food restaurant in Huntington Beach, California. Guests have the option to choose from its curated menu of plant-based wholesome grain bowls and gourmet toasts with fresh toppings to complement their frozen yogurt and toppings.

Yogurtland's mission is simple: to bring love, hope, and joy to the world, one spoonful at a time. A clean store with a friendly staff ensures a sense of pleasure for each guest visit. Yogurtland, through Yogurtland Cares®, is dedicated to supporting worldwide charities that benefit children and women seeking a better life.

Stop past one of the many Yogurtlands for a new flavor and a smile. 🍦

menchie's frozen yogurt
menchie's frozen yogurt
yogurt
NFYD
NATIONAL FROZEN YOGURT DAY
BUY ONE GET ONE FREE
DARK CHOCOLATE Mousse
MADE FROM ALMOND MILK
delivery
pickup
GRUBHUB
BEWARE: OPENING THIS DOOR MAY CAUSE SEVERE BOUTS OF HAPPINESS.
PULL
A

Menchie's Frozen Yogurt

SLOGAN: "Spreading Smiles"

ORIGINAL LOCATION: 4849 Laurel Canyon Blvd., Valley Village

OPENED: May 15, 2007

FOUNDERS: Adam and Danna Caldwell

CURRENT OWNERSHIP: Privately held company

CURRENTLY AT THE FIRST LOCATION: The first location is still in operation.

There are currently 351 locations in ten countries.

menchies.com

BEWARE:
OPENING THIS DOOR
MAY CAUSE SEVERE
BOUTS OF HAPPINESS.

HAPPINESS

ONE WORD ABOUT MENCHIE'S IS SMILES; they are "spreading smiles," one mix at a time. Everything is about happiness and smiles at their locations. Adam and Danna Caldwell went to a frozen-yogurt shop on a date in Orange County; it clicked. "Let's open up a frozen-yogurt shop," they said. Three years later, Menchie's was born. The name is the endearing nickname that Adam calls Danna.

After a year of steady sales, the Caldwells knew they needed to bring in a third party to grow their company. Amit Kleinberger was the choice. While growing up in Jerusalem, Amit saw the movie *The Secret of My Success* with Michael J. Fox, in which he was successful in the corporate world. Amit knew this was the career path he was destined for. At 18, Amit enlisted in the Israeli Defense Forces, learning from his commander that the way to lead is by example. After owning a few businesses, Amit became the CEO of Menchie's after six years of growing the company into 377 stores in 20 countries and 25 states.

In February 2012, Menchie's crossed the Pacific and opened its first store at the Ario Sapporo mall in Japan, which is owned and operated by the Japanese franchisor group NEO Corporation.

Menchie's sells not just yogurt but the entire experience, from the family-friendly atmosphere that is welcoming and warm, to the comfortable seating inside the shop and outside seating if room and weather permit. Some with larger spaces have party rooms for events and parties, chalkboards for children to color on, and upbeat fun music piped into the stores. They provide toys and activities also. Community means a lot to Menchie's family and franchisees. Each location donates products and cash annually to local schools and non-profits.

Opposite: Outside of Corona, CA location, (top): Door message: Opening this door may cause severe bouts of happiness

Private-Label Collection Flavors

Honeydew Sorbet
Mud Pie
Peanut Butter
Pistachio
Pure Chocolate
Purely Tart
Shredded Coconut
Vanilla Snow

Being a global brand-and-flavor profile from around the world, Menchie's creates yogurt flavors and toppings according to the preferences of the country in which that Menchie's is located, such as dragon fruit and lychee gummy worms in China. Menchie's is a leader in the frozen-yogurt business because they also use the highest quality dairy products from "happy" California cows at Scott Brothers Dairy in Chino. The four-generation Scott Brothers have been in business since 1913.

There's also a flavor for every smile! When you walk into Menchie's, you can sample as many flavors as you like, with over a hundred flavors, such as cake batter and homemade snickerdoodle cookies, to Live from N.Y. Cheesecake, to seasonal favorites such as Harvest Pumpkin and Spiced Gingerbread Cookie.

Their menu includes something for every dietary restriction, including vegan, dairy-free, gluten-free, and sugar-free options. A flavorful lower-calorie frozen treat once sold only at Disney resorts and the Dole Plantation in Hawaii is DoleWhip®. You can find one of the three citrus tart flavors at each store. Over 70 rotating toppings include cookie crumbles, brownie pieces, fresh fruits, nuts, candies, and more. Warm sauces include hot fudge, hard shell topping, marshmallow, and creamy peanut butter sauce.

Birthdays can be unique with Menchie's too. Some locations have a party room, and you can order a cake for any special event. The Fro-Yo cakes have a cake base with yogurt, fillings, and a topping, and are fully decorated. You can submit a picture to have duplicated or have one of the Fro-Yo artists create a cake from one of many famous superheroes or cartoon characters. In addition, Menchie's created a line of eight "Sweet Friends" images that are printed on T-shirts, stickers, and coloring pages. The Sweet Friends are sure to bring a smile from everyone.

First location in Valley Village, CA

(top): **Hidden Valley Corona, CA location,**
(bottom): **Menchie's yogurt cup**

Menchie's exclusive reward card is called "My Smile-age Club." It is all about the smile and the people in front of that smile. You can have the best product on the market, but it will fail if you don't have the best people selling it. 🧁

Sweet Friends

+ Menchie: A guitar-playing pink-and-green-swirled-hair guy.
+ Chip: Menchie's best friend who loves Peanut Butter.
+ Mookie: Loves "Moo-sic" and also Cookies and Crème Yogurt.
+ Sprinkle: Always looks on the bright side. Loves Cake Batter Yogurt.
+ Kiwi: The artist in the group.
+ Mellow: The tallest and strongest. Loves Chocolate Yogurt.
+ Barry: The wisest of the group. It can solve any puzzle. Loves Vanilla Yogurt.
+ P.B.: Always playing jokes, but does not joke about Red Velvet Yogurt.

Dog Haus

SLOGAN: "The Absolute Würst"

AKA: Dog Haus Biergarten

ORIGINAL LOCATION: 105 N. Hill Ave., Pasadena

OPENED: October 20, 2010

FOUNDERS: Hagop Giragossian, Vice President of Franchise Development; Quasim Riaz and Andre Vener, Partners

CURRENTLY AT THE FIRST LOCATION: The first location is in operation.

There are currently ninety-one locations in twenty-six states.

doghaus.com

THREE FRIENDS WITH VAST FOOD EXPERIENCE, from owning jazz clubs to pubs to coffee houses, shared a passion for great food, high-quality service, and commitment to the community. So those three friends, Hagop Giragossian, Quasim Riaz, and Andre Vener, devised a plan to open Dog Haus in Pasadena.

Dog Haus is different from other hot dog companies. The Dog Haus is a gourmet yet casual dining concept. The three founding partners knew their concept was not fast food or a fast-casual restaurant, so they called it Craft Casual. Also, a year after opening the first Dog Haus, Dog Haus Biergarten expanded the Dog Haus concept with a giant footprint that is more like a German beer garden.

Dog Haus is elevating dogs, sausages, and burgers to new levels, with quality, flavorful ingredients with a twist. A welcoming environment encourages people to linger to experience the laid-back atmosphere. Powder-coated metal tables and chairs line up with a welcoming bar and stained wooden flooring with black and white walls. The staff at the Dog Haus makes you feel very welcome, like at a neighborhood establishment, making it a place you want to return to—not just for the warm greetings but for the great food.

The first thing you'll notice about your hot dog or sausage is the sweet, perfectly toasted Hawaiian King's® Bun that encases your meal. Chef Adam Gertler, "Würstmacher," has appeared on numerous Food Network shows and paired with Dog Haus to create signature hot dogs and sausages. Some of his creations are regional, and many are rolled out nationwide. Gertler likes to work with various flavors when he creates sausages and the finished menu item. You can also make your

Opposite: Interior of Carson, CA location, (top): Dog Haus partners, left to right, Quasim Riaz, Andre Vener, and Hagop Giragossian

Time Line

2010: 1st Dog Haus opens in Pasadena, CA
2011: 1st Dog Haus Biergarten opens in Pasadena, CA
2013: Franchising begins
       Adam Gertler joins as Würstmacher Chef
       1st Franchise Territory sold
2014: 1st Franchise Location opens in Canoga Park
2015: Named one of 2015's Breakout Brands by NRN
       10th location opens in Centennial, Colorado
       100th Franchise sold: Las Vegas, NV
       Opened at the LA Coliseum for USC and LA Rams Games
2016: Signs a 305 Locations/12 State deal with American
       Development Partners
2017: Launches Mutha Clucka Chicken Sandwich
       25th Dog Haus location opening in Dallas "The Big D," Texas
       It opens in the Rose Bowl for Concerts and UCLA Games
       Serves Hormone, Antibiotic-Free Beef and Chicken
2018: Partners with No Kid Hungry
       30th location opens in Tennessee
       1st East Coast location opens in Maryland
       Opens in Mattress Firm Amphitheater, Chula Vista, CA
       Top Chef Ilan Hall to create the Huli Huli with proceeds
         for No Kid Hungry
2020: Haus Market introduced

(top): Double Burger with Tots, (middle): Dog Haus Sooo Cali, (bottom): Beer with assorted menu items

signature dog with over 30 condiments and ingredients.

The ingredients used are the industry's gold standard of Creekstone Farms Nature Premium Black Angus beef, Idaho Duroc Heritage pork, and hormone-and-antibiotic-free, vegetarian-fed poultry. Plant-based offerings are also on the menu, with proteins from Impossible Foods®and Beyond Meats®.

What goes best with hot dogs? Beer. Dog Haus focuses on local breweries in the region where they are open. Both Dog Haus and Biergartens offer a variety of beers and local breweries. You can also enjoy games on large-screen TVs with cable sports that add to the desire to stay a while. The Biergarten has interactive games on the patio, such as Corn Hole and board games.

Dog Haus goes beyond just feeding customers. They work with the communities in which they have locations through the No Kid Hungry program to educate and empower low-income families.

Dog Haus also created a Dine Out fundraising program, a way for nonprofits to raise money for their causes. Volunteers take orders, deliver food to the guests, and help on the evening of the event. In addition, Dog Haus donates 20 percent of sales after the evening's event.

Always thinking outside the box, Dog Haus, like all restaurants in 2020, had to discontinue dining but still could utilize pick-up. So Haus Market was formed, selling products from their back room and freezers, including cheese, hot dogs, sausages, tater tots, Kings® Hawaiian Rolls, and even scarce toilet paper.

Expansion is going fast; coast to coast, what started as one location in Pasadena is now nation-wide. 🌭

Flavors of Some Specialty Hot Dogs

+ Thai Curry Wurst: Spicy sausage with lime, Thai chilis, cilantro, and basil.
+ The "Big D" (Dallas Locations): King's® Hawaiian roll, relished peppers and onions, and sweet, spicy chipotle aioli.
+ The "Sooo Cali": Hot dog is topped with crispy onions, spicy basil aioli, avocado, and tomato.
+ "Lambda, Lambda. Lambda": Hot dog made with lamb and pork sausage, topped with tzatziki, feta, diced onion, tomato, and pickles.

Original first location of Lazy Dog, Pasadena, CA

A Few of the Awards

+ TimeOut: Listed as one of the "Best Hot Dogs" in America
+ Thrillist: The most creative and delicious hot dogs around
+ Zagat: High quality-loaded hot dogs, sausages, and burgers
+ CNN: Top 5 places to eat a hot dog in the U.S.
+ BuzzFeed: 10 out of 10, would eat again
+ Playboy: 11 restaurants so good, you wouldn't know they are a chain
+ Yelp: The real deal when it comes to hot dogs and burgers
+ Food & Wine: America's 20 Best Hot Dogs "Sooo Cali Dog"
+ Eater: Creative spins on the classic dog by using elevated ingredients

Acknowledgments

WHEN YOU WRITE A BOOK, you tend to worry about forgetting someone. I hope I remember everyone who has supported me with this book. First, my mom was one of the hardest-working car-hops in southern California in the 1950s. I think she could still carry five plates to a car. She has been and will continue to be my biggest supporter. My two sisters, Monica and Pattie, for caring for Mom while I am on the road and for all the love. Neil, my husband and travel companion for over 42 years, laughs at all my jokes and deals with my road trips. Trina Kaye of the Trina Kaye Organization has been my publicist and great friend for 15 years and ten books. Colleen Bates believed in this project and saw the first volume to fruition. Todd Bottorff, Publisher of Turner, for believing in this project to continue it; Amanda Chiu Krohn, Editor; Ashlyn Inman, Assistant Editor; Bill Ruoto, head of Design; Claire Ong, Production Manager; and Makala Marsee, Marketing Manager at Turner. Amy Inouye of Future Studio in Los Angeles for making this and my last four books works of art.

Many larger companies have historical research departments, while others have outside sources. I would like to thank everyone who answered my never-ending questions so I have the best answers possible. I have also included the passionate family members that hold the keys and facts to the early years of the companies their families started. Thank you to Pilar Almanza, Noah Alper, Daisy Alvarez, Wally Amos, Alexandra Baldwin, Jennifer Bispo, Ezra Cabral, Jordan Caravella, Barbara Caruso, Doug Cavanaugh, Elaina Chang, Nick Chang, Tom Chang, Lizzie Cloutier, Deanna Durst, Natalie Egan, Debbi Fields, Suzanne Fish, the Fraser Family, Ron Gelet, Cathie Haretakis, Lauren Healey, Brittany Heckman, Brad Hofman, Craig Hofman, Lauren Holzman, Jacob Jaber, Phil Jaber, Matt Kovacs, the Los Angeles Central Library, the Magnes Collection of Jewish Art and Life, Erin Mandzik, Leslie Mendoza, Michael, Mohammed, Anne Nero, Lily Newman, Chris Nichols, Amy Nickoloff, Craig Nickoloff, Kyle Okura, Naila Ortiz, Ashley Pedersen, Marilyn Perkins, E.G. Perry, Kevin Peters, Beatriz (Betty) Porto, Alethea Rowe, Sandova, Sherman Library and Gardens, Stacey, Dave Swart, Sara Swiger, Jill Teitelbaum, Jill Thrasher, Lincoln Watase, Jennifer Wells, Tara Woodall, Randy Wyner, and Anthony Zolezzi.

Photo Credits

Courtesy of Farmer Boy's Food Inc: 11

Courtesy of The Hofman Hospitality Group: 13, 14, 190, 191, 192, 193

From the collection of George Geary: 17, 18, 19, 20, 21, 22 (inset), 28, 29, 30, 31, 32, 34, 35, 36, 37, 38, 39, 42 (top), 44, 45, 52, 54, 55, 56, 57, 59, 61, 91 (top), 96, 97, 98, 99, 110, 112, 113, 114, 117, 122, 123, 124, 125, 128, 131, 139, 168, 169, 170, 172, 173, 182, 183, 185, 186, 189, 194, 197, 210, 212, 213, 218, 219, 220, 221

Courtesy of Xexperience Restaurant Group: 22 (top), 23, 154, 155, 156, 157

Courtesy of The Chang Family: 24, 25, 26

Courtesy of Southfield Mezzanine Capital: 41(top), 42 (bottom)

Courtesy of Yum Yum Donuts, Inc.: 46, 47

Courtesy of Rod Frazer Enterprises: 48, 49

Courtesy of Dave Swart: 60

Courtesy of Roscoe's: 70, 71, 72, 73

From The Porto Family Collection: 75, 76, 79

From Brian Feinzimer for The Portos Family: 75, 77 (bottom), 78, 79

Courtesy of CEC Holdings: 80, 81, 82, 83

From the Nickoloff family collection: 84, 85

From the Debbi Fields Rose collection: 90, 91 (bottom), 92, 94, 95

Courtesy of The Garden Fresh Restaurant Group: 100, 102

Courtesy of The Cheesecake Factory and the Overton Family: 104, 105, 106, 107, 108, 109

Courtesy of The Farmer Boys Food Inc.: 118, 119, 120, 121

From the Doug Cavanaugh family collection: 126, 129, 130

Courtesy of the Sacco Family collection: 132, 133, 134, 135

Courtesy of Panda Restaurant Group: 136, 137, 138

From the Ralph Rubio collection: 140, 141, 142

Courtesy of Mill Road Capitol: 143

Courtesy of Golden State Capitol: 148, 149, 150, 152, 153

Courtesy of Okura Family: 144, 145, 146

From the Jill Teitelbaum collection: 158, 159, 160, 161

Courtesy of JAB Holdings: 162

Courtesy of Noah Alper: 163

Courtesy of Lorne Goldberg Mandarin Holdings: 166

Courtesy of Wetzel Pretzel's: 178, 179, 180, 181

Courtesy of SJB Brands: 184

Courtesy of Randy Wyner: 196

From the Jaber Family collection: 198, 199, 200

About the Author

George Geary is the author of 16 books, from single-subject cookbooks to historical-driven California restaurant books, including *L.A.'s Landmark Restaurants* and *The Cheesecake Bible*. In addition, he is a cooking-school teacher, pastry chef, culinary travel guide, television personality, and in-demand public speaker on food and Hollywood/California history. A California native who has taught and traveled to 119 countries and every continent, he lives in southern California and owns a Mid-Century historical home with his husband of 43 years, Neil.